T0372460

Get the eBooks FREE!

(PDF, ePub, Kindle, and liveBook all included)

We believe that once you buy a book from us, you should be able to read it in any format we have available. To get electronic versions of this book at no additional cost to you, purchase and then register this book at the Manning website.

Go to https://www.manning.com/freebook and follow the instructions to complete your pBook registration.

That's it!
Thanks from Manning!

Functional Programming in C++

Functional Programming
in C++

IVAN ČUKIĆ

MANNING
SHELTER ISLAND

For online information and ordering of this and other Manning books, please visit www.manning.com.
The publisher offers discounts on this book when ordered in quantity.

For more information, please contact

Special Sales Department
Manning Publications Co.
20 Baldwin Road
PO Box 761
Shelter Island, NY 11964
Email: orders@manning.com

Manning Publications Co.
20 Baldwin Road
PO Box 761
Shelter Island, NY 11964

Development editor: Marina Michaels
Technical development editor: Mark Elston
Review editor: Aleksandar Dragosavljević
Project editor: Lori Weidert
Copy editor: Sharon Wilkey
Proofreader: Tiffany Taylor
Technical proofreader: Yongwei Wu
Typesetter: Happenstance Type-O-Rama
Cover designer: Leslie Haimes

ISBN 9781617293818
Printed and bound by CPI Group (UK) Ltd, Croydon, CR0 4YY
2 3 4 5 6 7 8 9 10 – CPI – 23 22 21 20 19 18

brief contents

contents

preface

Programming is one of the rare disciplines in which you can create something from absolutely nothing. You can create whole worlds that behave exactly as you want them to behave. The only thing you need is a computer.

When I was in school, most of my programming classes focused on imperative programming—first on procedural programming in C, and then on object-oriented programming in C++ and Java. The situation didn't change much at my university—the main paradigm was still object-oriented programming (OOP).

During this time, I almost fell into the trap of thinking that all languages are conceptually the same—that they differ only in syntax, and that after you learn the basics such as loops and branching in one language, you can write programs in all others with minor adjustments.

The first time I saw a functional programming language was at the university, when I learned LISP in one of my classes. My gut reaction was to use LISP to simulate `if-then-else` statements and `for` loops so that I could actually make it useful. Instead of trying to change my perspective to fit the language, I decided to bend the language to allow me to write programs in the same way I used to write them in C. Suffice it to say that back then, I saw no point whatsoever in functional programming—everything I could do with LISP, I could do with C much more easily.

It took a while before I started looking into FP again. The reason I did was that I was disappointed by the slow evolution of one particular language that I was required to use while working on a few projects. A `for-each` loop was added to the language, and it was advertised as if it were a huge deal: you just had to download the new compiler, and your life would become much easier.

That got me thinking. To get a new language construct like the `for-each` loop, I had to wait for a new version of the language and a new version of the compiler. But in LISP, I could implement the same `for` loop as a simple function. No compiler upgrade needed.

This was what first drew me to FP: the ability to extend the language without having to change the compiler. I was still in the "object-oriented" mindset, but I learned to use FP-style constructs to simplify my job of writing object-oriented code.

I started investing a lot of time in researching functional programming languages such as Haskell, Scala, and Erlang. I was astonished that some of the things that give object-oriented developers headaches can be easily handled by looking at the problem in a new way—the functional way.

Because most of my work revolves around C++, I had to find a way to use functional programming idioms with it. It turned out I'm not the only one; the world is filled with people who have similar ideas. I had the good fortune to meet some of them at various C++ conferences. This was the perfect opportunity to exchange ideas, learn new things, and share experiences about applying functional idioms in C++.

Most of these meetups ended with a common conclusion: it would be awesome if someone wrote a book on functional programming in C++. The problem was, all of us wanted someone else to write it, because we were looking for a source of ideas to try in our own projects.

When Manning approached me to write this book, I was torn at first—I thought I'd rather read a book on this topic than write it. But I realized if everyone thought that way, we'd never get a book on functional programming in C++. I decided to accept and embark on this journey: and you're reading the result.

acknowledgments

I'd like to thank everyone who made this book possible: my professor Saša Malkov, for making me love C++; Aco Samardžić, for teaching me the importance of writing readable code; my friend Nikola Jelić, for convincing me that functional programming is great; Zoltán Porkoláb, for supporting me in the notion that functional programming and C++ are a good mixture; and Mirjana Maljković, for help teaching our students modern C++ techniques, including functional programming concepts.

Also, big kudos to Sergey Platonov and Jens Weller, for organizing great C++ conferences for those of us who live in the *old world*. It's safe to say that without all these people, this book wouldn't exist.

I want to thank my parents, my sister Sonja, and my better half, Milica, for always supporting me in fun endeavors like this one; and I thank my long-time friends from KDE who helped me evolve as a developer during the past decade—most of all, Marco Martin, Aaron Seigo, and Sebastian Kügler.

A huge thank-you to the editorial team Manning organized for me: to Michael (Mike) Stephens, for the most laid-back initial interview I've ever had; to my amazing development editors Marina Michaels and Lesley Trites, who taught me how to write a book (thanks to them, I've learned much more than I expected); to my technical development editor Mark Elston, for keeping me grounded and practical; and to the great Yongwei Wu, who was officially my technical proofer but went far beyond that and helped me improve this manuscript in many ways. I hope I wasn't too much of a pain for any of them.

I'd also like to thank everyone who provided feedback on the manuscript: Andreas Schabus, Binnur Kurt, David Kerns, Dimitris Papadopoulos, Dror Helper, Frédéric Flayol, George Ehrhardt, Gianluigi Spagnuolo, Glen Sirakavit, Jean François Morin, Keerthi Shetty, Marco Massenzio, Nick Gideo, Nikos Athanasiou, Nitin Gode, Olve Maudal, Patrick Regan, Shaun Lippy, and especially Timothy Teatro, Adi Shavit, Sumant Tambe, Gian Lorenzo Meocci, and Nicola Gigante.

about this book

This book isn't meant to teach the C++ programming language. It's about functional programming and how it fits in with C++. Functional programming provides a different way to think about software design and a different way of programming, compared to the imperative, object-oriented styles commonly used with C++.

Many people who see the title of this book may find it strange, because C++ is commonly mistaken for an object-oriented language. Although C++ does support the object-oriented paradigm well, it goes much further than that. It also supports the procedural paradigm, and its support for generic programming puts most other languages to shame. C++ also supports most (if not all) functional idioms quite well, as you'll see. Each new version of the language has added more tools that make functional programming in C++ easier.

1.1 Who should read this book

This book is aimed primarily at professional C++ developers. I assume you have experience setting up a build system and installing and using external libraries. In addition, you should have a basic understanding of the standard template library, templates and template argument deduction, and concurrency primitives such as mutexes.

But the book won't go over your head if you're not an experienced C++ developer. At the end of each chapter, I link to articles explaining C++ features you may not yet be familiar with.

Roadmap

Functional Programming in C++ is intended to be read sequentially, because each chapter builds on the concepts learned in the previous ones. If you don't understand something after the first read, it's better to reread than to proceed, because the complexity of the concepts grows with each chapter. The only exception is chapter 8, which you can skip if you don't care about how persistent data structures are implemented.

The book is split into two parts. The first part covers functional programming idioms, and how they can be applied to C++:

- Chapter 1 gives a short introduction to FP, and what benefits it brings to the C++ world.
- Chapter 2 covers the higher-order functions—functions that accept other functions as arguments or return new functions. It demonstrates this concept with a few of the more useful higher-order functions found in the standard library of the C++ programming language.
- Chapter 3 talks about all the different things that C++ consider functions, or function-like—from ordinary C functions, to function objects and lambdas.
- Chapter 4 explains different ways to create new functions from the old ones. It explains partial function application using std::bind and lambdas, and it demonstrates a different way to look at functions called *currying*.
- Chapter 5 talks about the importance of immutable data—data that never changes. It explains the problems that arise from having mutable state, and how to implement programs without changing values of variables.
- Chapter 6 takes an in-depth look at lazy evaluation. It shows how lazy evaluation can be used for optimization—from simple tasks like string concatenation, to optimizing algorithms using dynamic programming.
- Chapter 7 demonstrates ranges—the modern take on standard library algorithms meant to improve usability and performance.
- Chapter 8 explains immutable data structures—data structures that preserve the previous versions of themselves any time they are modified.

The second part of the book deals with more advanced concepts, mostly pertaining to functional software design:

- Chapter 9 shows how sum types can be used to remove invalid states from programs. It shows how to implement sum types using inheritance and std::variant, and how to handle them by creating overloaded function objects.
- Chapter 10 explains functors and monads—abstractions that allow easier handling of generic types and that let you compose functions that work with generic types such as vectors, optionals, and futures.
- Chapter 11 explains the template metaprogramming techniques useful for FP in the C++ programming language. It covers static introspection techniques, callable objects, and how to use template metaprogramming in C++ to create domain-specific languages.

- Chapter 12 combines all that you have learned in the book to demonstrate a functional approach to designing concurrent software systems. This chapter explains how the continuation monad can be used to build reactive software systems.
- Chapter 13 presents the functional approach to program testing and debugging.

While you're reading this book, I advise you to try to implement all the presented concepts and to check out the accompanying code examples. Most of the techniques I cover can be used with older versions of C++, but doing so would require writing a lot of boilerplate code; so, I focus mostly on C++14 and C++17.

The examples assume you have a working C++17-compliant compiler. You can use either GCC (my personal choice) or Clang; the latest released versions of both support all the C++17 features we're going to use. All the examples have been tested with GCC 7.2 and Clang 5.0.

You can use an ordinary text editor and compile the examples manually by using the GNU `make` command (all the examples come with a simple Makefile), or you can fire up a full-fledged IDE such as Qt Creator (www.qt.io), Eclipse (www.eclipse.org), KDevelop (www.kdevelop.org), or CLion (www.jetbrains.com/clion) and import the examples into it. If you plan to use Microsoft Visual Studio, I advise installing the latest development version you can get your hands on; then you'll be able to use Clang as the default compiler instead of the Microsoft Visual C++ compiler (MSVC), which as of this writing is missing quite a few features.

Although most of the examples can be compiled without any external dependencies, some use third-party libraries such as range-v3, catch, and JSON, whose snapshots are provided along with the code examples in the common/3rd-party directory; or Boost libraries, which you can download from www.boost.org.

Code conventions and downloads

Source code for this book's examples is available from the publisher's website at www.manning.com/books/functional-programming-in-c-plus-plus and on GitLab at https://gitlab.com/manning-fpcpp-book.

The book contains many examples of source code, both in numbered listings and inline with normal text. In both cases, source code is formatted in a `fixed-width font like this` to separate it from ordinary text.

In many cases, the original source code has been reformatted; we've added line breaks and reworked indentation to accommodate the available page space in the book. In rare cases, even this was not enough, and listings include line-continuation markers (➥). Additionally, comments in the source code have often been removed from the listings when the code is described in the text. Code annotations accompany many of the listings, highlighting important concepts.

Coding styles are always a good opportunity for bike-shedding. This is even more true when C++ is concerned, because all projects tend to have their own style.

I tried to follow the styles used in other C++ books, but I want to state a couple of my choices here:

- Classes that model real-life entities such as people and pets have a _t suffix. This makes it easy to tell whether I'm talking about a real person or about the type—person_t is easier to read than *the person type*.
- Private member variables have an m_ prefix. This differentiates them from the static member variables, which have an s_ prefix.

Book forum

Purchase of *Functional Programming in C++* includes free access to a private web forum run by Manning Publications where you can make comments about the book, ask technical questions, and receive help from the author and from other users. To access the forum, go to https://forums.manning.com/forums/functional-programming-in -c-plus-plus. You can also learn more about Manning's forums and the rules of conduct at https://forums.manning.com/forums/about.

Manning's commitment to our readers is to provide a venue where a meaningful dialogue between individual readers and between readers and the author can take place. It is not a commitment to any specific amount of participation on the part of the author, whose contribution to the forum remains voluntary (and unpaid). We suggest you try asking the author some challenging questions lest his interest stray! The forum and the archives of previous discussions will be accessible from the publisher's website as long as the book is in print.

about the author

Ivan Čukić teaches modern C++ techniques and functional programming at the Faculty of Mathematics in Belgrade. He has been using C++ since 1998. He researched functional programming in C++ before and during his PhD studies, and he uses these FP techniques in real-world projects that are used by hundreds of millions of people around the world. Ivan is one of the core developers at KDE, the largest free/libre open source C++ project.

Introduction to functional programming

As programmers, we're required to learn more than a few programming languages during our lifetime, and we usually end up focusing on two or three that we're most comfortable with. It's common to hear somebody say that learning a new programming language is easy—that the differences between languages are mainly in the syntax, and that most languages provide roughly the same features. If we know C++, it should be easy to learn Java or C#, and vice versa.

This claim does have some merit. But when learning a new language, we usually end up trying to simulate the style of programming we used in the previous language. When I first worked with a functional programming language at my university, I began by learning how to use its features to simulate `for` and `while` loops and `if-then-else` branching. That was the approach most of us took, just to be able to pass the exam and never look back.

There's a saying that if the only tool you have is a hammer, you'll be tempted to treat every problem like a nail. This also applies the other way around: if you have a nail, you'll want to use whatever tool you're given as a hammer. Many programmers who check out a functional programming language decide that it isn't worth learning, because they don't see the benefits; they try to use the new tool the same way they used the old one.

This book isn't meant to teach you a new programming language, but it is meant to teach you an alternative way of using a language (C++): a way that's different enough that it'll often *feel* like you're using a new language. With this new style of programming, you can write more-concise programs and write code that's safer, easier to read and reason about, and, dare I say, more beautiful than the code usually written in C++.

1.1 What is functional programming?

Functional programming is an old programming paradigm that was born in academia during the 1950s; it stayed tied to that environment for a long time. Although it was always a hot topic for scientific researchers, it was never popular in the "real world." Instead, imperative languages (first procedural, later object-oriented) became ubiquitous.

It has often been predicted that one day functional programming languages will rule the world, but it hasn't happened yet. Famous functional languages such as Haskell and Lisp still aren't on the top-10 lists of the most popular programming languages. Those lists are reserved for traditionally imperative languages including C, Java, and C++. Like most predictions, this one needs to be open to interpretation to be considered fulfilled. Instead of functional programming languages becoming the most popular, something else is happening: the most popular programming languages have started introducing features inspired by functional programming languages.

What *is* functional programming (FP)? This question is difficult to answer because no widely accepted definition exists. There's a saying that if you ask two functional programmers what FP is, you'll get (at least) three different answers. People tend to define FP through related concepts including pure functions, lazy evaluation, pattern matching, and such. And usually, they list the features of their favorite language.

In order not to alienate anyone, we'll start with an overly mathematical definition from the functional programming Usenet group:

> *Functional programming is a style of programming that emphasizes the evaluation of expressions, rather than execution of commands. The expressions in these languages are formed by using functions to combine basic values. A functional language is a language that supports and encourages programming in a functional style.*
>
> —FAQ for comp.lang.functional

Over the course of this book, we'll cover various concepts related to FP. I'll leave it up to you to pick your favorites that you consider essential for a language to be called *functional*.

Broadly speaking, **FP** is a style of programming in which the main program building blocks are functions as opposed to objects and procedures. A program written in the functional style doesn't specify the commands that should be performed to achieve the result, but rather defines what the result is.

Consider a small example: calculating the sum of a list of numbers. In the imperative world, you implement this by iterating over the list and adding the numbers to the accumulator variable. You explain the step-by-step process of how to sum a list of numbers. On the other hand, in the functional style, you need to define only what a sum of a list of numbers is. The computer knows what to do when it's required to calculate a sum. One way you can do this is to say that the sum of a list of numbers equals the first element of the list added to the sum of the rest of the list, and that the sum is zero if the list is empty. You define what the sum is without explaining how to calculate it.

This difference is the origin of the terms *imperative* and *declarative* programming. *Imperative* means you command the computer to do something by explicitly stating each step it needs to perform in order to calculate the result. *Declarative* means you state what should be done, and the programming language has the task of figuring out how to do it. You define what a sum of a list of numbers is, and the language uses that definition to calculate the sum of a given list of numbers.

1.1.1 Relationship with object-oriented programming

It isn't possible to say which is better: the most popular imperative paradigm, object-oriented programming (OOP); or the most commonly used declarative one, the FP paradigm. Both have advantages and weaknesses.

The object-oriented paradigm is based on creating abstractions for data. It allows the programmer to hide the inner representation inside an object and provide only a view of it to the rest of the world via the object's API.

The FP style creates abstractions on the functions. This lets you create more-complex control structures than the underlying language provides. When C++11 introduced the range-based `for` loop (sometimes called `foreach`), it had to be implemented in every C++ compiler (and there are many of them). Using FP techniques, it was possible to do this without changing the compiler. Many third-party libraries implemented their own versions of the range-based `for` loop over the years. When we use FP idioms, we can create new language constructs like the range-based `for` loop and other, more advanced ones; these will be useful even when writing programs in the imperative style.

In some cases, one paradigm is more suitable than the other, and vice versa. Often, a combination of the two hits the sweet spot. This is evident from the fact that many old and new programming languages have become multiparadigm instead of sticking to their primary paradigm.

1.1.2 A concrete example of imperative vs. declarative programming

To demonstrate the difference between these two styles of programming, let's start with a simple program implemented in the imperative style, and convert it to its functional equivalent. One of the ways often used to measure the complexity of software is counting its lines of code (LOC). Although it's debatable whether this is a good metric, it's a perfect way to demonstrate the differences between imperative and FP styles.

Imagine that you want to write a function that takes a list of files and calculates the number of lines in each (see figure 1.1). To keep this example as simple as possible, you'll count only the number of newline characters in the file—assume that the last line in the file also ends with a newline character.

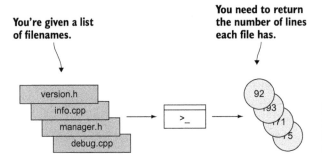

You're given a list of filenames.

You need to return the number of lines each file has.

version.h
info.cpp
manager.h
debug.cpp

92
93
71
75

Figure 1.1   The program input is a list of files. The program needs to return the number of newlines in each file as its output.

Thinking imperatively, you might analyze the steps in solving the problem as follows:

1 Open each file.
2 Define a counter to store the number of lines.
3 Read the file one character at a time, and increase the counter every time the newline character (\n) occurs.
4 At the end of a file, store the number of lines calculated.

The following listing reads files character by character and counts the number of newlines.

Listing 1.1   Calculating the number of lines the imperative way

```cpp
std::vector<int>
count_lines_in_files(const std::vector<std::string>& files)
{
    std::vector<int> results;
    char c = 0;

    for (const auto& file : files) {
        int line_count = 0;

        std::ifstream in(file);

        while (in.get(c)) {
            if (c == '\n') {
                line_count++;
            }
        }

        results.push_back(line_count);
    }

    return results;
}
```

You end up with two nested loops and a few variables to keep the current state of the process. Although the example is simple, it has a few places where you might make an error—an uninitialized (or badly initialized) variable, an improperly updated state, or a wrong loop condition. The compiler will report some of these mistakes as warnings, but the mistakes that get through are usually hard to find because our brains are hard-wired to ignore them, just like spelling errors. You should try to write your code in a way that minimizes the possibility of making mistakes like these.

More C++-savvy readers may have noticed that you could use the standard std::count algorithm instead of counting the number of newlines manually. C++ provides convenient abstractions such as stream iterators that allow you to treat the I/O streams similarly to ordinary collections like lists and vectors, so you might as well use them.

Listing 1.2 Using `std::count` to count newline characters

```cpp
int count_lines(const std::string& filename)
{
    std::ifstream in(filename);

    return std::count(
        std::istreambuf_iterator<char>(in),          // Counts newlines from the
        std::istreambuf_iterator<char>(),            // current position in the stream
        '\n');                                        // until the end of the file
}

std::vector<int>
count_lines_in_files(const std::vector<std::string>& files)
{
    std::vector<int> results;

    for (const auto& file : files) {
        results.push_back(count_lines(file));         // Saves the result
    }

    return results;
}
```

With this solution, you're no longer concerned about exactly how the counting is implemented; you're just declaring that you want to count the number of newlines that appear in the given input stream. This is always the main idea when writing programs in the functional style—use abstractions that let you define the *intent* instead of specifying *how* to do something—and is the aim of most techniques covered in this book. This is the reason FP goes hand in hand with generic programming (especially in C++): both let you think on a higher level of abstraction compared to the down-to-earth view of the imperative programming style.

Object-oriented?

I've always been amused that most developers say C++ is an object-oriented language. The reason this is amusing is that barely any parts of the standard library of the C++ programming language (commonly referred to as the *Standard Template Library*, or STL) use inheritance-based polymorphism, which is at the heart of the OOP paradigm.

The STL was created by Alexander Stepanov, a vocal critic of OOP. He wanted to create a generic programming library, and he did so by using the C++ template system combined with a few FP techniques.

This is one of the reasons I rely a lot on STL in this book—even if it isn't a *proper* FP library, it models a lot of FP concepts, which makes it a great starting point to enter the world of functional programming.

The benefit of this solution is that you have fewer state variables to worry about, and you can begin to express the higher-level intent of a program instead of specifying the exact steps it needs to take to find the result. You no longer care how the counting is implemented. The only task of the count_lines function is to convert its input (the filename) to the type that std::count can understand (a pair of stream iterators).

Let's take this even further and define the entire algorithm in the functional style—*what* should be done, instead of *how* it should be done. You're left with a range-based for loop that applies a function to all elements in a collection and collects the results. This is a common pattern, and it's to be expected that the programming language has support for it in its standard library. In C++, this is what the std::transform algorithm is for (in other languages, this is usually called map or fmap). The implementation of the same logic with the std::transform algorithm is shown in the next listing. std::transform traverses the items in the files collection one by one, transforms them using the count_lines function, and stores the resulting values in the results vector.

Listing 1.3   Mapping files to line counts by using `std::transform`

```
std::vector<int>
count_lines_in_files(const std::vector<std::string>& files)
{
    std::vector<int> results(files.size());

    std::transform(files.cbegin(), files.cend(),        Specifies which items
                   results.begin(),                     to transform
                   count_lines);                        Where to store the results

    return results;                                     Transformation function
}
```

This code no longer specifies the algorithm steps that need to be taken, but rather how the input should be transformed in order to get the desired output. It can be argued that removing the state variables, and relying on the standard library implementation of the counting algorithm instead of rolling your own, makes the code less prone to errors.

The problem is that the listing includes too much boilerplate code to be considered more readable than the original example. This function has only three important words:

- `transform`—What the code does
- `files`—Input
- `count_lines`—Transformation function

The rest is noise.

The function would be much more readable if you could write the important bits and skip everything else. In chapter 7, you'll see that this is achievable with the help of the ranges library. Here, I'm going to show what this function looks like when implemented with ranges and range transformations. Ranges use the | (pipe) operator to denote pushing a collection through a transformation.

Listing 1.4 Transformation using ranges

```
std::vector<int>
count_lines_in_files(const std::vector<std::string>& files)
{
    return files | transform(count_lines);
}
```

This code does the same thing as listing 1.3, but the meaning is more obvious. You take the input list, pass it through the transformation, and return the result.

Notation for specifying the function type

C++ doesn't have a single type to represent a function (you'll see all the things that C++ considers to be function-like in chapter 3). To specify just the argument types and return type of a function without specifying exactly what type it'll have in C++, we need to introduce a new language-independent notation.

When we write f: (arg1_t, arg2_t, ..., argn_t) → result_t, it means f accepts n arguments, where arg1_t is the type of the first argument, arg2_t is the type of the second, and so on; and f returns a value of type result_t. If the function takes only one argument, we omit the parentheses around the argument type. We also avoid using const references in this notation, for simplicity.

For example, if we say that the function repeat has a type of (char, int) → std::string, it means the function takes two arguments—one character and one integer—and returns a string. In C++, it would be written like this (the second version is available since C++11):

```
std::string repeat(char c, int count);
auto repeat(char c, int count) -> std::string;
```

This form also increases the maintainability of the code. You may have noticed that the `count_lines` function has a design flaw. If you were to look at just its name and type (`count_lines: std::string → int`), you'd see that the function takes a string, but it wouldn't be clear that this string represents a filename. It would be normal to expect that the function counts the number of lines in the passed string instead. To fix this issue, you can separate the function into two: `open_file: std::string → std::if-stream`, which takes the filename and returns the file stream; and `count_lines: std::ifstream → int`, which counts the number of lines in the given stream. With this change, it's obvious what the functions do from their names and involved types. Changing the range-based `count_lines_in_files` function involves just one additional transformation.

Listing 1.5   Transformation using ranges, modified

```
std::vector<int>
count_lines_in_files(const std::vector<std::string>& files)
{
    return files | transform(open_file)
                 | transform(count_lines);
}
```

This solution is much less verbose than the imperative solution in listing 1.1 and much more obvious. You start with a collection of filenames—it doesn't even matter which collection type you're using—and perform two transformations on each element in that collection. First you take the filename and create a stream from it, and then you go through that stream to count the newline characters. This is exactly what the preceding code says—without any excess syntax, and without any boilerplate.

1.2   *Pure functions*

One of the most significant sources of software bugs is the program state. It's difficult to keep track of all possible states a program can be in. The OOP paradigm gives you the option to group parts of the state into objects, thus making it easier to manage. But it doesn't significantly reduce the number of possible states.

Suppose you're making a text editor, and you're storing the text the user has written in a variable. The user clicks the Save button and continues typing. The program saves the text by writing one character at a time to storage (this is a bit oversimplified, but bear with me). What happens if the user changes part of the text while the program is saving it? Will the program save the text as it was when the user clicked Save, or save the current version, or do something else?

The problem is that all three cases are possible—and the answer will depend on the progress of the save operation and on which part of the text the user is changing. In the case presented in figure 1.2, the program will save text that was never in the editor.

Some parts of the saved file will come from the text as it was before the change occurred, and other parts will be from the text after it was changed. Parts of two different states will be saved at the same time.

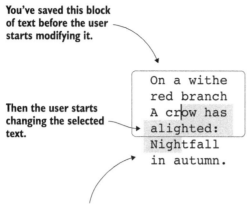

You've saved this block of text before the user starts modifying it.

```
On a withe
red branch
A crow has
alighted:
Nightfall
in autumn.
```

Then the user starts changing the selected text.

If you continue saving the file as if nothing has happened, you'll create a file that contains some chunks from the old version along with chunks from the new one, effectively creating a file that contains text that was never actually entered in the editor.

Figure 1.2   If you allow the user to modify the text while you're saving it, incomplete or invalid data could be saved, thus creating a corrupted file.

This issue wouldn't exist if the saving function had its own immutable copy of the data that it should write (see figure 1.3). This is the biggest problem of mutable state: it creates dependencies between parts of the program that don't need to have anything in common. This example involves two clearly separate user actions: saving the typed text and typing the text. These should be able to be performed independently of one another. Having multiple actions that might be executed at the same time and that share a mutable state creates a dependency between them, opening you to issues like the ones just described.

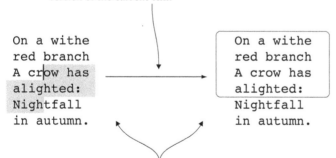

When the user triggers the action to save the file, the saving process will get an immutable version of the current text.

```
On a withe
red branch
A crow has
alighted:
Nightfall
in autumn.
```

```
On a withe
red branch
A crow has
alighted:
Nightfall
in autumn.
```

Because both processes have their own data, you can continue saving the file uninterrupted even if the user starts changing the text.

Figure 1.3   If you either create a full copy or use a structure that can remember multiple versions of data at the same time, you can decouple the processes of saving the file and changing the text in the text editor.

Michael Feathers, author of *Working Effectively with Legacy Code* (Prentice Hall, 2004), said, "OO makes code understandable by encapsulating moving parts. FP makes code understandable by minimizing moving parts." Even local mutable variables can be considered bad for the same reason. They create dependencies between different parts of the function, making it difficult to factor out parts of the function into a separate function.

One of FP's most powerful ideas is *pure functions*: functions that only use (but don't modify) the arguments passed to them in order to calculate the result. If a pure function is called multiple times with the same arguments, it must return the same result every time and leave no trace that it was ever invoked (no *side effects*). This all implies that pure functions are unable to alter the state of the program.

This is great, because you don't have to think about the program state. But, unfortunately, it also implies that pure functions can't read from the standard input, write to the standard output, create or delete files, insert rows into a database, and so on. If we wanted to be overly dedicated to immutability, we'd even have to forbid pure functions from changing the processor registers, memory, or anything else on the hardware level.

This makes this definition of pure functions unusable. The CPU executes instructions one by one, and it needs to track which instruction should be executed next. You can't execute anything on the computer without mutating at least the internal state of the CPU. In addition, you couldn't write useful programs if you couldn't communicate with the user or another software system.

Because of this, we're going to relax the requirements and refine our definition: a *pure function* is any function that doesn't have observable (at a higher level) side effects. The function caller shouldn't be able to see any trace that the function was executed, other than getting the result of the call. We won't limit ourselves to using and writing only pure functions, but we'll try to limit the number of nonpure ones we use.

1.2.1   *Avoiding mutable state*

We started talking about FP style by considering an imperative implementation of an algorithm that counts newlines in a collection of files. The function that counts newlines should always return the same array of integers when invoked over the same list of files (provided the files weren't changed by an external entity). This means the function could be implemented as a pure function.

Looking at our initial implementation of this function from listing 1.1, you can see quite a few statements that are impure:

```
for (const auto& file: files) {
    int line_count = 0;

    std::ifstream in(file);

    while (in.get(c)) {
        if (c == '\n') {
```

```
            line_count++;
        }
    }

    results.push_back(line_count);
}
```

Calling .get on an input stream changes the stream and the value stored in the variable c. The code changes the results array by appending new values to it and modifies line_count by incrementing it (figure 1.4 shows the state changes for processing a single file). This function definitely isn't implemented in a pure way.

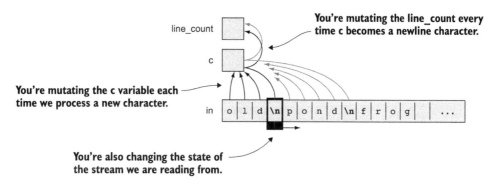

Figure 1.4 This example needs to modify a couple of independent variables while counting the number of newlines in a single file. Some changes depend on each other, and others don't.

But this isn't the only question you need to ask. The other important consideration is whether the function's impurities are observable from the outside. All mutable variables in this function are local—not even shared between possible concurrent invocations of the function—and aren't visible to the caller or to any external entity. Users of this function can consider it to be pure, even if the implementation isn't. This benefits the callers because they can rely on you not changing their state, but you still have to manage your own. And while doing so, you must ensure that you aren't changing anything that doesn't belong to you. Naturally, it would be better if you also limited your state and tried to make the function implementation as pure as possible. If you make sure you're using only pure functions in your implementation, you won't need to think about whether you're leaking any state changes, because you aren't mutating anything.

The second solution (listing 1.2) separates the counting into a function named count_lines. This function is also pure-looking from the outside, even if it internally declares an input stream and modifies it. Unfortunately, because of the API of std::ifstream, this is the best you can get:

```
int count_lines(const std::string& filename)
{
    std::ifstream in(filename);

    return std::count(
        std::istreambuf_iterator<char>(in),
```

```
            std::istreambuf_iterator<char>(),
        '\n');
}
```

This step doesn't improve the `count_lines_in_files` function in any significant manner. It moves some of the impurities to a different place but keeps the two mutable variables. Unlike `count_lines`, the `count_lines_in_files` function doesn't need I/O, and it's implemented only in terms of the `count_lines` function, which you (as a caller) can consider to be pure. There's no reason it would contain any impure parts. The following version of the code, which uses the range notation, implements the `count_lines_in_files` function without any local state—mutable or not. It defines the entire function in terms of other function calls on the given input:

```
std::vector<int>
count_lines_in_files(const std::vector<std::string>& files)
{
    return files | transform(count_lines);
}
```

This solution is a perfect example of what FP style looks like. It's short and concise, and what it does is obvious. What's more, it obviously doesn't do anything else—it has no visible side effects. It just gives the desired output for the given input.

1.3   *Thinking functionally*

It would be inefficient and counterproductive to write code in the imperative style first and then change it bit by bit until it became functional. Instead, you should think about problems differently. Instead of thinking of the algorithm steps, you should consider what the input is, what the output is, and which transformations you should perform to map one to the other.

In the example in figure 1.5, you're given a list of filenames and need to calculate the number of lines in each file. The first thing to notice is that you can simplify this problem by considering a single file at a time. You have a list of filenames, but you can process each of them independently of the rest. If you can find a way to solve this problem for a single file, you can easily solve the original problem as well (figure 1.6).

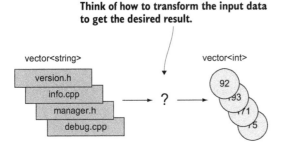

Figure 1.5   When thinking functionally, you consider the transformations you need to apply to the given input to get the desired output as the result.

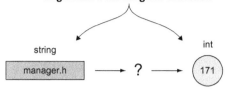

Simplifying the problem by analyzing
the needed transformation only for a
single item from the given collection

string   int

manager.h ⟶ ? ⟶ 171

Figure 1.6 You can perform the same transformation
on each element in a collection. This allows you to
look at the simpler problem of transforming a single
item instead of a collection of items.

Now, the main problem is to define a function that takes a filename and calculates the number of lines in the file represented by that filename. From this definition, it's clear that you're given one thing (the filename), but you need something else (the file's contents, so that you can count the newline characters). Therefore, you need a function that can give the contents of a file when provided with a filename. Whether the contents should be returned as a string, a file stream, or something else is up to you to decide. The code just needs to be able to provide one character at a time, so that you can pass it to the function that counts the newlines.

When you have the function that gives the contents of a file (`std::string` → `std::ifstream`), you can call the function that counts the lines on its result (`std::ifstream` → `int`). Composing these two functions by passing the `ifstream` created by the first as the input to the second gives the function you want (see figure 1.7).

You have one function that
takes the name of a file and
gives the contents.

The second function
just counts the number
of lines in its input.

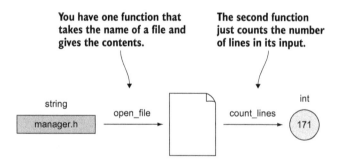

string   int

manager.h —open_file→ [file] —count_lines→ 171

Figure 1.7 You can decompose a bigger problem of counting
the number of lines in a file whose name you have into two
smaller problems: opening a file, given its name; and counting
the number of lines in a given file.

With this, you've solved the problem. You need to *lift* these two functions to be able to work not just on a single value, but on a collection of values. This is conceptually what `std::transform` does (with a more complicated API): it takes a function that can be applied to a single value and creates a transformation that can work on an entire collection of values (see figure 1.8). For the time being, think of *lifting* as a generic way to convert functions that operate on simple values of some type, to functions that work on more-complex data structures containing values of that type. Chapter 4 covers lifting in more detail.

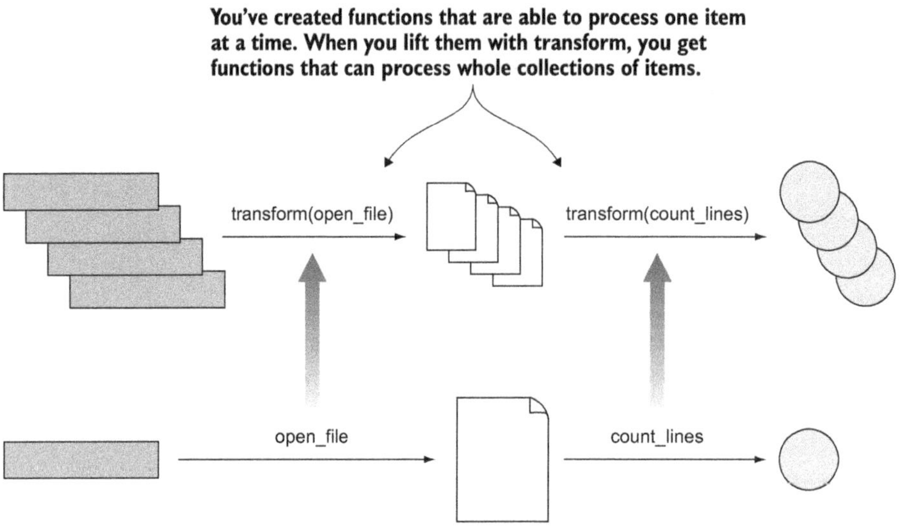

You've created functions that are able to process one item
at a time. When you lift them with transform, you get
functions that can process whole collections of items.

transform(open_file)   transform(count_lines)

open_file   count_lines

Figure 1.8 By using transform, **you can create functions that can process collections of
items from functions that can process only one item at a time.**

With this simple example, you've seen the functional approach to splitting bigger programming problems into smaller, independent tasks that are easily composed. One
useful analogy for thinking about function composition and lifting is a moving assembly line (see figure 1.9). At the beginning is the raw material from which the final
product will be made. This material goes through machines that transform it, and, in
the end, you get the final product. With an assembly line, you're thinking about the
transformations the product is going through instead of the steps the machine needs
to perform.

In this case, the raw material is the input you receive, and the machines are the functions applied to the input. Each function is highly specialized to do one simple task without concerning itself about the rest of the assembly line. Each function requires only
valid input; it doesn't care where that input comes from. The input items are placed on
the assembly line one by one (or you could have multiple assembly lines, which would
allow you to process multiple items in parallel). Each item is transformed, and you get a
collection of transformed items as a result.

1.4   *Benefits of functional programming*

Different aspects of FP provide different benefits. We'll cover them in due course, but
we'll start with a few primary benefits that most of these concepts aim to achieve.

The most obvious thing that most people notice when they start to implement programs in the functional style is that the code is much shorter. Some projects even have
official code annotations like "could have been one line in Haskell." This is because the
tools that FP provides are simple but highly expressive, and most functionality can be
implemented on a higher level without bothering with gritty details.

You have different transformations to apply one by one to the given input. This gives you a composition of all these transformation functions.

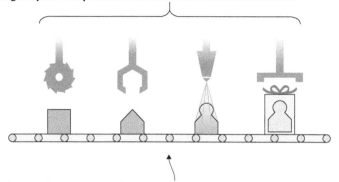

By placing multiple items onto the moving assembly line, you're lifting the composed transformation to work not only on a single value, but on a collection of values.

Figure 1.9   Function composition and lifting can be compared to a moving assembly line. Different transformations work on single items. By lifting these transformations to work on collections of items and composing them so that the result of one transformation is passed on to the next transformation, you get an assembly line that applies a series of transformations to as many items as you want.

This characteristic, combined with purity, has brought the FP style into the spotlight in recent years. Purity improves the correctness of the code, and expressiveness allows you to write less code (in which you might make mistakes).

1.4.1   *Code brevity and readability*

Functional programmers claim it's easier to understand programs written in the functional style. This is subjective, and people who are used to writing and reading imperative code may disagree. Objectively, it can be said that programs written in the functional style tend to be shorter and more concise. This was apparent in the earlier example: it started with 20 lines of code and ended up with a single line for `count_lines_in_files` and about 5 lines for `count_lines`, which mainly consisted of boilerplate imposed by C++ and STL. Achieving this was possible using higher-level abstractions provided by the FP parts of STL.

One unfortunate truth is that many C++ programmers stay away from using higher-level abstractions such as STL algorithms. They have various reasons, from being able to write more-efficient code manually, to avoiding writing code that their colleagues can't easily understand. These reasons are valid sometimes, but not in the majority of cases. Not availing yourself of more-advanced features of the programming language you're using reduces the power and expressiveness of the language and makes your code more complex and more difficult to maintain.

In 1987, Edsger Dijkstra published the paper "Go To Statement Considered Harmful." He advocated abandoning the GOTO statement, which was overused in that period, in favor of *structured programming* and using higher-level constructs including routines, loops, and `if-then-else` branching:

> The unbridled use of the go to statement has as an immediate consequence that it becomes terribly hard to find a meaningful set of coordinates in which to describe the process progress. ... The go to statement as it stands is just too primitive; it's too much an invitation to make a mess of one's program.[1]

In many cases, loops and branching are overly primitive. And just as with `GOTO`, loops and branching can make programs harder to write and understand and can often be replaced by higher-level FP constructs. We often write the same code in multiple places without even noticing that it's the same, because it works with different types or has behavior differences that could easily be factored out.

By using existing abstractions provided by STL or a third-party library, and by creating your own, you can make your code safer and shorter. But you'll also make it easier to expose bugs in those abstractions, because the same code will end up being used in multiple places.

1.4.2   Concurrency and synchronization

The main problem when developing concurrent systems is the shared mutable state. It requires you to pay extra attention to ensure that the components don't interfere with one another.

Parallelizing programs written with pure functions is trivial, because those functions don't mutate anything. There's no need for explicit synchronization with atomics or mutexes; you can run the code written for a single-threaded system on multiple threads with almost no changes. Chapter 12 covers this in more depth.

Consider the following code snippet, which sums the square roots of values in the xs vector:

```
std::vector<double> xs = {1.0, 2.0, ...};
auto result = sum(xs | transform(sqrt));
```

If the `sqrt` implementation is pure (there's no reason for it not to be), the implementation of the `sum` algorithm might automatically split the input into chunks and calculate partial sums for those chunks on separate threads. When all the threads finish, it would just need to collect the results and sum them.

Unfortunately, C++ doesn't (yet) have a notion of a pure function, so parallelization can't be performed automatically. Instead, you'd need to explicitly call the parallel version of the `sum` algorithm. The `sum` function might even be able to detect the number of CPU cores at runtime and use this information when deciding how many chunks to split the xs vector into. If you wrote the previous code with a `for` loop, you couldn't parallelize it as easily. You'd need to think about ensuring that variables weren't changed by different threads at the same time, and creating exactly the optimal number of threads

---

[1]   *Communications of the ACM* 11, no. 3 (March 1968).

for the system the program was running on, instead of leaving all that to the library providing the summing algorithm.

> **NOTE**   C++ compilers can sometimes perform automatic vectorization or other optimizations when they recognize that loop bodies are pure. This optimization also affects code that uses standard algorithms, because the standard algorithms are usually internally implemented with loops.

1.4.3   *Continuous optimization*

Using higher-level programming abstractions from STL or other trusted libraries carries another big benefit: your program will improve over time even if you don't change a single line. Every improvement in the programming language, the compiler implementation, or the implementation of the library you're using will improve the program as well. Although this is true for both functional and nonfunctional higher-level abstractions, FP concepts significantly increase the amount of code you can cover with those abstractions.

This seems like a no-brainer, but many programmers prefer to write low-level *performance-critical* code manually, sometimes even in assembly language. This approach can have benefits, but most of the time it just optimizes the code for a specific target platform and makes it borderline impossible for the compiler to optimize the code for another platform.

Let's consider the sum function. You might optimize it for a system that prefetches instructions by making the inner loop take two (or more) items in every iteration, instead of summing the numbers one by one. This would reduce the number of jumps in the code, so the CPU would prefetch the correct instructions more often. This would obviously improve performance for the target platform. But what if you ran the same program on a different platform? For some platforms, the original loop might be optimal; for others, it might be better to sum more items with every iteration of the loop. Some systems might even provide a CPU instruction that does exactly what the function needs.

By manually optimizing code this way, you miss the mark on all platforms but one. If you use higher-level abstractions, you're relying on other people to write optimized code. Most STL implementations provide specific optimizations for the platforms and compilers they're targeting.

1.5   *Evolution of C++ as a functional programming language*

C++ was born as an extension of the C programming language to allow programmers to write object-oriented code. (It was initially called "C with classes.") Even after its first standardized version (C++98), it was difficult to call the language *object-oriented*. With the introduction of templates into the language and the creation of STL, which only sparsely uses inheritance and virtual member functions, C++ became a proper multi-paradigm language.

Considering the design and implementation of STL, it can even be argued that C++ isn't primarily an object-oriented language, but a generic programming language. *Generic programming* is based on the idea that you can write code that uses general concepts and then apply it to any structure that fits those concepts. For example, STL provides the `vector` template that you can use over different types including ints, strings, and user types that satisfy certain preconditions. The compiler then generates optimized code for each of the specified types. This is usually called *static* or *compile-time polymorphism*, as opposed to the *dynamic* or *runtime polymorphism* provided by inheritance and virtual member functions.

For FP in C++, the importance of templates isn't (mainly) in the creation of container classes such as vectors, but in the fact that it allowed creation of STL algorithms—a set of common algorithm patterns such as sorting and counting. Most of these algorithms let you pass custom functions to customize the algorithms' behavior without resorting to function pointers and `void*`. This way, for example, you can change the sorting order, define which items should be included when counting, and so on.

The capability to pass functions as arguments to another function, and to have functions that return new functions (or, more precisely, things that *look* like functions, as we'll discuss in chapter 3), made even the first standardized version of C++ an FP language. C++11, C++14, and C++17 introduced quite a few features that make writing programs in the functional style much easier. The additional features are mostly syntactic sugar—but important syntactic sugar, in the form of the `auto` keyword and lambdas (discussed in chapter 3). These features also brought significant improvements to the set of standard algorithms. The next revision of the standard is planned for 2020, and it's expected to introduce even more FP-inspired features such as ranges, concepts, and coroutines, which are currently Technical Specifications.

ISO C++ standard evolution

The C++ programming language is an ISO standard. Every new version goes through a rigorous process before being released. The core language and the standard library are developed by a committee, so each new feature is discussed thoroughly and voted on before it becomes part of the final proposal for the new standard version. In the end, when all changes have been incorporated into the definition of the standard, it has to pass another vote—the final vote that happens for any new ISO standard.

Since 2012, the committee has separated its work into subgroups. Each group works on a specific language feature, and when the group deems it ready, it's delivered as a Technical Specification (TS). TSs are separate from the main standard and can later be incorporated into the standard.

The purpose of TSs is for developers to test new features and uncover kinks and bugs before the features are included in the main standard. The compiler vendors aren't required to implement TSs, but they usually do. You can find more information at https://isocpp.org/std/status.

Although most of the concepts we'll cover in this book can be used with older C++ versions, we'll mostly focus on C++14 and C++17.

1.6   *What you'll learn in this book*

This book is mainly aimed at experienced developers who use C++ every day and who want to add more-powerful tools to their toolbox. To get the most out of this book, you should be familiar with basic C++ features such as the C++ type system, references, const-ness, templates, operator overloading, and so on. You don't need to be familiar with the features introduced in C++14/17, which are covered in more detail in the book; these features aren't yet widely used, and it's likely that many readers won't be conversant with them.

We'll start with basic concepts such as higher-order functions, which allow you to increase the expressiveness of the language and make your programs shorter, and how to design software without mutable state to avoid the problems of explicit synchronization in concurrent software systems. After this, we'll switch to second gear and cover more-advanced topics such as ranges (the truly composable alternative to standard library algorithms) and algebraic data types (which you can use to reduce the number of states a program can be in). Finally, we'll discuss one of the most talked-about idioms in FP—the infamous *monad*—and how you can use various monads to implement complex, highly composable systems.

By the time you finish reading this book, you'll be able to design and implement safer concurrent systems that can scale horizontally without much effort, to implement the program state in a way that minimizes or even removes the possibility for the program to ever be in an invalid state due to an error or a bug, to think about software as a data flow and use the next big C++ thing—ranges—to define this data flow, and so on. With these skills, you'll be able to write terser, less error-prone code, even when you're working on object-oriented software systems. And if you take the full dive into the functional style, it'll help you design software systems in a cleaner, more composable way, as you'll see in chapter 13 when you implement a simple web service.

> **TIP** For more information and resources about the topics covered in this chapter, see https://forums.manning.com/posts/list/41680.page.

Summary

- The main philosophy of functional programming is that you shouldn't concern yourself with the way something should work, but rather with what it should *do*.
- Both approaches—functional programming and object-oriented programming—have a lot to offer. You should know when to use one, when to use the other, and when to combine them.
- C++ is a multiparadigm programming language you can use to write programs in various styles—procedural, object-oriented, and functional—and combine those styles with generic programming.

- Functional programming goes hand-in-hand with generic programming, especially in C++. They both inspire programmers not to think at the hardware level, but to move higher.
- Function lifting lets you create functions that operate on collections of values from functions that operate only on single values. With function composition, you can pass a value through a chain of transformations, and each transformation passes its result to the next.
- Avoiding mutable state improves the correctness of code and removes the need for mutexes in multithreaded code.
- Thinking functionally means thinking about the input data and the transformations you need to perform to get the desired output.

Getting started with functional programming

This chapter covers

- Understanding higher-order functions
- Using higher-order functions from the STL
- Problems with composability of STL algorithms
- Recursion and tail-call optimization
- The power of the folding algorithm

The previous chapter showed a few neat examples of how to improve your code by using simpler functional programming techniques. We focused on benefits such as greater code conciseness, correctness, and efficiency, but we haven't covered the special magic of functional programming languages that lets you write code in that manner.

The truth is, after you look behind the curtain, there's no magic—just simple concepts with big consequences. The first simple yet far-reaching concept we used in the previous chapter is the ability to pass one function as an argument to an algorithm from the Standard Template Library (STL). The algorithms in the STL are applicable to a multitude of problems mainly because you can customize their behavior.

2.1   *Functions taking functions?*

The main feature of all functional programming (FP) languages is that functions can be treated like ordinary values. They can be stored into variables, put into collections and structures, passed to other functions as arguments, and returned from other functions as results.

Functions that take other functions as arguments or that return new functions are called *higher-order functions*. They're probably the most important concept in FP. In the previous chapter, you saw how to make programs more concise and efficient by describing what the program should do on a higher level with the help of standard algorithms, instead of implementing everything by hand. Higher-order functions are indispensable for that task. They let you define abstract behaviors and more-complex control structures than those provided by the C++ programming language.

Let's illustrate this with an example. Imagine that you have a group of people, and need to write the names of all the females in the group (see figure 2.1).

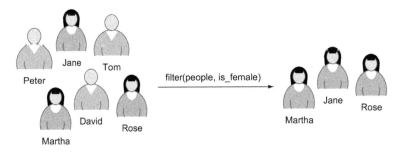

Figure 2.1   Filtering a collection of people based on the `is_female` predicate. It should return a new collection containing only females.

The first higher-level construct you could use here is collection filtering. Generally speaking, *filtering* is a simple algorithm that checks whether an item in the original collection satisfies a condition; if it does, the item is put into the result. The filtering algorithm can't know in advance what predicates users will use to filter their collections. Filtering could be done on a specific attribute (the example is filtering on a specific gender value), on multiple attributes at the same time (such as getting all females with black hair), or on a more complex condition (getting all females who recently bought a new car). So, this construct needs to provide a way for the user to specify the predicate. In this case, the construct needs to let you provide a predicate that takes a person and returns whether the person is female. Because filtering allows you to pass a predicate function to it, filtering is, by definition, a higher-order function.

More notation for specifying function types

When I want to denote an arbitrary collection containing items of a certain type T, I'll write collection<T> or just C<T>. To say that an argument for a function is another function, I'll write its type in the list of arguments.

The filter construct takes a collection and a predicate function (T → bool) as arguments, and it returns a collection of filtered items, so its type is written like this:

```
filter: (collection<T>, (T → bool)) → collection<T>
```

After the filtering is finished, you're left with the task of getting the names. You need a construct that takes a group of people and returns their names. Similar to filtering, this construct can't know in advance what information you want to collect from the original items. You might want to get a value of a specific attribute (the name, in this example), combine multiple attributes (perhaps fetch and concatenate both the first name and the surname), or do something more complex (get a list of children for each person). Again, the construct needs to allow the user to specify the function that takes an item from the collection, does something with it, and returns a value that will be put into the resulting collection (see figure 2.2).

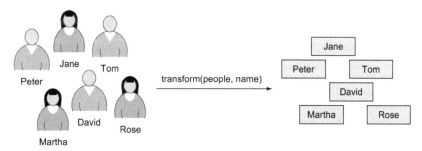

Figure 2.2   You have a collection of people. The transform algorithm should call the transformation function for each of them and collect the results. In this case, you're passing it a function that returns the name of a person. The transform algorithm collects the name of every person into a new collection.

Note that the output collection doesn't need to contain items of the same type as the input collection (unlike with filtering). This construct is called map or transform, and its type is as follows:

```
transform: (collection<In>, (In → Out)) → collection<Out>
```

When you compose these two constructs (see figure 2.3) by passing the result of one as the input for the other, you get the solution to the original problem: the names of all females in the given group of people.

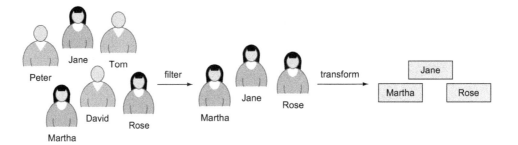

Figure 2.3   If you have one function that filters a collection of people to contain only females, and a second function that extracts the name of every person in a specified collection, you can compose the two functions into a function that gets the names of all females in a group of people.

Both `filter` and `transform` are common programming patterns that many programmers implement repeatedly in projects they work on. Small variations such as different filtering predicates—for example, filtering people based on gender or age—require writing the same code all over again. Higher-order functions allow you to factor out these differences and implement the general higher-level concept that's common to all of them. This also significantly improves code reuse and coverage.

2.2   Examples from the STL

The STL contains many higher-order functions disguised under the name *algorithms*. It provides efficient implementations of many common programming patterns. Using the standard algorithms instead of writing everything on a lower level with loops, branching, and recursion allows you to implement the program logic with less code and fewer bugs. We won't cover all higher-order functions that exist in the STL, but we'll look at a few interesting ones to pique your interest.

2.2.1   Calculating averages

Suppose you have a list of scores that website visitors have given a particular film, and you want to calculate the average. The imperative way of implementing this is to loop over all the scores, sum them one by one, and divide that sum by the total number of scores (see figure 2.4).

Listing 2.1   Calculating the average score imperatively

```
double average_score(const std::vector<int>& scores)
{
    int sum = 0;          ◀──── Initial value for summing

    for (int score : scores) {      ┌── Sums the scores
        sum += score;               │
    }

    return sum / (double)scores.size();   ◀──── Calculates the average score
}
```

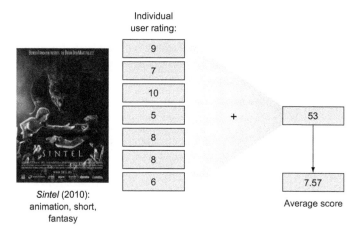

Figure 2.4 **Calculating the average score for a movie from a list of individual user ratings. You first sum all the individual ratings and then divide the sum by the number of users.**

Although this approach works, it's unnecessarily verbose. There are a few places where you might make a mistake such as using the wrong type while iterating over the collection, making a typo in the loop that would change the code semantics while still allowing it to compile, and so on. This code also defines an inherently serial implementation for summing, whereas summing can be easily parallelized and executed on multiple cores, or even on specialized hardware.

The STL provides a higher-order function that can sum all the items in a collection: the std::accumulate algorithm. It takes the collection (as a pair of iterators) and the initial value for summing, and it returns the sum of the initial value and all items in the collection. You just need to divide the sum by the total number of scores, as in the previous example. The following implementation doesn't specify how the summing should be performed—it states only what should be done. The implementation is as general as the problem presentation in figure 2.4.

Listing 2.2 **Calculating the average score functionally**

```
double average_score(const std::vector<int>& scores)
{
    return std::accumulate(
            scores.cbegin(), scores.cend(),      Sums all the scores in the collection
            0                                     Initial value for summing
    ) / (double)scores.size();                    Calculates the average score
}
```

Although the std::accumulate algorithm is also a serial implementation of summation, it would be trivial to replace it with a parallel version. On the other hand, making a parallelized version of the initial implementation would be nontrivial.

Parallel versions of standard algorithms

Since C++17, many STL algorithms let you specify that their execution should be parallelized. The algorithms that can be parallelized accept the execution policy as an additional argument. If you want the algorithm execution to be parallelized, you need to pass
it the `std::execution::par` policy. For more information on execution policies, check
out the C++ Reference entry at http://mng.bz/EBys.

The `std::accumulate` algorithm is special. It guarantees that the items in a collection
will be accumulated sequentially from the first to last, which makes it impossible to parallelize without changing its behavior. If you want to sum all elements but make the process parallelized, use the `std::reduce` algorithm:

```
double average_score(const std::vector<int>& scores)
{
    return std::reduce(
            std::execution::par,
            scores.cbegin(), scores.cend(),
            0
          ) / (double) scores.length();
}
```

If you have an older compiler and an STL implementation that doesn't fully support
C++17, you can find the `reduce` algorithm in the `std::experimental::parallel`
namespace, or you can use a third-party library like HPX or Parallel STL (see my article
"C++17 and Parallel Algorithms in STL—Setting Up" at http://mng.bz/8435).

But something is missing in listing 2.2. I said that the `std::accumulate` algorithm is a
higher-order function, yet you didn't pass it another function as an argument, nor did
it return a new function.

By default, `std::accumulate` sums the items, but you can provide it with a custom
function if you want to change that behavior. If you needed to calculate the product of
all the scores for some reason, you could pass `std::multiplies` as the last argument of
`std::accumulate` and set the initial value to 1, as shown in the next listing. We'll cover
function objects such as `std::multiplies` in detail in the next chapter. At this point,
it's only important to note that it takes two values of a certain type and returns their
product.

Listing 2.3 Calculating the product of all scores

```
double scores_product(const std::vector<int>& scores)
{
    return std::accumulate(                          ⟵ Calculates the product
            scores.cbegin(), scores.cend(),              of all the scores
            1,                          ⟵ Initial value for
            std::multiplies<int>()         calculating the product
        );
}
```

Multiplies the scores instead of summing → `std::multiplies<int>()`

Being able to sum a collection of integers with a single function call has its benefits, but it isn't that impressive if you limit yourself to calculating sums or products. On the other hand, replacing addition and multiplication with something more interesting *does* lead to impressive possibilities.

2.2.2 Folding

We often need to process a collection of items one item at a time, in order to calculate something. The result might be as simple as a sum or a product of all items in the collection (as in the previous examples), or a number of all items that have a specific value or that satisfy a predefined predicate. The result might also be something more complex, such as a new collection that contains only a part of the original (filtering), or a new collection with the original items reordered (for sorting or partitioning).

The std::accumulate algorithm is an implementation of a general concept called *folding* (or *reduction*). This is a higher-order function that abstracts the process of iterating over recursive structures such as vectors, lists, trees, and so on and lets you gradually build the result you need. In the previous example, you used folding to sum a collection of movie ratings. The std::accumulate algorithm first sums the initial value passed to it and the first item in the collection. That result is then summed with the next item in the collection, and so on. This is repeated until you reach the end of the collection (see figure 2.5).

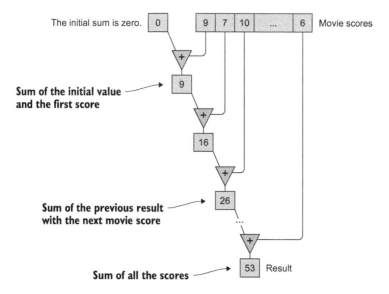

Figure 2.5 Folding calculates the sum of all movie scores in a collection by adding the first score to the initial value used for summation (zero), adding the second score to the previously calculated sum, and so on.

In general, folding doesn't require that the arguments and the result of the binary function passed to it have the same type. Folding takes a collection that contains items of type T, an initial value of type R (which doesn't need to be the same as T), and a function f: (R, T) → R. It calls the specified function on the initial value and the first item in the collection. The result is then passed to the function f along with the next item in the collection. This is repeated until all items from the collection are processed. The algorithm returns the value of type R: the value that the last invocation of function f returned (see figure 2.6). In the previous code example, the initial value was 0 (or 1 in the case of multiplication), and the binary function f was addition (or multiplication).

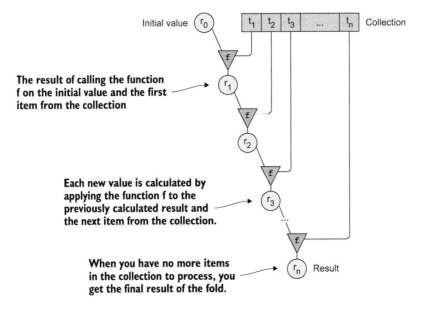

Figure 2.6   In general, folding takes the first element in a collection and applies the specified binary function f to it and the initial value for folding (r0); then it takes the second element from the collection and calls f on it and the previously calculated result. This is repeated until you get to the last item in the collection.

As a first example of when a function f might return a different type than the type of the items in the collection over which you're folding, you'll implement a simple function that counts the number of lines in a string by counting the number of occurrences of the newline character in it, using std::accumulate. As a reminder, you used std::count to do this in chapter 1.

From the requirements of the problem, you can deduce the type of the binary function f that you'll pass to the std::accumulate algorithm. std::string is a collection of characters, so type T will be char; and because the resulting number of newline characters is an integer, type R will be int. This means the type of the binary function f will be (int, char) → int.

You also know that the first time f is called, its first argument will be 0, because you're just starting to count. When it's invoked the last time, it should return the final count as the result. Moreover, because f doesn't know whether it's currently processing the first, the last, or any other random character in the string, it can't use the character position in its implementation. It knows only the *value* of the current character and the result that the previous call to f returned. This forces the meaning of the first argument of the binary function passed to std::accumulate to be *the number of newlines in the previously processed part of the string.* From this point on, the implementation is straightforward: if the current character isn't a newline, return the same value that was passed to you as the previous count; otherwise, increment that value and return it. A concrete example for this evaluation is shown in the following listing and figure 2.7.

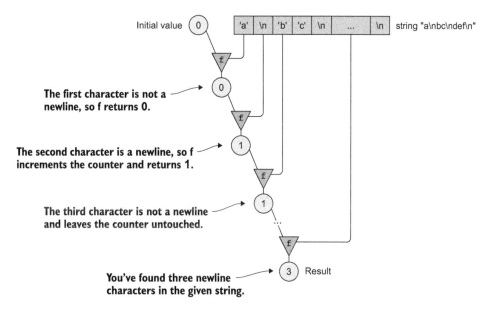

Figure 2.7   You can count the number of newline characters in a given string by folding a string with a simple function that increments the count each time it encounters a newline.

Listing 2.4   Counting newline characters with `std::accumulate`

```
int f(int previous_count, char c)
{
    return (c != '\n') ? previous_count           Increases the count if the current
                       : previous_count + 1;       character is a newline
}

int count_lines(const std::string& s)
{
    return std::accumulate(
            s.cbegin(), s.cend(),          Folds the entire string
            0,              Starts the count with 0
            f
        );
}
```

An alternative way to look at folding is to alter your perception of the binary function f passed to the `std::accumulate` algorithm. If you consider it to be a normal left-associative binary operator such as + that you can write in the infix notation, then folding is equivalent to putting this operator between every element in the collection. In the example of summing the movie scores, it would be equivalent to writing all the scores, one after the other, and putting + between them (see figure 2.8). This would be evaluated from left to right, just like the fold performed by `std::accumulate`.

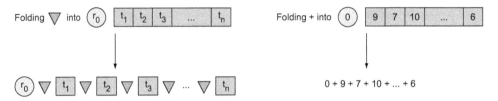

Figure 2.8   Folding on a left-associative operator is the same as writing all the items in the collection one after another, and putting the operator between them.

This type of folding—where you start processing the items from the first item—is called a *left fold*. There's also a *right fold*, where processing starts with the last element in a collection and moves toward the beginning. A right fold corresponds to the evaluation of the infix notation shown in figure 2.8 when the operator is right-associative (see figure 2.9). C++ doesn't provide a separate algorithm for right folding, but you could pass reverse iterators (`crbegin` and `crend`) to `std::accumulate` to achieve the same effect.

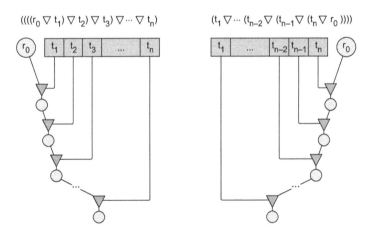

Figure 2.9   The main difference between left and right folding is that a left fold starts from the first element and moves toward the end of the collection, whereas a right fold starts at the end and moves toward the beginning.

Folding seems simple at first—summing a bunch of numbers in a collection. But when you accept the idea that addition can be replaced with an arbitrary binary operation that can even produce a result of a different type than the items in the collection, folding becomes a power tool for implementing many algorithms. You'll see another concrete example later in this chapter.

Associativity

An operator ∇ is left-associative if a ∇ b ∇ c = (a ∇ b) ∇ c, and right-associative if a ∇ b ∇ c = a ∇ (b ∇ c). Mathematically, addition and multiplication are both left- and right-associative—it doesn't matter whether you start multiplying arguments from the left or from the right. But in C++, addition and multiplication are specified as left-associative so that the language can guarantee the order of evaluation for the expression.

This still doesn't mean C++ guarantees the order of evaluation of the arguments in most cases; it just guarantees the order in which the operator will be applied to them. For example, in the expression a * b * c (where a, b, and c are nested expressions), you don't know which one will be evaluated first, but you know exactly the order in which the multiplication will be performed: the product of a and b will be multiplied by c.[a]

Most binary operators in C++ are left-associative (arithmetic, logical, comparison), whereas the assignment operators are right-associative (direct and compound assignments).

---

[a] C++17 does define the order of argument evaluation in some cases (see Gabriel Dos Reis, Herb Sutter, and Jonathan Caves, "Refining Expression Evaluation Order for Idiomatic C++," *open-std.org*, June 23, 2016, http://mng.bz/gO5J), but it leaves unspecified the order of argument evaluation for operators like summing and multiplication.

2.2.3 String trimming

Suppose you're given a string and need to strip the whitespace from its start and end. For example, you might want to read a line of text from a file and write it centered on the screen. If you kept the leading and trailing spaces, the text would appear misaligned.

STL doesn't have functions to remove the whitespace from the beginning and the end of a string. But it does provide algorithms you can use to implement something like this.

The algorithm you need is `std::find_if`. It searches for the first item in the collection that satisfies the specified predicate. In this case, you're going to search for the first character in the string that isn't whitespace. The algorithm returns the iterator pointing to the first element in the string that satisfies the predicate. It's sufficient to remove all elements from the beginning up to that element, thus stripping the whitespace from the start of the string:

```cpp
std::string trim_left(std::string s)
{
    s.erase(s.begin(),
            std::find_if(s.begin(), s.end(), is_not_space));
    return s;
}
```

As usual, the algorithm takes a pair of iterators to define the collection. If you pass it the reverse iterators, it'll search from the end toward the beginning of the string. This way, you can trim the whitespace from the right:

```
std::string trim_right(std::string s)
{
    s.erase(std::find_if(s.rbegin(), s.rend(), is_not_space).base(),
            s.end());
    return s;
}
```

Passing by value

In the previous example, it's better to pass the string by value instead of passing it as a const reference, because you're modifying it and returning the modified version. Otherwise, you'd need to create a local copy of the string inside the function. That might be slower if the user calls the function with a temporary value (rvalue) that will be copied instead of being moved into the function. The only downside of passing by value here is that if the copy constructor for the string throws an exception, the backtrace may be confusing to the user of the function.[b]

---

[b] For more information about copying and moving, see Alex Allain, "Move Semantics and rvalue References in C++11," *Cprogramming.com*, http://mng.bz/JULm.

Composing these two functions gives you the full trim function:

```
std::string trim(std::string s)
{
    return trim_left(trim_right(std::move(s)));
}
```

This example showed you a possible use for the std::find_if higher-order function. You used it to find the first non-whitespace character, searching from the start of the string and then from the end of the string. You also saw how a composition of two smaller functions (trim_left and trim_right) gives a function that solves the original problem.

2.2.4 *Partitioning collections based on a predicate*

Before we move on to something more involved, imagine that you have a collection of people, and your task is to move all females to the beginning of the collection. To do this, you can use the std::partition algorithm and its variant, std::stable_partition.

Both algorithms take a collection and a predicate. They reorder the items in the original collection so that the items that satisfy the specified predicate are separated from those that don't. The items that satisfy the predicate are moved to the beginning of the collection, and the items that don't are moved to the back. The algorithm returns an iterator to the first element in the second group (to the first element that doesn't satisfy the predicate). The returned iterator can be paired with the begin iterator of the original collection to provide a collection of elements that satisfy the predicate, or it can be paired with the end iterator of the original collection to provide a collection of all elements that don't satisfy the predicate. This is true even if any of these collections are empty.

The difference between these two algorithms is that `std::stable_partition` retains the ordering between elements from the same group. The following example uses `std::partition`—Rose ends up in front of Martha even though she was after her in the original list (see figure 2.10).

Listing 2.5   Females first

```
std::partition(
        people.begin(), people.end(),
        is_female
    );
```

Figure 2.10   Partitioning a group of people based on a predicate that checks whether a person is female. As the result, all females are moved to the start of the collection.

Although this example may seem contrived, imagine that you have a list of items in a UI. The user can select items and drag them to a specific place. If that place is the beginning of a list, you have a problem equivalent to the previous one; but instead of moving females to the beginning, you're moving selected items. If you need to move the selected items to the end, it's equivalent to moving those who aren't selected to the top.

If you need to move selected items to the middle of the list, you can split the list into the part above the destination point and the part below. Then, you have one list in which the selected items should go to the bottom and one list in which they should go to the top.

When users drag selected items, they expect the items' order to remain intact. The same is true for the items that aren't selected: moving a few items shouldn't arbitrarily change the order of the rest of the list. Thus you need to use the `std::stable_partition` algorithm instead of `std::partition`, even if the latter is more efficient (see figure 2.11).

Listing 2.6   Moving selected items to a specific point

```
std::stable_partition(first, destination, is_not_selected);
std::stable_partition(destination, last,  is_selected);
```

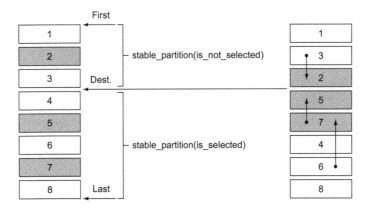

Figure 2.11   Moving selected items to a specified position with the help of `std::stable_partition`. **Selected items that are above the destination location should move down, and selected items that come after the destination location should move up.**

2.2.5   Filtering and transforming

Let's try to implement the problem from the beginning of this chapter by using STL algorithms. As a reminder, the task is to get the names of all females in a given group of people (see figure 2.12).

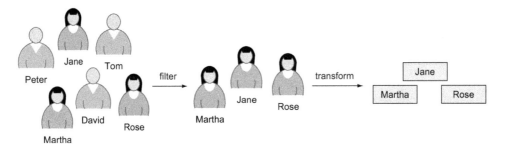

Figure 2.12   Getting the names of all females in a group

A person has the type `person_t`, and you'll use `std::vector` as the collection type. To make the implementation simpler, let's say `is_female`, `is_not_female`, and `name` are non-member functions:

```
bool is_female(const person_t& person);
bool is_not_female(const person_t& person);
std::string name(const person_t& person);
```

As you saw earlier, the first thing you need to do is filter the collection to get a vector that contains only females. You have two ways to achieve this using STL algorithms. If you're allowed to change the original collection, you can use the `std::remove_if` algorithm with the erase-remove idiom to remove all persons who aren't female.

Listing 2.7 Filtering items by removing undesired ones

```
people.erase(                                    ◄─────────── Removes the marked items
    std::remove_if(people.begin(), people.end(),
                   is_not_female),               ├─ Marks items for removal
    people.end());
```

The erase-remove idiom

If you want to use STL algorithms to remove from a collection elements that satisfy a predicate, or all elements that have a specific value, you can use `std::remove_if` and `std::remove`. Unfortunately, because these algorithms operate on a range of elements defined by a pair of iterators and don't know what the underlying collection is, they can't remove the elements from the collection. The algorithms only move all elements that don't satisfy the criteria for removal to the beginning of the collection.

Other elements are left in an unspecified state. The algorithm returns the iterator to the first of them (or to the end of the collection if no elements should be removed). You need to pass this iterator to the `.erase` member function of the collection, which performs the removal.

Alternatively, if you don't want to change the original collection—which should be the right way to go, because you aim to be as pure as possible—you can use the `std::-copy_if` algorithm to copy all the items that satisfy the predicate you're filtering on to the new collection. The algorithm requires you to pass it a pair of iterators that define the input collection: one iterator that points to the destination collection you want to copy the items to, and a predicate that returns whether a specific item should be copied. Because you don't know the number of females in advance (you can try to predict a number based on statistical data, but that's outside the scope of this example), you need to create an empty vector `females` and use `std::back_inserter(females)` as the destination iterator.

Listing 2.8 Filtering items by copying them to a new collection

```
std::vector<person_t> females;                   ◄─┤ Creates a new collection in which
                                                   │ to store the filtered items

std::copy_if(people.cbegin(), people.cend(),
             std::back_inserter(females),        ─┤ Copies the items that satisfy the
             is_female);                          │ condition to the new collection
```

The next step is to get the names of the people in the filtered collection. You can use `std::transform` to do this. You need to pass it the input collection as a pair of iterators, the transformation function, and where the results should be stored. In this case, you know that the number of names is the same as the number of females, so you can immediately create the names vector to be the size required to store the result and use `names.begin()` as the destination iterator instead of relying on `std::back_inserter`. This way, you'll eliminate the potential memory reallocations needed for vector resizing.

Listing 2.9   Getting the names

```
std::vector<std::string> names(females.size());

std::transform(females.cbegin(), females.cend(),        What you're transforming
               names.begin(),                           Where to store the results
               name);
                                                        Transformation function
```

You've split a larger problem into two smaller ones. This way, instead of creating one highly specialized function that will be of limited use, you create two separate, much more broadly applicable functions: one that filters a collection of people based on a predicate, and one that retrieves the names of people in a collection. The code reusability is thus much higher.

2.3 *Composability problems of STL algorithms*

The solution from the previous section is valid and will work correctly for any type of input collection that can be iterated on, from vectors and lists to sets, hash maps, and trees. It also shows the exact intent of the program: to copy all females from the input collection and then get their names.

Unfortunately, this approach isn't as efficient or simple as a handwritten loop:

```
std::vector<std::string> names;

for (const auto& person : people) {
    if (is_female(person)) {
        names.push_back(name(person));
    }
}
```

The STL-based implementation makes unnecessary copies of people (which might be an expensive operation or could even be disabled if the copy constructor was deleted or private), and it creates an additional vector that isn't needed. You could try to compensate for these problems by using references or pointers instead of copies, or by creating smart iterators that skip all persons who aren't females, and so on. But the need to do this extra work is a clear indication that STL loses in this case; the handwritten loop is better and requires less effort.

What went wrong? Recall the signatures for transform and filter. They're designed to be composable. You call one on the result of the other:

```
filter    : (collection<T>, (T → bool)) → collection<T>
transform : (collection<T>, (T → T2)) → collection<T2>

transform(filter(people, is_female), name)
```

The std::copy_if and std::transform algorithms don't fit into these types. They require the same basic elements, but in a significantly different manner. They take the input collection through a pair of input iterators, which makes it impossible to invoke them on a result of a function that returns a collection without first saving that result to a variable. And they don't return the transformed collection as the result of the algorithm call, but they require the iterator to the output collection to be passed in as the algorithm argument. The result of the algorithm is an output iterator to the element in the destination range, one past the last element stored:

```
OutputIt copy_if(InputIt first, InputIt last,
                 OutputIt destination_begin,
                 UnaryPredicate pred);

OutputIt transform(InputIt first, InputIt last,
                   OutputIt destination_begin,
                   UnaryOperation transformation);
```

This effectively kills the ability to compose these two algorithms without creating intermediary variables as you saw in the previous section.

Although this might seem like a design issue that shouldn't have happened, there are practical reasons behind these problems. First, passing a collection as a pair of iterators allows you to invoke the algorithm on parts of a collection instead of on the whole thing. Passing the output iterator as an argument instead of the algorithm returning the collection lets you have different collection structures for input and output. (For example, if you wanted to collect all the different female names, you might pass the iterator to a `std::set` as the output iterator.)

Even having the result of the algorithm as an iterator to the element in the destination range, one past the last element stored, has its merits. If you wanted to create an array of all people but order them such that females were first, followed by others (like `std::stable_partition`, but creating a new collection instead of changing the old one), it would be as simple as calling `std::copy_if` twice: once to copy all the females, and again to get everyone else. The first call would return the iterator to the place where you should start putting nonfemales.

Listing 2.10   Females first

```
std::vector<person_t> separated(people.size());

const auto last = std::copy_if(          ◄——┤ Returns the location after the
        people.cbegin(), people.cend(),       last person copied
        separated.begin(),
        is_female);

std::copy_if(
        people.cbegin(), people.cend(),
        last,          ◄——————————————————— Stores the rest after all the females
        is_not_female);
```

Although the standard algorithms provide a way to write code in a more functional manner than doing everything with handwritten loops and branches, they aren't designed to be composed in a way common to other FP libraries and languages. In chapter 7, you'll see a more composable approach that's used in the ranges library.

2.4   *Writing your own higher-order functions*

Many algorithms are implemented in the STL and freely available third-party libraries such as Boost, but you'll often need to implement something domain specific. Sometimes you need a specialized version of a standard algorithm, and other times you need to implement something from scratch.

2.4.1   *Receiving functions as arguments*

In the previous example, you wanted to get the names of all females in a collection. Suppose you have a collection of people and often need to get the names that satisfy a certain predicate, but you don't want to limit yourself to a predefined predicate such as is_female. You want to support any predicate that takes a person_t. The user might want to separate the people based on their age, hair color, marital status, and so on.

Creating a function that you could call multiple times would be useful. The function would need to accept a vector of people and a predicate function to be used for filtering, and it would return a vector of strings containing the names of people satisfying that predicate.

This example may seem overly specific. It would be much more useful if this function could work with any type of collection and any collected type so that it wasn't limited just to vectors of people. It would also be better if the function could extract any kind of data about a person, not just the name. You could make it more generic, but here you'll keep it simple in order to focus on what's important.

You know that you should pass the vector of people as a const reference, but what do you do with the function? You could use function pointers, but that would be overly limiting. In C++, many things can behave like functions, and you have no universal type that can hold any function-like thing without incurring performance penalties. Instead of trying to guess which type would be best, you can make the function type the template parameter and leave it up to the compiler to determine the exact type:

```
template <typename FilterFunction>
std::vector<std::string> names_for(
        const std::vector<person_t>& people,
        FilterFunction filter)
```

This will allow the user to pass in anything that can behave like a function, and you'll be able to call it as if it were an ordinary function. We'll cover everything that C++ considers function-like in the next chapter.

2.4.2   *Implementing with loops*

You've seen how you could implement the names_for function by using STL algorithms. Although you're advised to use STL algorithms whenever possible, this isn't an unbreakable rule. But if you do break it, you should have a good reason to do so, and you should be aware that you're opening yourself to the possibility of more bugs in your code. In this case, because using STL algorithms would incur unnecessary memory allocations, it might be smarter if you just implemented the previous example as a handwritten loop (see listing 2.11).

Ranges to the rescue

The issue of unnecessary memory allocation arises from the composability problem of STL algorithms. This problem has been known for some time, and a few libraries have been created to fix it.

Chapter 7 covers a concept called *ranges* in detail. Ranges are currently published as a Technical Specification and are planned for inclusion in C++20. Until ranges become part of the STL, they're available as a third-party library that can be used with most C++11-compatible compilers.

Ranges let you have your cake and eat it too, by creating composable smaller functions without any performance penalties.

Listing 2.11   Implementing the function by using a handwritten loop

```
template <typename FilterFunction>
std::vector<std::string> names_for(
        const std::vector<person_t>& people,
        FilterFunction filter)
{
    std::vector<std::string> result;

    for (const person_t& person : people) {
        if (filter(person)) {
            result.push_back(name(person));
        }
    }

    return result;
}
```

Implementing a function as simple as this one by using a handwritten loop isn't a huge issue. The names of the function and its parameters are sufficient to make it obvious what the loop does. Most STL algorithms are implemented as loops, just like this function.

If STL algorithms are implemented as loops, why is it a bad idea to implement everything with loops? Why bother learning STL at all?

There are several reasons. The first is simplicity. Using code that somebody else wrote saves time. This also leads to the second benefit: correctness. If you need to write the same thing over and over again, it's reasonable to expect that at some point you'll slip up and make a mistake. STL algorithms are thoroughly tested and will work correctly for any given input. This is the same reason you might implement frequently used functions with handwritten loops: they'll often be tested.

Although many STL algorithms aren't pure, they're built as higher-order functions, and this allows them to be more generic and thus applicable to more scenarios. And if something is used frequently, it's less likely to contain previously unseen bugs.

2.4.3   *Recursion and tail-call optimization*

The previous solution is pure from the outside, but its implementation isn't. It changes the result vector every time it finds a new person who matches the criteria. In pure FP languages, where loops don't exist, functions that iterate over collections are usually implemented using recursion. We won't dive too deeply into recursion, because you won't use it that often, but we need to cover a few important things.

You can process a non-empty vector recursively by first processing its *head* (the first element) and then processing its *tail* (all other elements), which can also be seen as a vector. If the head satisfies the predicate, you include it in the result. If you get an empty vector, there's nothing to process, so you also return an empty vector.

Suppose you have a `tail` function that takes a vector and returns its tail. You also have a `prepend` function that takes an element and a vector and returns a copy of the original vector, with the specified element prepended to it.

Listing 2.12   Naive recursive implementation

```
template <typename FilterFunction>
std::vector<std::string> names_for(
        const std::vector<person_t>& people,
        FilterFunction filter)
{
    if (people.empty()) {
        return {};                              ◄─── If the collection is empty,
                                                     returns an empty result

    } else {
        const auto head = people.front();
        const auto processed_tail = names_for(  ◄─── Calls the function recursively to
                tail(people),                        process the collection's tail
                filter);

        if (filter(head)) {                          ┐ If the first element
            return prepend(name(head), processed_tail); │ satisfies the predicate,
        } else {                                        │ includes it in the result.
            return processed_tail;                      ┘ Otherwise, skips it.
        }
    }
}
```

This implementation is inefficient. First, there's a reason a `tail` function for vectors doesn't exist: it would require creating a new vector and copying all the data from the old vector into it (other than the first element). The problem with the `tail` function can be remedied by using a pair of iterators instead of a vector as the input. In that case, getting the tail becomes trivial—you just have to move the iterator that points to the first element.

Listing 2.13   Recursive implementation

```
template <typename FilterFunction, typename Iterator>
std::vector<std::string> names_for(
        Iterator people_begin,
        Iterator people_end,
        FilterFunction filter)
```

```
{
        ...
        const auto processed_tail = names_for(
                people_begin + 1,
                people_end,
                filter);
        ...
}
```

The second issue in this implementation is that you're prepending items to the vector. You can't do much about that. You also had this situation in the handwritten loop, albeit with appending, which is more efficient than prepending when vectors are concerned.

The last and probably most important issue is that you can have problems if you call the function with a large collection of items. Every recursive call takes memory on the stack, and at some point the stack will overflow and the program will crash. Even if the collection isn't big enough to cause the stack to overflow, function calls aren't free; simple jumps to which a for loop is compiled are significantly faster.

Although the previous issues could be easily fixed, this one can't be. Here you need to rely on your compiler to transform the recursion into loops. And in order for the compiler to do so, you must implement a special form of recursion called *tail recursion*. With tail recursion, the recursive call is the last thing in the function: the function mustn't do anything after recursing.

In the previous example, the function isn't tail recursive because you're getting the result of the recursive call; and, in the case where filter(head) is true, you're adding an element to it and only then returning the result. Changing the function to be tail recursive isn't as trivial as the previous changes were. Because the function must return the final result, you must find another way to collect the intermediary results. You'll have to do it by using an additional argument that you'll pass from call to call.

Listing 2.14   Tail-recursive implementation

```
template <typename FilterFunction, typename Iterator>
std::vector<std::string> names_for_helper(
        Iterator people_begin,
        Iterator people_end,
        FilterFunction filter,
        std::vector<std::string> previously_collected)
{
    if (people_begin == people_end) {
        return previously_collected;

    } else {
        const auto head = *people_begin;

        if (filter(head)) {
            previously_collected.push_back(name(head));
        }
```

```
        return names_for_helper(
                people_begin + 1,
                people_end,
                filter,
                std::move(previously_collected));
    }
}
```

Now you're returning an already-calculated value or exactly what the inner recursive call returned to you. A minor issue is that you need to call this function with an additional argument. Because of this, it's named names_for_helper; the main function can be trivially implemented by calling the helper function and passing it an empty vector for the previously_collected parameter.

Listing 2.15   Calling the helper function

```
template <typename FilterFunction, typename Iterator>
std::vector<std::string> names_for(
        Iterator people_begin,
        Iterator people_end,
        FilterFunction filter)
{
    return names_for_helper(people_begin,
                            people_end,
                            filter,
                            {});
}
```

In this case, compilers that support tail-call optimization (TCO) will be able to convert the recursive function to a simple loop and make it as efficient as the code you started with (listing 2.11).

> **NOTE** The C++ standard makes no guarantees that tail-call optimization will be performed. But most modern compilers, including GCC, Clang, and MSVC, support this. They can even sometimes optimize mutually recursive calls (when function a calls function b, and b also calls a) and some functions that aren't strictly tail-recursive functions but are close enough.

Recursion is a powerful mechanism that lets you implement iterative algorithms in languages that don't have loops. But recursion is still a low-level construct. You can achieve true inner purity with it, but in many cases doing so makes no sense. I said that you want to be pure so you can make fewer mistakes while writing code, because you don't need to think about the mutable state. But by writing tail-recursive functions like the one in listing 2.14, you're simulating the mutable state and loops another way. It's a nice exercise for the gray cells, but not much more than that.

    Recursion, like handwritten loops, has its place in the world. But in most cases in C++, it should raise a red flag during code review. It needs to be checked for correctness and to be sure it covers all the use cases without overflowing the stack.

2.4.4 Implementing using folds

Because recursion is a low-level construct, implementing it manually is often avoided even in pure FP languages. Some may say that higher-level constructs are especially popular in FP exactly because recursion is so convoluted.

You've seen what folding is, but you still don't know its roots. *Folding* takes one element at a time and applies a specified function to the previously accumulated value and the currently processed element, thus producing a new accumulated value. If you read the previous section, you probably noticed that this is exactly what the tail-recursive implementation of the `names_for_helper` function did in listing 2.14. In essence, folding is nothing more than a nicer way to write tail-recursive functions that iterate over a collection. The common parts are abstracted out, and you need to specify only the collection, the starting value, and the essence of the accumulation process without having to write recursive functions.

If you wanted to implement the `names_for` function with folding (`std::accumulate`), it would be trivial now that you know how to do so in a tail-recursive way. You start with an empty vector of strings and append a new name if the person satisfies the predicate, and that's it.

> **Listing 2.16 Implementation using folding**

```
std::vector<std::string> append_name_if(
        std::vector<std::string> previously_collected,
        const person_t& person)
{
    if (filter(person)) {
        previously_collected.push_back(name(person));
    }
    return previously_collected;
}

...

return std::accumulate(
        people.cbegin(),
        people.cend(),
        std::vector<std::string>{},
        append_name_if);
```

> **Too many copies**
>
> If you run the function in listing 2.16 on a large collection, you'll see that it's slow. The reason is that `append_name_if` receives a vector by value, which induces a copy whenever `std::accumulate` calls `append_name_if` and passes it the value it accumulated so far.
>
> Always creating copies in this case is an unnecessary pessimization that will be fixed in C++20. Until then, you can roll your own variant of `std::accumulate`, which will trigger the C++ move semantics on the accumulated value instead of creating copies (just as `std::accumulate` will do in C++20). You can find the implementation of `moving_accumulate` in the examples that accompany this book.

Folding is a powerful concept. So far, you've seen that it's expressive enough to implement counting, transformation (or mapping), and filtering (the last example implemented a combination of `transform` and `filter`). Folding can be used to implement more than a few standard algorithms. It would be a nice exercise to implement algorithms such as `std::any_of`, `std::all_of`, and `std::find_if` by using `std::accumulate`; check whether these implementations are as fast as the original algorithms, and, if not, investigate why. Another algorithm that could serve as a great exercise to implement using `std::accumulate` is insertion sort.

> **TIP** For more information and resources about the topics covered in this chapter, see https://forums.manning.com/posts/list/41681.page.

Summary

- By passing specific predicate functions to algorithms such as `transform` and `filter`, you change their behavior and make a general algorithm work for a specific problem you have.
- The `std::accumulate` algorithm lives in the `<numeric>` header, but it's applicable to many more areas than just performing simple calculations.
- `std::accumulate` implements a concept called *folding* that isn't limited to addition and multiplication and can be used to implement many standard algorithms.
- If you don't want to change the order of selected elements in a list while dragging them, it's better to use the `std::stable_partition` algorithm instead of `std::partition`. Similarly, in a UI, `std::stable_sort` is often preferable to `std::sort`.
- Although STL algorithms are meant to be composed, they aren't meant to be composed the same way as algorithms in other functional programming languages. This will be easily remedied when you start using ranges.
- The fact that most standard algorithms are implemented as loops isn't a reason to use handwritten loops instead. In the same way, `while`, `if`, and others are implemented using `goto`s (jumps)—but you don't use `goto` statements, because you know better.

Function objects

You saw how to create functions that can accept other functions as their arguments
in the previous chapter. Now you'll check out the other side of the coin—to see all
the things that you can use as functions in C++. This topic is a bit dry, but it's necessary for the deeper understanding of functions in C++ and for achieving that sweet
spot of using higher-level abstractions without incurring performance penalties. If
you want to be able to use all the power that C++ gives you during your functional
programming adventures, you need to know all the things that C++ can treat as
functions—and which of them to prefer, and which of them to avoid.

Using *duck-typing* (if it walks like a duck and quacks like a duck, it's a duck), we can say that anything that can be called like a function is a function object. Namely, if we can write the name of an entity followed by arguments in parentheses, such as f(arg1, arg2, …, argn), that entity is a function object. We'll cover all the things that C++ considers to be function objects in this chapter.

> **DEFINITION**   To differentiate between ordinary C++ functions and all the things that can be used as functions, I'll call the latter *function objects* when I want to make an explicit distinction.

3.1   *Functions and function objects*

A *function* is a named group of statements that can be invoked from other parts of the program or from the function itself in the case of recursive functions. C++ provides several slightly different ways to define a function:

```
int max(int arg1, int arg2) { … }          ◄──────┘ Old C-like syntax

auto max(int arg1, int arg2) -> int { … }        ◄──────┘ With a trailing return type
```

Although some people prefer to write functions with the trailing return type even when it isn't necessary, this isn't a common practice. This syntax is mainly useful when writing function templates in which the return type depends on the types of the arguments.

Trailing return type definition

In the previous code snippet, it doesn't matter whether the return type is specified before the function name and its arguments, or after. Specifying the return type after the function name and the arguments is required when you're writing a function template and need to deduce the return type based on the types of the arguments.

Some people prefer to always use the trailing return type because they consider it to be much less important than the function name and its arguments and think it should therefore come after. Although this notion is valid, the traditional approach is still omnipresent.

3.1.1   *Automatic return type deduction*

Since C++14, we've been allowed to omit the return type and rely on the compiler to deduce it automatically from the expression in the return statement. The type deduction in this case follows the rules of template-argument deduction.

The following example has an integer named answer and two functions ask1 and ask2. Both functions have the same body; they return answer. But their return types are specified differently. The first function returns a value whose type is automatically deduced, and the second function returns a const-ref to a type that's automatically

deduced. The compiler will check the type of the variable you pass to the return statement, which is int, and replace the keyword auto with it:

```
int answer = 42;
auto ask1() { return answer; }          Return type is int
const auto& ask2() { return answer; }    Return type is const int&
```

Although the template-argument deduction (and therefore the return type deduction) rules are more complex than just *replace the auto keyword with a type*, they behave
intuitively, and I don't cover them here.[1]

In the case of functions with multiple return statements, all of them need to return
results of the same type. If the types differ, the compiler will report an error. In the following snippet, you have a function that takes a bool flag and, depending on the value
of that flag, returns an int or a std::string. The compiler will complain that it first
deduced the return type to be an integer and that the second return statement returns
a different type:

```
auto ask(bool flag)
{
    if (flag) return 42;
    else      return std::string("42");     Error: inconsistent deduction for
}                                            'auto': 'int' and then 'std::string'
```

After the return type is deduced, it can be used in the rest of the function. This lets you
write recursive functions with automatic return type deduction, as shown next:

```
auto factorial(int n)
{
    if (n == 0) {                Deduces the return
        return 1;                type to be int
    } else {                                      You know factorial returns an
        return factorial(n - 1) * n;             int, and multiplying two ints
    }                                            returns an int, so you're OK.
}
```

Swapping the if and else branches would result in an error because the compiler
would arrive at the recursive call to factorial before the return type of the function
was deduced. When writing recursive functions, you need to either specify the return
type or first write the return statements that don't recurse.

As an alternative to auto, which uses the template argument type deduction rules for
the resulting type, it's also possible to use decltype(auto) as the return type specification. In that case, the function return type will be decltype of the returned expression:

```
Returns an
int: decltype(answer)

    decltype(auto) ask() { return answer; }
    decltype(auto) ask() { return (answer); }       Returns a reference to int:
    decltype(auto) ask() { return 42 + answer; }    decltype( (answer) ), whereas
                                                    auto would deduce just int

                                                    Returns an
                                                    int: decltype(42 + answer)
```

---

[1] You can find a detailed explanation of template argument deduction rules in the C++ reference:
http://mng.bz/YXIU.

This is useful when you're writing generic functions that forward the result of another function without modifying it. In this case, you don't know in advance what function will be passed to you, and you can't know whether you should pass its result back to the caller as a value or as a reference. If you pass it as a reference, it might return a reference to a temporary value that will produce undefined behavior. And if you pass it as a value, it might make an unnecessary copy of the result. Copying will have performance penalties and is sometimes semantically wrong—the caller may expect a reference to an existing object.

If you want to perfectly forward the result (to return the result returned to you without any modifications), you can use `decltype(auto)` as the specification of the return type:

```
template <typename Object, typename Function>
decltype(auto) call_on_object(Object&& object, Function function)
{
    return function(std::forward<Object>(object));
}
```

In this code snippet, you have a simple function template that takes an object, and a function that should be invoked on that object. You're perfectly forwarding the `object` argument to the `function`; and by using `decltype(auto)` as the return type, you're perfectly forwarding the result of the `function` back to your caller.

PERFECT FORWARDING FOR ARGUMENTS

You sometimes need to write a function that wraps in another function. The only thing it should do is call the wrapped function with some arguments modified, added, or removed. In that case, you have the problem of how to pass the arguments from the wrapper to the function you need to call.

If you have the same setup as in the previous snippet, the user is passing you a function you know nothing about. You don't know how it expects you to pass it the argument.

The first option is to make your `call_on_object` function accept the `object` argument by value and pass it on to the wrapped function. This will lead to problems if the wrapped function accepts a reference to the object, because it needs to change that object. The change won't be visible outside the `call_on_object` function because it'll be performed on the local copy of the object that exists only in the `call_on_object` function:

```
template <typename Object, typename Function>
decltype(auto) call_on_object(Object object,
                              Function function)
{
    return function(object);
}
```

The second option is to pass the object by reference. This would make the changes to the `object` visible to the caller of your function. But you'll have a problem if `function` doesn't actually change the `object` but accepts the argument as a const-reference. The caller won't be able to invoke `call_on_object` on a constant object or a temporary value. The idea to accept the object as an ordinary reference still isn't right. And you can't make that reference const, because the `function` may want to change the original `object`.

Some pre-C++11 libraries approached this problem by creating overloads for both const and non-const references. This isn't practical because the number of overloads grows exponentially with the number of arguments that need to be forwarded.

This is solved in C++11 with *forwarding references* (formerly known as *universal references*[2]). A forwarding reference is written as a *double reference* on a templated type. In the following code, the fwd argument is a forwarding reference to type T, whereas value isn't (it's a normal *rvalue* reference):

```
template <typename T>
void f(T&& fwd, int&& value) { … }
```

The forwarding reference allows you to accept both const and non-const objects, and temporaries. Now you only need to pass that argument, and pass it in the same value category as you've received it, which is exactly what std::forward does.

3.1.2 Function pointers

A *function pointer* is a variable that stores the address of a function that can later be called through that pointer. C++ inherited this low-level construct from the C programming language to allow polymorphic code. The (runtime) polymorphism is achieved by changing which function the pointer points to, thus changing the behavior when that function pointer is called.

Function pointers (and references) are also function objects, because they can be called like ordinary functions. Additionally, all types that can be implicitly converted to a function pointer are also function objects, but this should be avoided. You should prefer proper function objects (which you'll see in a few moments) because they're more powerful and easier to deal with. Objects that can be converted to function pointers can be useful when you need to interface with a C library that takes a function pointer and you need to pass it something more complex than a simple function.

The following example demonstrates calling function pointers, function references, and objects convertible to function pointers:

```
int ask() { return 42; }

typedef decltype(ask)* function_ptr;

class convertible_to_function_ptr {
public:
    operator function_ptr() const
    {
        return ask;
    }
};
```

The casting operator can return only a pointer to a function. Although it can return different functions depending on certain conditions, it can't pass any data to them (without resorting to dirty tricks).

```
int main(int argc, char* argv[])
{
    auto ask_ptr = &ask;
    std::cout << ask_ptr() << '\n';
```

Pointer to the function

---

2 As named by Scott Meyers in "Universal References in C++11," *Standard C++ Foundation*, Nov. 1, 2012, http://mng.bz/Z7nj.

```
auto& ask_ref = ask;
std::cout << ask_ref() << '\n';
```
⊢───── **Reference to the function**

```
convertible_to_function_ptr ask_wrapper;
std::cout << ask_wrapper() << '\n';
```
⊢───── **Object that can be implicitly converted to a function pointer**
```
}
```

This example demonstrates that you can create a function pointer (ask_ptr) that points to an ordinary function, and a function reference (ask_ref) that references the same function, and that you can call them as if they were functions themselves—with the usual function call syntax. It also demonstrates that you can create an object that's convertible to a function pointer and call that object as if it were a normal function without any complications.

3.1.3   *Call operator overloading*

Instead of creating types that can be implicitly converted to function pointers, C++ provides a much nicer way to create new types that behave like functions: by creating classes and overloading their call operators. Unlike other operators, a *call operator* can have an arbitrary number of arguments, and the arguments can have any type, so you can create a function object of any signature you like.

The syntax for overriding the call operator is as simple as defining a member function—just with a special name of operator(). You specify the return type and all the arguments the function needs:

```
class function_object {
public:
    return_type operator()(arguments) const
    {
        ...
    }
};
```

These function objects have one advantage compared to the ordinary functions: each instance can have its own state, whether mutable or not. The state is used to customize the behavior of the function without the caller having to specify it.

Say you have a list of people, as in the examples from the previous chapter. Each person has a name, an age, and a few characteristics you don't care about at the moment. You want to allow the user to count the number of people who are older than a specified age (see figure 3.1).

If the age limit was fixed, you could create an ordinary function to check whether the person was older than that predefined value:

```
bool older_than_42(const person_t& person)
{
    return person.age > 42;
}

std::count_if(persons.cbegin(), persons.cend(),
              older_than_42);
```

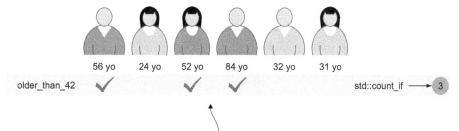

The older_than_42 predicate returns true
for people who are older than 42 years, and
the std::count_if algorithm will count them.

Figure 3.1 You can use an ordinary function that checks whether a person is more than
42 years old when you want to count the number of people over that age limit. But with this
approach, you have the ability to check the age against a single predefined value.

This solution isn't scalable because you'd need to create separate functions for all age
limits you needed or use an error-prone hack, such as saving the age limit you were
currently testing against in a global variable.

Instead, it's much wiser to create a proper function object that keeps the age limit
as its inner state. This will allow you to write the implementation of the predicate only
once and instantiate it several times for different age limits:

```
class older_than {
public:
    older_than(int limit)
        : m_limit(limit)
    {
    }

    bool operator()(const person_t& person) const
    {
        return person.age() > m_limit;
    }

private:
    int m_limit;
};
```

You can now define multiple variables of this type and use them as functions:

```
older_than older_than_42(42);
older_than older_than_14(14);

if (older_than_42(person)) {
    std::cout << person.name() << " is more than 42 years old\n";
} else if (older_than_14(person)) {
    std::cout << person.name() << " is more than 14 years old\n";
} else {
    std::cout << person.name() << " is 14 years old, or younger\n";
}
```

DEFINITION   Classes with the overloaded call operator are often called *functors*. This term is highly problematic because it's already used for something different in category theory. Although we could ignore this fact, category theory is important for functional programming (and programming in general), so I'll keep calling them *function objects*.

The `std::count_if` algorithm doesn't care what you've passed to it as a predicate function, as long as it can be invoked as a normal function—and by overloading the call operator, you do just that:

```
std::count_if(persons.cbegin(), persons.cend(),
        older_than(42));
std::count_if(persons.cbegin(), persons.cend(),
        older_than(16));
```

You're relying on the fact that function templates such as `std::count_if` don't require arguments of specific types to be passed to them. They require only that the argument has all the features needed by the function template implementation. In this case, `std::count_if` requires the first two arguments to behave as forward iterators and the third argument to behave as a function. Some people call this a *weakly typed* part of C++, but that's a misnomer. This is still strongly typed; it's just that templates use duck-typing. There are no runtime checks of whether the type is a function object; all the needed checks are performed at compile-time.

3.1.4   *Creating generic function objects*

In the previous example, you created a function object that checks whether a person is older than a predefined age limit. This solved the problem of needing to create different functions for different age limits, but it's still overly restrictive: it accepts only persons as input.

Quite a few types could include age information—from concrete things like cars and pets to more abstract ones like software projects. If you wanted to count the number of cars that were older than 5 years (see figure 3.2), you couldn't use the preceding function object because it's defined only for people.

Again, instead of writing a different function object for each type, you want to be able to write the function object once and use it for any type that has the age information. You could solve this in an object-oriented way by creating a superclass with a virtual `.age()` member function, but that approach would have runtime performance penalties and would force all the classes that want to support the `older_than` function object to inherit from that superclass. This ruins encapsulation, so we won't bother with it.

The first valid approach you could take would be to turn the `older_than` class into a class template. It would be templated on the type of the object whose age you want to check:

```
template <typename T>
class older_than {
public:
    older_than(int limit)
```

```
        : m_limit(limit)
    {
    }

    bool operator()(const T& object) const
    {
        return object.age() > m_limit;
    }

private:
    int m_limit;
};
```

You can use `older_than` for any type that has the `.age()` getter:

```
std::count_if(persons.cbegin(), persons.cend(),
              older_than<person_t>(42));
std::count_if(cars.cbegin(), cars.cend(),
              older_than<car_t>(5));
std::count_if(projects.cbegin(), projects.cend(),
              older_than<project_t>(2));
```

Unfortunately, this approach forces you to specify the type of the object whose age you want to check when you instantiate the function object. Although this is sometimes useful, in most cases it's tedious. It might also lead to problems if the specified type didn't exactly match the type passed to the call operator.

Instead of creating the class template, you can make the call operator a template member function, as shown in the following listing (and found in the book's sample code in example:older-than-generic/main.cpp). This way, you won't need to specify the type when you instantiate the `older_than` function object, and the compiler will automatically deduce the type of the argument when invoking the call operator.

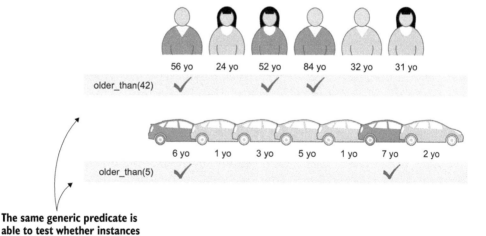

The same generic predicate is able to test whether instances of different types are above that required age limit.

Figure 3.2 When creating the predicate, it's useful not only to allow the specification of different age limits, but also to support different types that have the age information.

Listing 3.1   Creating a function object with a generic call operator

```
class older_than {
public:
    older_than(int limit)
        : m_limit(limit)
    {
    }

    template <typename T>
    bool operator()(T&& object) const
    {
        return std::forward<T>(object).age() > m_limit;
    }

private:
    int m_limit;
};
```

You forward the object because it can have separate overloads on the age member function for lvalue and rvalue instances. This way, the correct overload will be called.

You can now use the older_than function object without explicitly stating the type of the object you'll be calling it on. You can even use the same object instance for different types (if you want to check all objects against the same age limit):

Listing 3.2   Using a function object with a generic call operator

```
older_than predicate(5);

std::count_if(persons.cbegin(), persons.cend(), predicate);
std::count_if(cars.cbegin(), cars.cend(), predicate);
std::count_if(projects.cbegin(), projects.cend(), predicate);
```

A single instance of the older_than type checks whether the age of the object passed to it is greater than 5. The same instance implements this check for any type that has the .age() member function that returns an integer or something comparable to an integer. You've created a proper generic function object.

So far, you've seen how to write different types of function objects in C++. Function objects like these are perfect for passing to the algorithms from the standard library or to your own higher-order functions. The only problem is that their syntax is a bit verbose and that you need to define them outside the scope you're using them in.

3.2   *Lambdas and closures*

The previous examples have relied on the fact that the function you pass to the algorithm already exists outside the function you're using the algorithm in. Having to write a proper function, or even a whole class, is sometimes tedious, just to be able to call an algorithm from the standard library or some other higher-order function. It can also be seen as bad software design, because you're forced to create and name a function that may not be useful to anyone else and is used in only one place in the program: as an argument to an algorithm call.

Fortunately, C++ has *lambdas,* which are syntactic sugar for creating anonymous (unnamed) function objects. Lambdas allow you to create function objects inline—at the place where you want to use them—instead of outside the function you're currently writing. Let's see this in an example from earlier: you have a group of people, and you want to collect only females from that group (see figure 3.3).

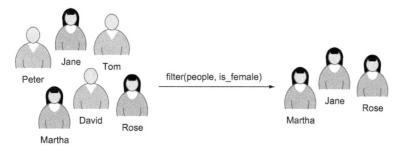

Figure 3.3 Getting all females from a group of people. You've been using a predicate called is_female, which is a non-member function for this. Now you're going to do the same with a lambda.

In chapter 2, you saw how to use `std::copy_if` to filter a collection of people based on their gender. You relied on the fact that the function `is_female` exists as a non-member function that accepts a `person_t` and returns `true` if that person is female. Because the `person_t` type has a member function that returns its gender, it's overkill to have to define non-member predicate functions for all the possible genders, just to be able to use those predicates when calling an STL algorithm.

Instead, you can use a lambda to achieve the same effect while keeping the code localized and not polluting the program namespace:

```
std::copy_if(people.cbegin(), people.cend(),
        std::back_inserter(females),
        [](const person_t& person) {
            return person.gender() == person_t::female;
        }
    );
```

You call `std::copy_if` just as in the original example. But instead of passing an existing predicate function, you tell the compiler to create an anonymous function object that's used only here—a function that takes a constant reference to a person and returns whether that person is a female—and to pass that function object to the `std::copy_if` algorithm.

3.2.1 Lambda syntax

Syntactically, lambda expressions in C++ have three main parts—a head, an argument list, and the body:

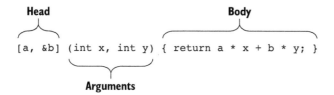

The head of the lambda specifies which variables from the surrounding scope will be visible inside the lambda body. The variables can be captured as values (the variable a in the preceding snippet), or by references (specified by prefixing the variable name with an ampersand—variable b in the preceding snippet). If the variables are passed in as values, their copies will be stored inside the lambda object itself, whereas if they're passed in as references, only a reference to the original variable will be stored.

You're also allowed to not specify all the variables that need to be captured, but to tell the compiler to capture all variables from the outer scope that are used in the body. If you want to capture all variables by value, you can define the lambda head to be [=], and if you want to catch them by reference, you can write [&].

Let's see a few examples of lambda heads:

- [a, &b]—Lambda head from the previous example; a is captured by value, and b is by reference.
- []—A lambda that doesn't use any variable from the surrounding scope. These lambdas don't have any internal state and can be implicitly cast to ordinary function pointers.
- [&]—Captures all variables that are used in the lambda body by reference.
- [=]—Captures all variables that are used in the lambda body by value.
- [this]—Captures the this pointer by value.
- [&, a]—Captures all variables by reference, except a, which is captured by value.
- [=, &b]—Captures all variables by value, except b, which is captured by reference.

Explicitly enlisting all the variables that need to be used in the lambda body and not using *wildcards* such as [&] and [=] may be tedious but is the preferred approach when creating lambdas because it stops you from accidentally using a variable that you didn't intend to use. (The usual problem is the this pointer, because you might use it implicitly by accessing a class member or by calling a class member function.)

3.2.2   *Under the hood of lambdas*

Although lambdas do provide a nice inline syntax to create function objects, they aren't magic. They can't do anything you weren't able to do without them. They are just that—a nicer syntax to create and instantiate a new function object.

Let's see this in an example. You're still going to work with a list of people, but this time they'll be employees in a company. The company is separated into teams, and each team has a name. You're going to represent a company by using a simple compa-ny_t class. This class will have a member function to get the name of the team that each employee belongs to. Your task is to implement a member function that will accept the team name and return the number of employees it contains. Here's the setup:

```
class company_t {
public:
    std::string team_name_for(const person_t& employee) const;

    int count_team_members(const std::string& team_name) const;
```

```
private:
    std::vector<person_t> m_employees;
    ...
};
```

You need to implement the `count_team_members` member function. You can do it by checking which team each employee belongs to, and counting only those whose team matches the function arguments (figure 3.4).

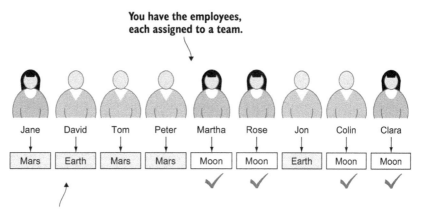

You have the employees, each assigned to a team.

The lambda checks the team name for an employee to see whether it's the same team whose employees you're asked to count.

Figure 3.4 You're passing a lambda as a predicate to the `std::count_if` algorithm. The lambda receives a single employee and checks whether a person belongs to the team you're checking the count for. The `std::count_if` algorithm will count all the yeses and return the answer.

As before, you'll use `std::count_if`, but you'll pass a more-complicated lambda as the predicate function (see example:counting-team-members/main.cpp).

Listing 3.3 Counting the number of employees in a given team

```
int company_t::count_team_members(
        const std::string& team_name) const
{
    return std::count_if(
            m_employees.cbegin(), m_employees.cend(),
            [this, &team_name]
                (const person_t& employee)
            {
                return team_name_for(employee) ==
                    team_name;
            }
        );
}
```

You need to capture "this" because you're implicitly using it when calling the team_name_for member function, and you've captured team_name because you need to use it for comparison.

As before, this function object has only one argument: an employee. You'll return whether they belong to the specified team.

What happens in C++ when you write this? When compiled, the lambda expression will turn into a new class that has two member variables—a pointer to the `company_t` object and a reference to a `std::string`—one member for each captured variable. This class will have the call operator with the same arguments and the same body of the lambda. You'll get a class equivalent to the following.

Listing 3.4 Lambda converted to a class

```
class lambda_implementation {
public:
    lambda_implementation(
            const company_t* _this,
            const std::string& team_name)
        : m_this(_this)
        , m_team_name(team_name)
    {
    }

    bool operator()(const person_t& employee) const
    {
        return m_this->team_name_for(employee) == m_team_name;
    }

private:
    const company_t* m_this;
    const std::string& m_team_name;
};
```

In addition to creating a class, evaluating the lambda expression also creates an instance of that class called a *closure*: an object containing some state or environment along with code that should be executed on that state.

One thing worth noting is that the call operator of lambdas is constant by default (contrary to the other parts of the language, where you need to explicitly specify that something is `const`). If you want to change the value of the captured variables, when they're captured by value and not by reference, you'll need to declare the lambda as `mutable`. In the following example, you use the `std::for_each` algorithm to write all words beginning with an uppercase letter, and you use the `count` variable to count the number of words you wrote. This is sometimes useful for debugging, but mutable lambdas should be avoided. Obviously, there are better ways to do this, but the point here is to demonstrate how mutable lambdas work.

Listing 3.5 Creating a mutable lambda

```
int count = 0;
std::vector<std::string> words{"An", "ancient", "pond"};

std::for_each(words.cbegin(), words.cend(),
        [count]
        (const std::string& word)
        mutable
        {
            if (isupper(word[0])) {
                std::cout << word
                    << " " << count <<std::endl;
```

You're capturing "count" by value; all changes to it are localized and visible only from the lambda.

mutable comes after the argument list and tells the compiler that the call operator on this lambda shouldn't be const.

```
                count++;
            }
        }
    );
```

Lambdas don't allow you to do anything that you weren't able to do before. But they do free you from writing too much boilerplate code and allow you to keep the logic of your code localized instead of forcing you to create functions or function objects outside the function in which they're used. In these examples, the boilerplate code would be larger than the code that does something useful.

> **NOTE** When a lambda is created, the compiler creates a class with a call operator and gives that class an internal name. That name isn't accessible to the programmer, and different compilers give it different names. The only way to save a lambda (without excess baggage of the `std::function` that you'll see in a moment) is to declare the variable by using `auto`.

3.2.3 *Creating arbitrary member variables in lambdas*

So far, you've created lambdas that can access the variables from the surrounding scope by either storing the references to the used variables or storing the copies of them inside of the closure object. On the other hand, by writing your own classes with the call operator, you're able to create as many member variables as you want, without needing to tie them to a variable in the surrounding scope. You can initialize them to a fixed value or initialize them to a result of a function call. Although this might sound like it isn't a big deal (you could always declare a local variable with the desired value before creating the lambda, and then capture it), in some cases it's essential.

If you had the ability to only capture objects by value or by reference, you wouldn't be able to store objects that are move-only inside a lambda (instances of classes that define the move constructor, but that don't have the copy constructor). The most obvious example of this issue arises when you want to give the ownership of a `std::unique_ptr` to a lambda.

Say you want to create a network request, and you have the session data stored in a unique pointer. You're creating a network request and scheduling a lambda to be executed when that request is completed. You still want to be able to access the session data in the completion handler, so you need to capture it in the lambda.

Listing 3.6 Error when trying to capture a move-only type

```
std::unique_ptr<session_t> session = create_session();

auto request = server.request("GET /", session->id());

request.on_completed(                      Error: there's no copy-constructor
        [session]          ◀──────────────  for std::unique_ptr<session_t>.
        (response_t response)
        {
            std::cout << "Got response: " << response
                      << " for session: " << session;
        }
    );
```

In cases like these, you can use the extended syntax (generalized lambda captures). Instead of specifying which variables you want to capture, you can define arbitrary member variables by specifying the variable name and its initial value separately. The type of the variable is automatically deduced from the specified value.

Listing 3.7 Generalized lambda captures

```
request.on_completed(
        [ session = std::move(session),              Moves the ownership of
          time = current_time()                      session into the lambda
        ]
        (response_t response)          Creates a time lambda
        {                              member variable and sets
            std::cout                  its value to the current time
                    << "Got response: " << response
                    << " for session: " << session
                    << " the request took: "
                    << (current_time() - time)
                    << "milliseconds";
        }
    );
```

Using this approach allows you to move objects from the surrounding scope into the lambda. By using `std::move` in the preceding example, you're calling the move constructor for the `session` member variable of the lambda, and it'll take ownership over the session object.

You also create a new member variable called `time`, which doesn't capture anything from the outer scope. It's a completely new variable whose initial value is the result of the `current_time` function that's evaluated when lambda is constructed.

3.2.4 *Generic lambdas*

So far, you've seen that with lambdas, you can do most of the things you were able to do with normal function objects. Earlier in this chapter, you implemented a generic function object that allowed you to count the number of items in a given collection that were older than a predefined age limit, without caring about the type of those items, by making the call operator be a function template (listing 3.2).

Lambdas also allow you to create generic function objects by specifying the argument types to be `auto`. You can easily create a generic lambda that can accept any object that has an `.age()` member function checking whether the age of a given object is greater than a predefined limit, as shown in the following listing.

Listing 3.8 Generic lambda that accepts objects with `age()`

```
auto predicate = [limit = 42](auto&& object) {
    return object.age() > limit;
};
```

You don't have a name for the type of the object argument, so you can't use it for perfect forwarding. You'd need to write std::forward<decltype(object)>(object) instead.

```
std::count_if(persons.cbegin(), persons.cend(),
              predicate);
std::count_if(cars.cbegin(), cars.cend(),
              predicate);
std::count_if(projects.cbegin(), projects.cend(),
              predicate);
```

It's important to note that a generic lambda is a class on which the call operator is templated, not a class template that has a call operator. The lambda will deduce the type for each of its arguments that were declared as `auto` when it's called, not when it's constructed, and the same lambda can be used on completely different types.

More-generic lambdas in C++20

If you create a lambda with multiple arguments declared as `auto`, the types of all those arguments will be deduced separately when the lambda is called. If you want to create a generic lambda that has all the arguments of the same type, but for that type to be deduced automatically, you need to resort to trickery and use `decltype` to define the types of lambda arguments.

For example, you might want to create a generic lambda that gets two values of the same type and checks whether they're equal. You could specify the type of the first argument to be `auto` and use `decltype(first)` to specify the type of the second argument, like so:

```
[] (auto first, decltype(first) second) { … }
```

When the lambda is called, the type for the first argument will be deduced, and the second argument will have the same type.

In C++20, the lambda syntax will be extended to allow specifying the template parameters explicitly. Instead of relying on the `decltype` trick, you'll be able to write this:

```
[] <typename T> (T first, T second) { … }
```

Although this new syntax is planned for inclusion in C++20, it's already supported by GCC, and other compilers will likely be quick to support it as well.

3.3 *Writing function objects that are even terser than lambdas*

As you saw, lambdas are nice and remove the need to write large chunks of boilerplate code when creating function objects. On the other hand, they introduce new boiler-plate code (albeit a much smaller amount) to the call site. Consider the example in figure 3.5.

You're writing a web client, and you've sent a few requests to the server and received a collection of responses (with a type named `response_t`) in return. Because every request can fail, `response_t` provides the `.error()` member function that will provide some information in the case of failure. If the request has failed, this function will return `true` (or an object that when cast to a `bool` returns `true`). It'll be `false` otherwise.

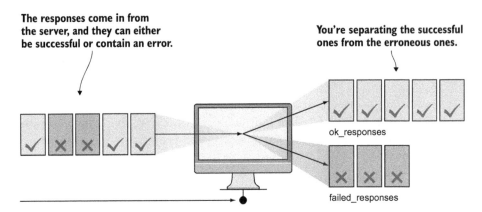

Figure 3.5. You're filtering the responses based on whether they contain an error, in order to process them separately.

You want to filter the given collection depending on whether the responses were erroneous. You want to create one collection that will contain the valid responses and one containing the invalid ones. You can easily pass a lambda to the previously defined `filter` function:

```
ok_responses = filter(responses,
        [](const response_t& response) {
            return !response.error();
        });
failed_responses = filter(responses,
        [](const response_t& response) {
            return response.error();
        });
```

If you had to do this often, and for various other types that have an `.error()` member function that returns a `bool` value (or some other type that's convertible to a `bool`), the amount of boilerplate code would significantly surpass the boilerplate you'd have if you wrote the function object by hand. It would be ideal if you had a terse syntax for creating lambdas that would allow you to write something like this:

```
ok_responses     = filter(responses, _.error() == false);
failed_responses = filter(responses, _.error());
```

Unfortunately, this isn't valid C++, but you now know enough to be able to create something similar.

What you want to create is a function object that will be able to work on any class that provides an `.error()` member function and that will provide you with a nice, terse syntax. Although you can't achieve the same syntax as in the previous code snippet, you can do something even better: you can provide the user with a few ways of writing the predicate (different people prefer different notations when testing bools), which will look like regular C++ code without any boilerplate at all:

```
ok_responses     = filter(responses, not_error);
   // or           filter(responses, !error);
   // or           filter(responses, error == false);
```

```
failed_responses = filter(responses, error);
    // or          filter(responses, error == true);
    // or even     filter(responses, not_error == false);
```

To achieve this, you only need to implement a simple class with an overloaded call operator. It needs to store a single `bool` value that will tell you whether you're looking for correct or erroneous responses (or other objects).

Listing 3.9   Basic implementation of a predicate to test for errors

```
class error_test_t {
public:
    error_test_t(bool error = true)
        : m_error(error)
    {
    }

    template <typename T>
    bool operator()(T&& value) const
    {
        return m_error ==
                (bool)std::forward<T>(value).error();
    }

private:
    bool m_error;
};


error_test_t error(true);
error_test_t not_error(false);
```

> This usage of std::forward may seem strange, but it's nothing more than perfectly forwarding the argument passed to the call operator as the forwarding reference. You do the perfect forwarding because error() could be implemented differently for lvalue and rvalue references.

This will allow you to use `error` and `not_error` as predicates. To support the alternative syntax options you saw earlier, you need to provide `operator==` and `operator!`.

Listing 3.10   Defining convenient operators for the predicate function object

```
class error_test_t {
public:
    ...

    error_test_t operator==(bool test) const
    {
        return error_test_t(
                test ? m_error : !m_error
            );
    }

    error_test_t operator!() const
    {
        return error_test_t(!m_error);
    }

    ...
};
```

> If the test is true, you're returning the same predicate you currently have. If it's false, you're returning its negation.

> You're returning the negation of the current predicate.

Although this seems like an awful lot of code to write just to make creating a predicate function at the call site simpler than writing a lambda, it pays off when the same predicate is used often. And it isn't difficult to imagine that a predicate that tests for errors might be used often.

My advice is to never refrain from simplifying the important parts of code. By creating the error_test_t predicate function object, you're writing a large chunk of code in a separate header file that (if tested properly) nobody will ever need to open while debugging the main parts of the program. Simplifying will make these main parts of the program shorter and easier to understand, thus also making them easier to debug.

3.3.1 Operator function objects in STL

As mentioned in the previous chapter, you can customize the behavior of many algorithms from the standard library. For example, std::accumulate lets you replace addition with another operation, and std::sort lets you change the comparison function used to order the elements.

You can write a function or a lambda and pass it to the algorithm, but that's overkill in some cases. For this reason, as when you implement the error_test_t function object, the standard library provides wrappers over all common operators; see the list in table 3.1. For example, if you want to multiply a collection of integers, you can write your own function that multiplies two numbers and returns a result, but you can also rely on the operator wrapper from the STL called std::multiplies:

```
std::vector<int> numbers{1, 2, 3, 4};

product = std::accumulate(numbers.cbegin(), numbers.cend(), 1,
                          std::multiplies<int>());

// product is 24
```

In the same manner, if you want to use std::sort to order elements in descending order, you might want to use std::greater as the comparison function:

```
std::vector<int> numbers{5, 21, 13, 42};

std::sort(numbers.begin(), numbers.end(), std::greater<int>());

// numbers now contain {42, 21, 13, 5}
```

Table 3.1 Operator wrappers available in the standard library

Group	Wrapper name	Operation
Arithmetic operators	std::plus	arg_1 + arg_2
	std::minus	arg_1 - arg_2
	std::multiplies	arg_1 * arg_2

Table 3.1 Operator wrappers available in the standard library *(continued)*

Group	Wrapper name	Operation
Arithmetic operators (continued)	`std::divides`	`arg_1 / arg_2`
	`std::modulus`	`arg_1 % arg_2`
	`std::negates`	`- arg_1` (a unary function)
Comparison operators	`std::equal_to`	`arg_1 == arg_2`
	`std::not_equal_to`	`arg_1 != arg_2`
	`std::greater`	`arg_1 > arg_2`
	`std::less`	`arg_1 < arg_2`
	`std::greater_equal`	`arg_1 >= arg_2`
	`std::less_equal`	`arg_1 <= arg_2`
Logical operators	`std::logical_and`	`arg_1 && arg_2`
	`std::logical_or`	`arg_1 || arg_2`
	`std::logical_not`	`!arg_1` (a unary function)
Bitwise operators	`std::bit_and`	`arg_1 & arg_2`
	`std::bit_or`	`arg_1 | arg_2`
	`std::bit_xor`	`arg_1 ^ arg_2`

The diamond alternative

Since C++14, you can omit the type when using the operator wrappers from the standard library. Instead of writing `std::greater<int>()`, you can write just `std::greater<>()`, which automatically deduces the argument type when called.

For example, when calling `std::sort`, you can write this:

```
std::sort(numbers.begin(), numbers.end(),
        std::greater<>());
```

If you have a C++14-compliant compiler and the standard library, this version is the preferred one unless you want to force the conversion to a specific type before the comparison takes place.

3.3.2   *Operator function objects in other libraries*

Although the operator wrappers from the STL can cover the most rudimentary cases, they're a bit awkward to write and aren't easily composed. A few libraries have been created as a part of the Boost project to remedy this problem (and a few outside Boost).

Boost libraries

Initially, Boost libraries were created as a test bed for features planned for inclusion in future versions of the C++ STL. Afterward, the collection of libraries grew, and they now cover many common and niche programming domains. Many C++ developers consider them to be an integral part of the C++ ecosystem and a *go-to* place when they need something that's missing in the standard library.

I'm going to show a few examples of creating function objects by using the Boost.Phoenix library.[2] I don't cover this library in detail, but the provided examples should be enough to serve as teasers for you to investigate it further or to implement your own version of the same concepts.

Let's start with a small motivator example. You want to use the `std::partition` algorithm on a collection of numbers to separate those that are less than or equal to 42 from those that aren't.

You saw that the STL provides the `std::less_equal` function object. But you can't use it with `std::partition`. The partitioning algorithm expects a unary function that returns a Boolean result, whereas `std::less_equal` requires two arguments. Although the standard library does provide a way to bind one of those arguments to a fixed value (you'll see how to do it in the next chapter), it isn't pretty and has significant downsides.

Libraries such as Boost.Phoenix provide an alternative way of defining function objects that heavily relies on operator overloading. This library defines *magic* argument placeholders, and operators that allow you to compose them. Solving your problem becomes rather trivial:

```
using namespace boost::phoenix::arg_names;

std::vector<int> numbers{21, 5, 62, 42, 53};

std::partition(numbers.begin(), numbers.end(),
               arg1 <= 42);

// numbers now contain {21, 5, 42,    62, 53}
//                               <= 42        > 42
```

`arg1` is a placeholder defined in the Boost.Phoenix library that binds itself to the first argument passed to the function object. When you call `operator<=` on the placeholder, it won't compare the `arg1` object to the value 42, but will return a unary function object. When that function object is called, it'll return whether the passed argument is less than or equal to 42. This behavior is similar to the `operator==(bool)` you created for the `error_test_t` class.

---

[2] Boost.Phoenix library documentation is available at http://mng.bz/XR7E.

You could create much more intricate function objects in this manner. You could, for example, easily calculate the sum of half-squares of all numbers in a collection (if you'd ever need to do something this strange):

```
std::accumulate(numbers.cbegin(), numbers.cend(), 0,
                arg1 + arg2 * arg2 / 2);
```

◄── Reminder: when folding, the first argument is the accumulated value, and the second argument is the value you're currently processing

The expression `arg1 + arg2 * arg2 / 2` produces a function object that takes two arguments, squares the second one, divides it by two, and adds it to the first argument, as shown in figure 3.6.

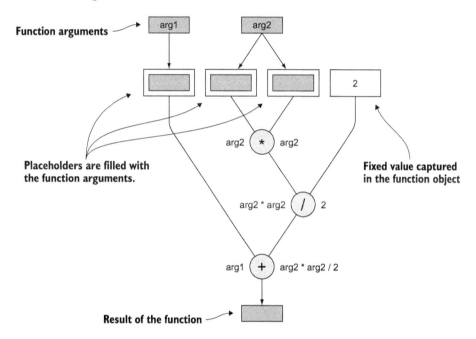

Figure 3.6 The Phoenix expression is composed of captured values and placeholders that represent the function arguments. When the arguments are provided by calling the function object, the expression is evaluated and the calculated value returned as the result of the function.

You can even replace the operator wrappers provided by the standard library that you used earlier:

```
product = std::accumulate(numbers.cbegin(), numbers.cend(), 1,
                          arg1 * arg2);

std::sort(numbers.begin(), numbers.end(), arg1 > arg2);
```

Although these let you create complex function objects, they're most useful for writing simple ones. It you need to create something complex, you should always turn to lambdas. If a function is big enough, the boilerplate that lambdas introduce become insignificant, and lambdas make it easier for the compiler to optimize the code.

The main downside of libraries such as Boost.Phoenix is that they slow the compilation time significantly. If that proves to be a problem for your project, you should revert to using lambdas, or create your own simpler function objects such as the `error` object you implemented in this chapter.

3.4 *Wrapping function objects with std::function*

So far, you've relied on automatic type deduction when you wanted to either accept a function object as an argument (by making the function object type parameterized with a template) or create a variable to store a lambda (by using `auto` instead of specifying the type explicitly). Although this is the preferred and optimal way, it's sometimes not possible. When you need to save a function object as a member in a class that can't be templated on the type of that function object (thus having to explicitly specify its type), or when you want to use a function between separate compilation units, you need to be able to provide a concrete type.

Because there's no supertype for all kinds of function objects that you could use in these cases, the standard library provides a class template `std::function` that can wrap any type of function object:

```
std::function<float(float, float)> test_function;    ◄── The result of the function is
                                                          written first, followed by
                                                          the list of arguments inside
                                                          the parentheses.

test_function = std::fmaxf;    ◄── Ordinary function

test_function = std::multiplies<float>();    ◄── Class with a call operator

test_function = std::multiplies<>();    ◄── Class with a generic call operator

test_function = [x](float a, float b) { return a * x + b; };    ◄── Lambda

test_function = [x](auto a, auto b) { return a * x + b; };    ◄── Generic lambda

test_function = (arg1 + arg2) / 2;    ◄── boost.phoenix expression

test_function = [](std::string s) { return s.empty(); } // ERROR!    ◄── Lambda with a
                                                                         wrong signature
```

The `std::function` isn't templated on the contained type, but on the signature of the function object. The template argument specifies the return type of the function and its arguments. You're able to use the same type to store ordinary functions, function pointers, lambdas, and other callable objects (as shown in the previous snippet)—anything that has the signature specified in the `std::function` template parameter.

You can even go a bit further. You can store some things that don't provide the usual call syntax, such as class member variables and class member functions. For example, the C++ core language stops you from calling the `.empty()` member function of `std::string` as if it were a non-member function (`std::string::empty(str)`), and because of that, you don't consider data members and member functions to be function objects. But if you store them in a std::function object, you can call it with the normal call syntax:[3]

```
std::string str{"A small pond"};
std::function<bool(std::string)> f;

f = &std::string::empty;

std::cout << f(str);
```

We'll refer to function objects (as previously defined) together with pointers to member variables and functions, as *callables*. You'll see how to implement functions that can call any callable object, not only function objects, in chapter 11, where I explain the usage of the std::invoke function.

Although all the preceding factors make std::function useful, it shouldn't be overused because it introduces noticeable performance penalties. To be able to hide the contained type and provide a common interface over all callable types, std::function uses a technique known as *type erasure*. We aren't going to dive deeper into this, but it's enough to be aware that type erasure is usually based on virtual member function calls. Because virtual calls are resolved at runtime, the compiler can't inline the call and has limited optimization opportunities.

An additional issue of std::function is that although its call operator is marked as const, it can invoke a nonconstant callable. This can lead to all kinds of problems in multithreaded code.

Small-function-object optimization

When the wrapped callable is a function pointer or a std::reference_wrapper (as produced by the std::ref function), small-object optimization is guaranteed to be performed. These callables are stored directly inside the std::function object, without the need for any dynamic memory allocation.

Larger objects may be constructed in dynamically allocated memory and accessed by the std::function object through a pointer. This has a performance impact on the construction and destruction of the std::function object, and when its call operator is invoked. The maximum size of the callable object for which the small-function-object optimization will be performed varies among different compilers and standard library implementations.

TIP For more information and resources about the topics covered in this chapter, see https://forums.manning.com/posts/list/41682.page.

---

[3] If you're using Clang, you might get a linking error due to a libc++ bug that doesn't export the std::string::empty symbol.

Summary

- It's possible to use objects that are castable to function pointers as if they were ordinary functions, but the call operator is the preferred way of creating function objects.

- For functions whose return type isn't important enough to be explicitly stated, you can let the compiler deduce it from the value you're returning by using the `auto` keyword.

- Using the automatic return type deduction avoids any type of conversion or narrowing that might arise when you specify the type explicitly (for example, returning a `double` value in a function that should return an `int`).

- If you want to create a function object that can work on a multitude of types, you should make its call operator a function template.

- Lambdas are useful syntactic sugar for creating function objects. Using them is usually better than writing whole classes with call operators by hand.

- Lambdas in C++14 have become a true replacement for most function objects that you could write by hand. They add new possibilities when capturing variables, and they support creating generic function objects.

- Although the lambdas provide terser syntax for creating function objects, they're still overly verbose for some cases. In those situations, you can use the libraries such as Boost.Phoenix, or roll out your own function objects.

- The `std::function` is a useful, but it comes with a performance penalty equivalent to a virtual function call.

Creating new functions from the old ones

4

This chapter covers

- Understanding partial function application

- Fixing function arguments to specific values with `std::bind`

- Using lambdas for partial function application

- Are all functions in the world unary?

- Creating functions that operate on collections of items

Most programming paradigms tend to provide a way to increase code reusability. In the object-oriented world, we create classes we can later use in various situations. We can use them directly or combine them to implement more-complex classes. The possibility of breaking complex systems into smaller components that can be used and tested separately is a powerful one.

In the same way that OOP gives you the tools to combine and modify types, the functional programming paradigm gives you ways to easily create new functions by combining the functions we've already written, by *upgrading* specialized functions to cover more-general use cases, or, the other way around, by taking more-general functions and simplifying them to perfectly fit a specific use case.

4.1   *Partial function application*

In the previous chapter, you counted the number of objects in a collection that were older than a certain predefined age limit. If you think about that example, you conceptually have a function that takes two arguments: an object (for example, a person or a car) and a value that will be compared against the age of that object, as shown in figure 4.1. This function returns `true` if the age of the object is greater than that value.

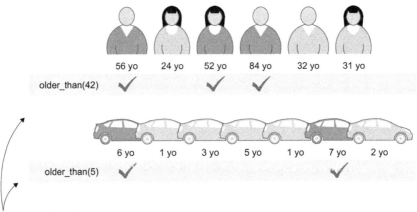

The same generic predicate is able to test whether instances of different types are above the required age limit.

Figure 4.1   On a higher level, you have a function of two arguments: one object, and an integer value representing the age limit. The function returns whether the object is older than that age limit. When you fix the age limit to a specific value, you get a unary function that compares the object's age against that predefined value.

Because the `std::count_if` algorithm expects you to give it a unary predicate, you have to create a function object that stores the age limit inside itself, and use that value when it gets the object whose age needs to be checked. The notion that you don't need to pass in at once all the arguments a function requires is something we'll explore a bit more in this section.

Let's look at a simpler version of the example from the previous chapter. Instead of checking whether a person's age is greater than a specified value, you'll take the general *greater-than* operator (a function that takes two arguments) and bind its second argument to a fixed value, thus creating a unary function (see figure 4.2).

You're creating an ordinary function object that gets a single integer value on its construction, stores it inside the function object, and then uses it to compare the values passed to its call operator against it.

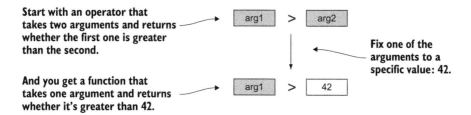

Figure 4.2 Fixing the second argument of the greater-than comparison operator to 42 turns it into a unary predicate that tests whether a value is greater than 42.

Instances of this class can be used with any higher-order function that takes a predicate (such as `std::find_if`, `std::partition`, or `std::remove_if`), given that it'll call that predicate on integer values (or values that can be implicitly converted to an integer).

Listing 4.1 Comparing an argument to a predefined value

```
class greater_than {
public:
    greater_than(int value)
        : m_value
    {
    }

    bool operator()(int arg) const
    {
        return arg > m_value;
    }

private:
    int m_value;
};

...

greater_than greater_than_42(42);

greater_than_42(1);  // false
greater_than_42(50); // true

std::partition(xs.begin(), xs.end(), greater_than(6));
```

You can create an instance of this object and use it multiple times to check whether other specific values are greater than 42.

And you can create an instance directly when calling a specific algorithm such as std::partition to separate items greater than 6 from those that are less.

You don't do anything overly complicated here. You take a binary function—operator> : (int, int) → bool—and create a new unary function object from it that does the same thing as the greater-than operator, but with the second argument fixed to a specific value (see figure 4.2).

This concept of creating a new function object from an existing one by fixing one or more of its arguments to a specific value is called *partial function application*. The word *partial* in this case means you provide some, but not all, arguments needed to calculate the result of the function.

4.1.1   *A generic way to convert binary functions into unary ones*

Let's try to make the previous implementation more generic. You want to create a function object that can wrap any binary function that the user passes to it, and bind one of its arguments. For consistency's sake, you're going to bind the second argument, as the greater_than class did.

> **NOTE**   The standard library used to contain a function called std::bind2nd, which implemented the same concept as the one presented in this section. Although this function has been removed from the standard in favor of lambdas and std::bind (which are covered in the next section), it's a nice example of how partial application can be implemented in C++.

The function object needs to be able to store a binary function and one of its arguments. Because you don't know in advance the types of the function and the second argument, you need to create a class templated on these two types. The constructor will need to only initialize the members and nothing more. Note that you're going to capture both the function and the second argument that will later be passed to it by value for simplicity.

Listing 4.2   Basic structure of the templated class

```
template <typename Function, typename SecondArgType>
class partial_application_on_2nd_impl {
public:
    partial_application_bind2nd_impl(Function function,
                                     SecondArgType second_arg)
        : m_function(function)
        , m_value(second_arg)
    {
    }

    ...

private:
    Function m_function;
    SecondArgType m_second_arg;
};
```

You don't know the type of the first argument in advance, so you need to make the call operator a template as well. The implementation is straightforward: you call the function that you've stored in the m_function member and forward it the argument passed to the call operator as the first argument, along with the value stored in the m_second_arg member as the second argument.

Listing 4.3   Call operator for partial function application

```
template <typename Function, typename SecondArgType>
class partial_application_bind2nd_impl {
public:
    ...

    template <typename FirstArgType>
    auto operator()(FirstArgType&& first_arg) const
        -> decltype(m_function(
                std::forward<FirstArgType>(first_arg),
                m_second_arg))
    {
        return m_function(
                std::forward<FirstArgType>(first_arg),
                m_second_arg);
    }

    ...
};
```

If you don't have a compiler that supports automatic return type deduction, you need to use decltype to achieve the same effect. Otherwise, you could have written decltype(auto).

The argument of the call operator is passed to the function as the first argument.

The saved value is passed as the second argument to the function.

NOTE Just a quick reminder: because you're using the regular function call syntax, the class from the listing 4.3 will work only with function objects, not other callables such as pointers to member functions and member variables. If you want to support them as well, you need to use `std::invoke`, which is explained in chapter 11.

Now that you've defined the complete class, you need one more thing to make it useful. If you want to use it directly from your code, you must specify the template argument types explicitly when creating an instance of this class. This would be ugly, and in some cases impossible (for example, you don't know the type of the lambda).

NOTE The requirement of class template instantiation for the template arguments to be explicitly defined has been removed in C++17. But because this standard hasn't yet been widely accepted, these examples don't rely on this feature.

To have the compiler deduce the types automatically, create a function template whose job is only to make an instance of this class. Because template-argument deduction[1] works when calling functions, you don't need to specify the types when calling it. The function calls the constructor for the class you defined previously and forwards its arguments to the constructor. It's mostly boilerplate that the language forces you to write in order to have a way to instantiate a class template without having to explicitly specify the template arguments.

---

[1] Check out http://mng.bz/YXIU for more information regarding template-argument deduction.

Listing 4.4   **Wrapper function for creating the previous function object**

```
template <typename Function, typename SecondArgType>
partial_application_bind2nd_impl<Function, SecondArgType>
bind2nd(Function&& function, SecondArgType&& second_arg)
{
    return partial_application_bind2nd_impl<Function, SecondArgType>(
            std::forward<Function>(function),
            std::forward<SecondArgType>(second_arg));
}
```

Now, let's use the newly created function to replace the usage of greater_than in the initial example.

Listing 4.5   **Using** bind2nd **to create the function object**

```
auto greater_than_42 = bind2nd(std::greater<int>(), 42);

greater_than_42(1);  // false
greater_than_42(50); // true

std::partition(xs.begin(), xs.end(), bind2nd(std::greater<int>(), 6));
```

You've created a more general function that can be used in many more places than greater_than, and trivially replaced all usages of greater_than with that new function. To show that it's truly more general, the following short example uses the newly created bind2nd function for multiplication rather than the greater-than relation.

Imagine you have a collection of angle sizes given in degrees, but the rest of your code relies on angles being given in radians. This problem appears every so often in many graphics programs—graphics libraries usually define angles for rotation in degrees, whereas most math libraries used alongside these graphics libraries require radians. Converting one to another is simple: the value in degrees needs to be multiplied by $\pi/180$ (see figure 4.3).

Listing 4.6   **Using** bind2nd **to convert from degrees to radians**

```
std::vector<double> degrees = {0, 30, 45, 60};
std::vector<double> radians(degrees.size());

std::transform(degrees.cbegin(), degrees.cend(),
            radians.begin(),
            bind2nd(std::multiplies<double>(),
                PI / 180));
```

Saves the converted results to the radians vector

Passes multiplication with the second argument bound to $\pi/180$ as the transformation function

Iterates through all elements in the degrees vector

This example shows that you aren't limited to creating only predicate functions (functions that return bool values); you can take any binary function and turn it into a unary one by binding its second argument to a specific value. This allows you to use that binary function in contexts requiring unary functions, as in the preceding example.

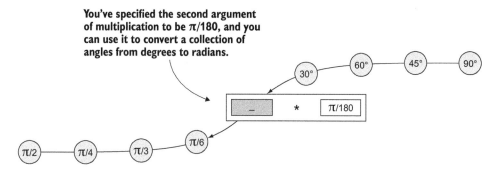

Figure 4.3 Binding one argument of multiplication to π/180 gives you a function that converts degrees to radians.

4.1.2 *Using std::bind to bind values to specific function arguments*

Pre-C++11, the standard library provided two functions similar to the function you created in the previous section. These functions, std::bind1st and std::bind2nd, provided a way to turn a binary function into a unary one by binding its first or second argument to a specific value—much like bind2nd.

In C++11, these two functions were deprecated (they were removed in C++17) in favor of a much more general one called std::bind. The std::bind function isn't limited to only binary functions and can work with functions that have an arbitrary number of arguments. It also doesn't limit the user regarding which arguments can be bound; you can bind any number of arguments, in any order, while leaving the rest unbound.

Let's start with a basic example of using std::bind: binding all arguments of a function to specific values, but without invoking it. The first argument of std::bind is the function whose arguments you want to bind to specific values, and the other arguments are the values the function arguments will be bound to. You'll bind the arguments of the std::greater comparator function to fixed values: 6 and 42. Technically, this isn't partial function application, because you're binding all the arguments of a function, but it's a good start to introduce the syntax of std::bind.

Listing 4.7 Binding all arguments of a function with std::bind

Only when calling the bound function object are the elements 6 and 42 compared.

The std::greater function isn't yet invoked; you've created a function object that will call std::greater with the specified values 6 and 42.

```
auto bound =
    std::bind(std::greater<double>(), 6, 42);

bool is_6_greater_than_42 = bound();
```

By providing values for all needed arguments when binding a function, you create a new function object that saves the function whose arguments you're binding (the std::greater comparator, in this case) and all the passed values (see figure 4.4). Binding defines the values for the arguments, but it doesn't invoke the function. The function is invoked only when someone calls the function object returned by std::bind. In the example, the std::greater comparator is called only when calling bound().

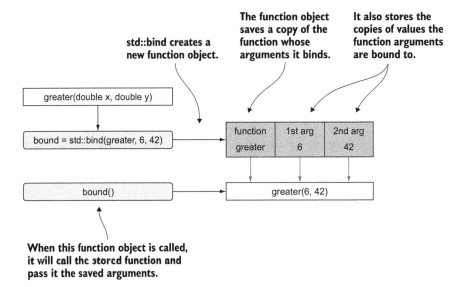

Figure 4.4 The two-argument function tests whether its first argument is greater than its second. Binding both arguments to specific values such as 6 and 42 creates a nullary function object that, when called, returns the result of greater(6, 42).

Now, let's see how you can leave one of the arguments unbound while binding the other one. You can't just define one value and skip the other, because std::bind wouldn't know which argument you want to bind—the first or the second. Therefore, std::bind introduces the concept of *placeholders*. If you want to bind an argument, you pass a value for it to std::bind as you did in the preceding example. But if you want to say that an argument should remain unbound, you have to pass a placeholder instead.

The placeholders look and behave similarly to the function objects you created in the previous chapter using the Boost.Phoenix library. This time, they have names that are a bit different: _1 instead of arg1, _2 instead of arg2, and so on.

> **NOTE** The placeholders are defined in the <functional> header in the std::placeholders namespace. This is one of the rare cases in which you won't explicitly specify the namespace, because that would significantly hinder the readability of the code. For all the std::bind examples, you'll consider that the namespace std::placeholders is used.

Let's take the previous example and modify it to bind only one of the arguments. You want to create one predicate that tests whether a number is greater than 42, and one predicate that tests whether a number is less than 42—both by using only std::bind and the std::greater comparator. In the first case, you'll bind the second argument to the specified value while passing a placeholder as the first; and vice versa for the second case.

Listing 4.8   Binding arguments of a function with `std::bind`

```
auto is_greater_than_42 =
    std::bind(std::greater<double>(), _1, 42);
auto is_less_than_42 =
    std::bind(std::greater<double>(), 42, _1);

is_less_than_42(6);    // returns true
is_greater_than_42(6); // returns false
```

What's going on here? You're taking a two-argument function—the `std::greater` comparator—and binding one of its arguments to a value and one to a placeholder. Binding an argument to a placeholder effectively states that you don't have a value for that argument at the moment, and you're leaving a hole that you're going to fill later.

When you call the function object returned by `std::bind` with a specific value, that value is used to fill that hole defined by the `_1` placeholder (see figure 4.5). If you bind several arguments to the same placeholder, all of these arguments will be filled with the same value.

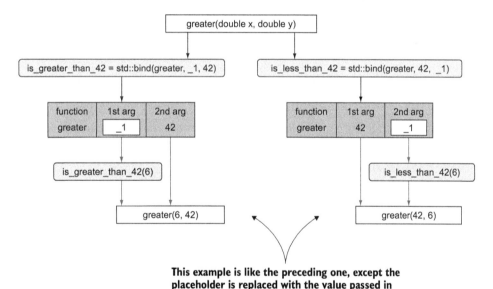

This example is like the preceding one, except the placeholder is replaced with the value passed in when calling the function object.

Figure 4.5 The two-argument function tests whether its first argument is greater than its second. Binding one of the arguments to a value and the other to a placeholder creates a unary function object that, when called with a single argument, uses that argument to fill the hole defined by the placeholder.

4.1.3 Reversing the arguments of a binary function

You've seen that you can bind all arguments to specific values, or leave one of the arguments unbound by using the `_1` placeholder. Can you use multiple placeholders at the same time?

Say you have a vector of doubles that you want to sort in ascending order. Usually, you'd do this with `std::less` (which is the default behavior of `std::sort`), but this time, just for demonstration purposes, you'll do it with `std::greater` (see figure 4.6). To do so, you can create a function object by using `std::bind` that reverses the arguments before they're passed to `std::greater`.

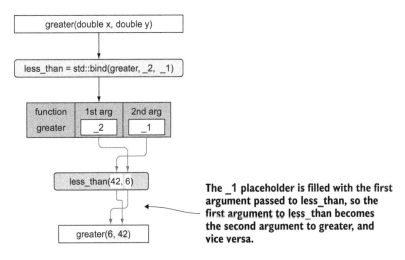

Figure 4.6   You specify the first placeholder to be the second argument passed to `greater`, and vice versa. This results in a new function that's the same as `greater`, but with the arguments switched.

You're creating a two-argument function object (because the highest-numbered placeholder is _2) that, when called, invokes `std::greater` with the same arguments it received, but swapped. You can use it to implement sorting of the scores in ascending order.

> **Listing 4.9   Sorting film scores in ascending order**

```
std::sort(scores.begin(), scores.end(),
        std::bind(std::greater<double>(), _2, _1));
```

The arguments are reversed: you pass the _2 placeholder first and the _l placeholder second.

Now that you have a basic grasp of `std::bind` and what it can do, let's move on to more-complex examples.

4.1.4   Using std::bind on functions with more arguments

You'll use the collection of people yet again, but this time you want to write all the people to the standard output or some other output stream. You'll start by defining a non-member function that will write the person information in one of the predefined formats. The function will have three arguments—a person, a reference to the output stream, and the desired output format:

```
void print_person(const person_t& person,
                std::ostream& out,
                person_t::output_format_t format)
```

```
{
    if (format == person_t::name_only) {
        out << person.name() << '\n';

    } else if (format == person_t::full_name) {
        out << person.name() << ' '
            << person.surname() << '\n';

    }
}
```

Now, if you wanted to write out all people in the collection, you could do it by passing print_person to the std::for_each algorithm, with the out and format arguments bound (see figure 4.7).

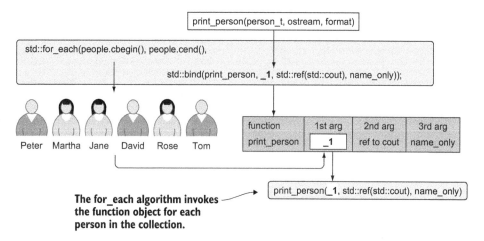

Figure 4.7 You want to create a function that prints names of people to the standard output. You have a function that can write a person's information in multiple formats and to different output streams. You specify the output stream and the format while leaving the person empty, to be defined by the std::for_each algorithm.

By default, std::bind stores the copies of the bound values in the function object it returns. Because copying is disabled on std::cout, you need to bind the out argument to a reference to std::cout and not its copy. For this, you use the std::ref helper function (see example:printing-people/main.cpp).

Listing 4.10 Binding the arguments of print_person

```
std::for_each(people.cbegin(), people.cend(),
        std::bind(print_person,
            _1,
            std::ref(std::cout),
            person_t::name_only
        ));
```

> Creates a unary function that prints the name of a person to the standard output

```
std::for_each(people.cbegin(), people.cend(),
        std::bind(print_person,
```

```
        _1,
        std::ref(file),                    ┌──── Prints the name and the surname
        person_t::full_name    ─┤          └──── of a person to the specified file
    ));
```

You started with a function that needs three arguments—the person, the output stream, and the output format—and used it to create two new ones. Each takes a person as its argument but behaves differently. One writes the first name of a person to the standard output, and the other writes the person's full name to the specified file. And you did this without writing the new functions by hand; you used the existing function, bound a couple of its arguments, and got a unary function that you can use in the std::for_each algorithm as the result.

So far, you've preferred non-member functions or static member functions to proper class member functions, because class member functions aren't considered function objects—they don't support the function call syntax.

This limitation is artificial. Member functions are essentially the same as ordinary ones, except they have an implicit first argument this that points to the instance of the class the member function was called on.

You have a print_person function that takes three arguments: person t, an output stream, and a format. You can replace this function with a member function inside the person_t type, like this:

```
class person_t {
    …

    void print(std::ostream& out, output_format_t format) const
    {
        …
    }

    …
};
```

In essence, there's no difference between the print_person and person_t::print functions except that C++ doesn't allow you to call the latter by using the usual call syntax. The print member function also has three arguments—an implicit argument this that refers to a person, and two explicit arguments out and format—and it does the same thing as print_person.

Fortunately, std::bind can bind arguments of any callable, and it treats print_person and person_t::print the same. If you want to convert the previous example to use this member function, you need to replace print_person with a pointer to the person_t::print member function.

```
std::for_each(people.cbegin(), people.cend(),
        std::bind(&person_t::print,    ◄────┐ You're creating a unary
                _1,                          │ function object from a
                std::ref(std::cout),         │ member function pointer.
                person_t::name_only
        ));
```

NOTE It would be a nice exercise to check which non-member functions in the previous examples could be easily replaced by member functions with the help of std::bind.

You've seen that std::bind allows you to perform partial function application by binding some arguments, and also to reorder the function arguments. It has slightly unorthodox syntax for the object-oriented world, but it's terse and easy to understand. It supports any callable object, making it easy to use both normal function objects and member variable and function pointers with standard algorithms and other higher-order functions.

4.1.5 *Using lambdas as an alternative for std::bind*

Although std::bind provides a nice, terse syntax for creating function objects that bind or reorder arguments of existing functions, it comes with a cost: it makes the job of the compiler much more difficult, and it's harder to optimize. It's implemented on the library level, and it uses many complex template metaprogramming techniques to achieve its goal.

An alternative to using std::bind is to use lambdas for partial function application. Lambdas are a core-language feature, which means the compiler can optimize them more easily. The syntax will be a bit more verbose, but it'll allow the compiler more freedom to optimize the code.

Turning all std::bind calls to lambda is simple (see figure 4.8):

- Turn any argument bound to a variable or a reference to a variable into a captured variable
- Turn all placeholders into lambda arguments
- Specify all the arguments bound to a specific value directly in the lambda body

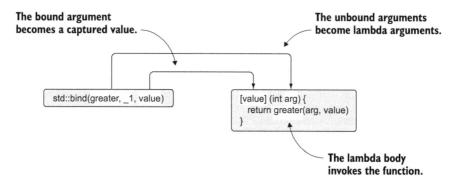

Figure 4.8 If you want to use lambdas instead of std::bind, you need to convert bound arguments to captured values; the unbound arguments will become lambda arguments.

Let's see what the examples from the previous section look like. First you had a two-argument function and bound both its arguments to a specific value. No arguments are bound to variables, so you don't need to capture anything. There are no placeholders, so the lambda won't have any arguments. And you pass the bound values directly when calling the std::greater comparator:

```
auto bound = [] {
        return std::greater<double>()(6, 42);
    };
```

This could be even shorter if you replaced the std::greater call with the operator >. But let's leave it as is because not all functions can be replaced with infix operators, and I'm demonstrating the general approach of replacing std::bind with lambdas.

The next example was to bind one of the arguments to a specific value while binding the other argument to a placeholder. This time, because you have a single placeholder, the lambda will have a single argument. You still don't need to capture any variables:

```
auto is_greater_than_42 =
    [](double value) {
        return std::greater<double>()(value, 42);
    };
auto is_less_than_42 =
    [](double value) {
        return std::greater<double>()(42, value);
    };

is_less_than_42(6);    // returns true
is_greater_than_42(6); // returns false
```

As before, you pass the bound values directly in the lambda body when calling the std::greater comparator.

Going further, you want to reimplement the example of sorting a vector of scores in ascending order by using std::greater. In this example, you swap the arguments when calling the comparator. You now have two placeholders, so the lambda will have two arguments:

```
std::sort(scores.begin(), scores.end(),
        [](double value1, double value2) {
            return std::greater<double>()(value2, value1);
        });
```

As in the example with std::bind, you're calling std::sort with a function object that will, when called with two arguments, pass those arguments to std::greater in reverse order.

In the last example, you used std::for_each to print the names of people contained in a collection. In this example, you need to consider a few entities:

- You have a single _1 placeholder, so you'll create a unary lambda.
- You're binding the values person_t::name_only and person_t::full_name, which you can pass in directly when calling the print_person function.
- You're using a reference to std::cout, which you don't need to capture because it'll be visible in the lambda anyway.
- You have a reference to the output stream called file, which you need to capture by reference in the lambda:

```
std::for_each(people.cbegin(), people.cend(),
        [](const person_t& person) {
            print_person(person,
                            std::cout,
                            person_t::name_only);
        });

std::for_each(people.cbegin(), people.cend(),
        [&file](const person_t& person) {
            print_person(person,
                            file,
                            person_t::full_name);
        });
```

All these examples have been generally identical to those that used `std::bind`, with a different, slightly more verbose syntax. But other subtle differences exist. `std::bind` stores the copies of all values, references, and functions in the function object it creates. It even needs to store the information about which placeholders are used. Lambdas, on the other hand, store only what you want them to. This can make `std::bind` slower than an ordinary lambda if the compiler doesn't manage to optimize it properly.

You've seen a few approaches to partial function application in C++. You performed partial application of operators such as multiplication and comparison by using the Boost.Phoenix library (as you saw in the previous chapter), which gave you nice, terse syntax. You also used partial application of any function you want by using the `std::bind` function or lambdas. Lambdas and `std::bind` give you similar levels of expressiveness, but with a different syntax. Lambdas tend to be more verbose but are more likely to lead to more efficient code (benchmarking your particular use cases is always worthwhile).

4.2 *Currying: a different way to look at functions*

You've seen what partial function application is and how to use it in C++. Now, let's move on to something that has a strange name—*currying*—and that often looks much like partial function application to the untrained eye. In order not to confuse these two, I'll first define the concept and then show a few examples.

> **NOTE** *Currying* is named after Haskell Curry, a mathematician and logician who perfected this concept from the ideas first introduced by Gottlob Frege and Moses Schönfinkel.

Say you're working in a programming language that doesn't let you create functions that have more than a single argument. Although this seems limiting at first, you'll see that it allows you all the expressiveness you have with proper unary functions with a simple, yet clever trick.

Instead of creating a function that takes two arguments and returns a single value, you can create a unary function that returns a second unary function. When this second function is called, this means you've received both needed arguments and can return the resulting value. If you had a function that took three arguments, you could convert it into a unary function that returned the previously defined curried version of the two-argument function—and so on for as many arguments as you wanted.

Let's see this idea in a simple example. You have a function called `greater` that takes two values and checks whether the first one is greater than the second. On the other hand, you have its curried version, which can't return a `bool` value because it only knows the value of the first argument. It returns a unary lambda that captures the value of that argument. The resulting lambda will compare the captured value with its argument when it gets invoked (see figure 4.9).

Listing 4.12   The `greater` function and its curried version

```
// greater : (double, double) → bool
bool greater(double first, double second)
{
    return first > second;
}

// greater_curried : double → (double → bool)
auto greater_curried(double first)
{
    return [first](double second) {
        return first > second;
    },
}

// Invocation
greater(2, 3);                 |  Returns false
greater_curried(2);
greater_curried(2)(3);         |  Returns a unary function object that
                                  checks whether its argument is less than 2
                               |  Returns false
```

If you have a function with more arguments, you can keep nesting as many lambdas as you need until you gather all the arguments required to return a proper result.

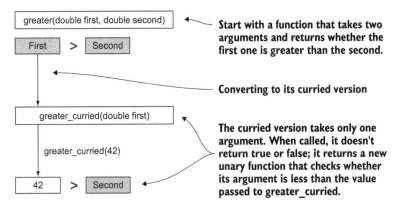

Start with a function that takes two arguments and returns whether the first one is greater than the second.

Converting to its curried version

The curried version takes only one argument. When called, it doesn't return true or false; it returns a new unary function that checks whether its argument is less than the value passed to greater_curried.

Figure 4.9   The function takes two arguments, and you're converting it to a unary function that returns not a value, but a new unary function. This allows you to pass in the arguments one at a time rather than all at once.

4.2.1 Creating curried functions the easier way

As you may recall, the function `print_person` took three arguments: a person, the output stream, and the output format. If you want to call that function, you need to pass all three arguments at once, or to perform partial function application in order to separate the arguments into those that you can define immediately and those that you will define later:

```
void print_person(const person_t& person,
                  std::ostream& out,
                  person_t::output_format_t format);
```

You can call it like so:

```
print_person(person, std::cout, person_t::full_name);
```

You can convert this function to its curried version in the same way you did for `greater`—by nesting enough lambda expressions to capture all the arguments needed to execute `print_person` one by one (see figure 4.10):

```
auto print_person_cd(const person_t& person)
{
    return [&](std::ostream& out) {
        return [&](person_t::output_format_t format) {
            print_person(person, out, format);
        };
    };
}
```

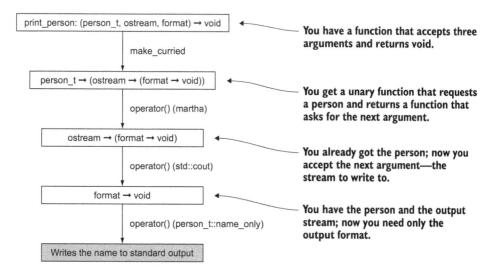

Figure 4.10 You started with a function of three arguments and converted it to its curried version. The curried version is a function that accepts a person and returns a function that takes an output stream. That function, again, returns a new function that takes the output format and prints the person's info.

Because writing code like this is tedious, you're going to use a helper function called `make_curried` from now on. This function can convert any function into its curried version. Even more, the resulting curried function will provide you with syntactic sugar, which will allow you to specify more than one argument at a time if needed. This is syntactic sugar; the curried function is still just a unary function, as I said before, just more convenient to use.

> **NOTE**   You'll see how to implement a function like this in chapter 11. At this point, the implementation isn't important; you just need it to do what you want.

Before we move on to the possible uses of currying in C++, let's first demonstrate what you can do with the `make_curried` function and what the usage syntax is like.

> **Listing 4.13   Using the curried version of `print_person`**

Returns a function object that can print martha's info to the standard output with the format you choose

```
using std::cout;

auto print_person_cd = make_curried(print_person);

print_person_cd(martha, cout, person_t::full_name);
print_person_cd(martha)(cout, person_t::full_name);
print_person_cd(martha, cout)(person_t::full_name);
print_person_cd(martha)(cout)(person_t::full_name);

auto print_martha = print_person_cd(martha);
print_martha(cout, person_t::name_only);

auto print_martha_to_cout =
        print_person_cd(martha, cout);
print_martha_to_cout(person_t::name_only);
```

All of these write the martha name and surname to the standard output. You can choose how many arguments to provide in the single call.

Returns a curried function object that will write martha's info to an output stream you pass it to, in the format you specify

Is this only a cool idea that some mathematician came up with because it was easier to think about unary functions instead of having to consider those with more arguments? Or is it useful in our lives as programmers?

4.2.2   Using currying with database access

Let's consider a real-world example. You're writing an application that connects to a database and performs queries on it. Maybe you want to get a list of all people who rated a particular movie.

You're using a library that allows you to create multiple database connections, to initiate connection subsessions (for handling database transactions and such), and, obviously, to query the stored data. Let's say the main query function looks like this:

```
result_t query(connection_t& connection,
               session_t& session,
               const std::string& table_name,
               const std::string& filter);
```

It queries all the rows in a given table that match the given filter. All the queries need to have the connection and session specified so the library can tell which database to query and what to include in a single database transaction.

Many applications don't need to create multiple connections, but only a single one for all queries (see figure 4.11). One approach that library developers use in this case is to make the query function a member function in the connection_t type. Another viable alternative would be to create an overloaded query function that wouldn't have the connection as one of the arguments; it would use the default system connection instead.

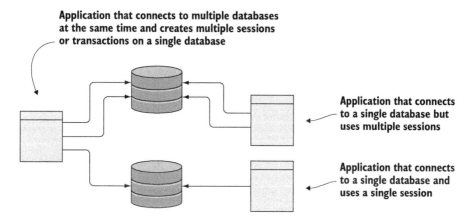

Figure 4.11   Different applications have different needs; some may want to connect to multiple databases, some may need multiple sessions, and some need just a single session while connected to a single database.

This situation becomes more entangled when you consider the possibility that some users don't need multiple sessions. If they access a read-only database, there isn't much point in defining transactions. The library author can also add a query function to a session object, which the user will use throughout the application, or you can get another overload of the original query function, this time without both session and connection arguments.

After this, it would also be easy to imagine that parts of a user's application might need access to only a single table (in this case, you just need a table that contains the user scores). The library might then provide a table_t class that has its own query member function, and so on.

It isn't easy to predict all the use cases a user might have. Those we've predicted make the library more complex than it needs to be. Let's see whether having a single query function—like the preceding one, but curried—can be sufficient to cover all these cases without making the library developer go nuts over all the overloads and classes you force them to create for your use cases.

If users need multiple database connections, they can either use the query function directly, by always specifying the connection and session, or create a separate function for each connection that will apply the first argument of the curried function. The latter will also be useful if only one database connection is needed for the entire application.

If only a single database is needed, and a single session, it's easy to create a function that covers that case exactly; you need to call the curried `query` function and pass it the connection and session, and it will return a function that you can use from there. And if you need to query a single table multiple times, you can bind the table argument as well.

Listing 4.14   Solving the API boom with curried functions

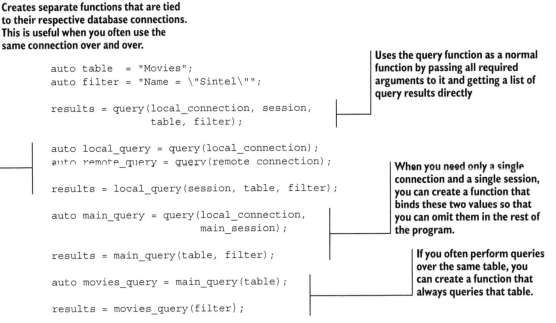

Creates separate functions that are tied to their respective database connections. This is useful when you often use the same connection over and over.

```
auto table  = "Movies";
auto filter = "Name = \"Sintel\"";

results = query(local_connection, session,
                table, filter);

auto local_query = query(local_connection);
auto remote_query = query(remote_connection);

results = local_query(session, table, filter);

auto main_query = query(local_connection,
                        main_session);

results = main_query(table, filter);

auto movies_query = main_query(table);

results = movies_query(filter);
```

Uses the query function as a normal function by passing all required arguments to it and getting a list of query results directly

When you need only a single connection and a single session, you can create a function that binds these two values so that you can omit them in the rest of the program.

If you often perform queries over the same table, you can create a function that always queries that table.

By providing a curried version of the `query` function, you allow users to create exactly the functions needed for their particular use case, without complicating your API. This is a big improvement in code reusability because you aren't creating separate classes that might end up with separate bugs that are discovered only when a particular use case appears and that specific class is used. Here, a single implementation can be used in all the use cases.

4.2.3   *Currying and partial function application*

Currying and partial function application look similar at first. They both seem to let you create new functions by binding a few arguments to specific values while leaving other arguments unbound. So far, you've seen only that they have different syntax and that currying is more limiting in the sense that it must bind the arguments in order: first argument first, last argument last.

These approaches are similar and allow you to achieve similar things. You might even implement one by using the other. But they have an important distinction that makes them both useful.

The advantage of using `std::bind` over currying is obvious: you can take the `query` function and bind any of its arguments, whereas the curried function first binds the first argument.

> **Listing 4.15 Binding arguments with curried functions and `std::bind`**

```
                                                    ┌─ Binds only the connection
auto local_query = query(local_connection);   ◄─────┤  argument to be local_connection

auto local_query = std::bind(                       ┌─ You can bind the first
        query, local_connection, _1, _2, _3);       │  argument, but you
auto session_query = std::bind(                      ┤  aren't required to.
        query, _1, main_session, _2, _3);           │  You can bind just the
                                                     └─ second one.
```

You might think that `std::bind` is better and just has syntax that's a bit more complex. But it has one important drawback that should be obvious from the preceding example. To use `std::bind`, you need to know exactly how many arguments the function you're passing to `std::bind` has. You need to bind each argument to either a value (or a variable, a reference) or a placeholder. With the curried `query` function, you don't need to care about that; you define the value for the first function argument, and `query` returns a function that accepts all other arguments, no matter how many there are.

This might seem like only a syntactic difference—you need to type less—but it isn't just that. In addition to `query`, you'd probably want to have an `update` function. The function would update the values of rows matched by a filter. It would accept the same arguments as `query`, plus an additional one: the instruction indicating how each matching result should be updated:

```
result_t update(connection_t& connection,
                session_t& session,
                const std::string& table_name,
                const std::string& filter,
                const std::string& update_rule);
```

You'd expect to have to create the same functions for `update` as for `query`. If you have only one connection, and you've created a specialized `query` function that works with that connection, it's to be expected that you'll need to do the same for `update`. If you wanted to do it with `std::bind`, you'd need to pay attention to the number of arguments, whereas with the curried versions of those functions, you just copy and paste the previous definition and replace `query` with `update`:

```
auto local_query  = query(local_connection);
auto local_update = update(local_connection);
```

You may say this is still only a syntactic difference; you know how many arguments a function has, and you can always define enough placeholders to bind them to. But what happens when you don't know the exact number of arguments? If the preceding approach of creating many functions for which only the first argument is bound to a specific database connection is a common use case, you might want to create a generic function that automatically binds `local_connection` to the first argument of any function you pass to it.

With `std::bind`, you'd need to use clever metaprogramming to create various implementations depending on the number of arguments. With curried functions, that's trivial:

```
template <typename Function>
auto for_local_connection(Function f) {
    return f(local_connection);
}

auto local_query = for_local_connection(query);
auto local_update = for_local_connection(update);
auto local_delete = for_local_connection(delete);
```

As you've seen, although similar, currying and partial function application have their advantages and disadvantages. And both have their use cases. Partial function application is useful when you have a specific function whose arguments you want to bind. In this case, you know how many arguments the function has, and you can choose exactly which arguments you want bound to a specific value. Currying is particularly useful in generic contexts when you can be given a function with any number of arguments. In this case, `std::bind` isn't useful, because if you don't know how many arguments a function has, you can't know how many arguments you need to bind to a placeholder; you don't even know how many placeholders you'll need.

4.3   *Function composition*

Back in 1986, the famous Donald Knuth was asked to implement a program for the "Programming Pearls" column in the *Communications of the ACM* journal.[2] The task was to "read a file of text, determine the *n* most frequently used words, and print out a sorted list of those words along with their frequencies." Knuth produced a solution in Pascal that spanned 10 pages. It was thoroughly commented and even contained a novel data structure for managing the word-count list.

In response, Doug McIlroy wrote a UNIX shell script that solved the same problem, but in only six lines:

```
tr -cs A-Za-z '\n' |
    tr A-Z a-z |
    sort |
    uniq -c |
    sort -rn |
    sed ${1}q
```

Although we don't care about shell scripting, this is a nice example of the functional way of problem solving. First, it's surprisingly short. It doesn't define the algorithm steps, but rather the transformations that need to be done on the input so you can get the desired output. It also has no state; there aren't any variables. It's a pure implementation of the given problem.

---

[2]   *Communications of the ACM* is the monthly magazine of the Association for Computing Machinery (ACM).

McIlroy separated the given problem into a set of simpler but powerful functions that somebody else wrote (UNIX commands, in this case) and passed results that one function returned to another function. This ability to compose functions is exactly what gives you the expressiveness to solve problems elegantly in a few lines of code.

Because most of us don't speak "shell" on the same level as McIlroy, we're going to analyze this problem from scratch, to see how you can decompose it in C++. We won't deal with the letter capitalization, because that's the least interesting part of this example.

The process, depicted in figure 4.12, consists of the following transformations:

1 You have a file. You can easily open it and read the text it contains. Instead of a single string, you want to get a list of words that appear in that string.

2 Put all those words into a `std::unordered_map<std::string, unsigned int>`, where you'll keep a count for each word you find. (You're using `std::unordered_map` because it's faster than `std::map` and you don't need the items to be sorted at this point.)

3 Iterate through all items in the map (the items will be instances of `std::pair<const std::string, unsigned int>`), and swap each pair around to have the count first and then the word.

4 Sort the collection of pairs lexicographically (first on the first item of the pair, but descending, and then on the second). This gives you the most frequent words first and the least frequent ones last.

5 Print out the words.

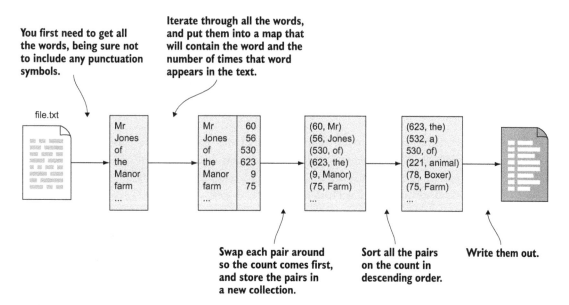

Figure 4.12 You're transforming the original text to a list of words, assigning a count to each word, and then sorting the words based on the number of times they appear in the text.

Looking at this example, you need to create five functions. All functions should do only one simple thing and be created in a way that makes them compose easily. The output of one function can be easily passed as the input of another. The original file can be seen as a collection of characters—say, a `std::string`—so your first function, let's call it `words`, needs to be able to receive the `std::string` as its argument. Its return type should be a collection of words, so you can use `std::vector<std::string>`. (You could also use something more efficient that would avoid making unnecessary copies, but that's out of the scope of this chapter. We'll return to it in chapter 7.)

```
std::vector<std::string> words(const std::string& text);
```

The second function—let's call it `count_occurrences`—gets a list of words, so, again a `std::vector<std::string>`. It creates a `std::unordered_map<std::string, unsigned int>` that stores all the words and the number of times each word appears in the text. You can even make it a function template so it can be used for other things, not just strings:

```
template <typename T>
std::unordered_map<T, unsigned int> count_occurrences(
    const std::vector<T>& items);
```

> ### With a bit of light template magic
> You also could make a template for the collection, not only the contained type:
>
> ```
> template <typename C,
>           typename T = typename C::value_type>
> std::unordered_map<T, unsigned int> count_occurrences(
>     const C& collection)
> ```
>
> This function would be able to accept any collection that allows you to deduce the type of the contained items (`C::value_type`). You could invoke it to count occurrences of characters in a string, strings in a vector of strings, integer values in a list of integers, and so on.

The third function takes each pair of values from the container and creates a new pair with the elements reversed. It needs to return a collection of newly created pairs. Because you're planning to sort it later, and you want to create easily composable functions, you can return it as a vector:

```
template <typename C,
          typename P1,
          typename P2>
std::vector<std::pair<P2, P1>> reverse_pairs(
    const C& collection);
```

After that, you only need a function that sorts a vector (`sort_by_frequency`) and a function that can write that vector to the standard output (`print_pairs`). When you compose these functions, you get the final result. Generally, function composition in

C++ is done by composing the functions at the point in code where you want to call them on a specific original value. In this case, it looks like this:

```
void print_common_words(const std::string& text)
{
    return print_pairs(
        sort_by_frequency(
            reverse_pairs(
                count_occurrences(
                    words(text)
                )
            )
        )
    );
}
```

In this example, you've seen how a problem that takes more than a few pages when implemented in the imperative style can be split into a few functions that are fairly small and easy to implement. You started with a bigger problem and, instead of analyzing the steps you need to perform to achieve the result, began thinking about what transformations you need to perform on the input. You created a short and simple function for each of those transformations. And, finally, you composed them into one bigger function that solves the problem.

4.4 Function lifting, revisited

We touched on the topic of lifting in chapter 1, and this is the perfect place to expand on it. Broadly speaking, *lifting* is a programming pattern that gives you a way to transform a given function into a similar function that's applicable in a broader context. For example, if you have a function that operates on a string, lifting allows you to easily create functions that operate on a vector or a list of strings, on pointers to strings, on a map that maps integers to strings, and on other structures that contain strings.

Let's start with a simple function that takes a string and converts it to uppercase:

```
void to_upper(std::string& string);
```

If you have a function that operates on a string (such as to_upper), what does it take to implement a function that operates on a pointer to a string (and transforms the string that the pointer points to if the pointer isn't null)? What about using that function to transform all people names stored in a vector of strings or in a map that maps movie identifiers to their names? You can easily create all these functions, as shown in the following listing.

Listing 4.17 Functions that operate on a collection of strings

```
void pointer_to_upper(std::string* str)
{
    if (str) to_upper(*str);
}
```

You can see a pointer to a string as a collection that contains either one element or nothing. If the pointer points to a string, that string will be transformed.

```
void vector_to_upper(std::vector<std::string>& strs)
{
    for (auto& str : strs) {
        to_upper(str);
    }
}
```

A vector can contain as many strings as you want. This function converts them all to uppercase.

```
void map_to_upper(std::map<int, std::string>& strs)
{
    for (auto& pair : strs) {
        to_upper(pair.second);
    }
}
```

The map contains pairs of <const int, std::string>. You're leaving the integer values untouched while converting all strings to uppercase.

It's worth noting that these functions would be implemented the exact same way if to_upper was replaced with something else. The implementation does, however, depend on the container type, so you have three implementations: for a pointer to a string, a vector of strings, and a map (see figure 4.13).

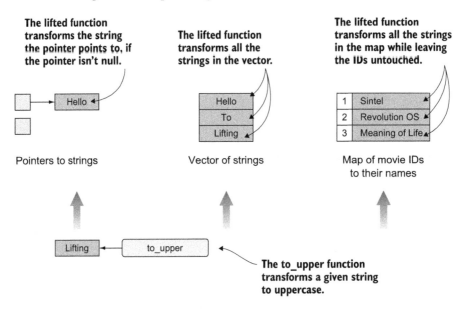

Figure 4.13   You're lifting a function that transforms a single string to a few functions that transform strings contained in various container-like types.

You could create a higher-order function that takes any function that operates on a single string, and creates a function that operates on a pointer to a string. You'd create a separate function that operates on a vector of strings and on a map. These functions are called *lifting functions* because they lift the function that operates on a certain type to a structure or a collection containing that type.

Let's implement these using C++14 features for the sake of brevity. It would be easy to implement them as regular classes with the call operator, as you saw in the previous chapter.

Listing 4.18 Lifting functions

```
template <typename Function>
auto pointer_lift(Function f)
{
    return [f](auto* item) {
        if (item) {
            f(*item);
        }
    };
}
```

You're using auto* as the type specifier. So, you can use this function not only for pointers to strings, but for pointers to any type you want.

```
template <typename Function>
auto collection_lift(Function f)
{
    return [f](auto& items) {
        for (auto& item : items) {
            f(item);
        }
    };
}
```

The same goes for this function: you can use it not only for vectors of strings, but for any iterable collection holding any type.

You could easily do the same for any other container-like type: structures that have a few strings in them; smart pointers such as `std::unique_ptr` and `std::shared_ptr`, for tokenized input streams; as well as some of the more unorthodox container types we'll cover later. This would allow you to always implement the simplest case possible and then lift it up to the structure you need to use it on.

4.4.1 Reversing a list of pairs

Now that you've seen what lifting is, let's return to the Knuth problem. One of the transformation steps was to reverse a collection of pairs, and you used the `reverse_pairs` function to do that. Let's look a bit deeper into this function; see figure 4.14.

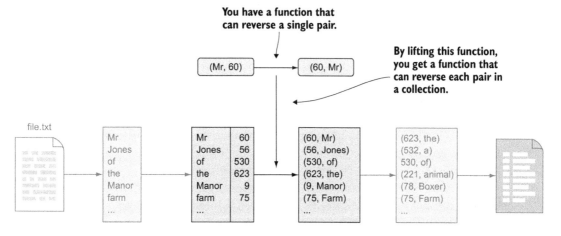

Figure 4.14 You have a collection of pairs that you want to reverse and a function that's capable of reversing a single pair. By lifting the function, you get a function that can reverse each pair in a collection.

As in the previous case, you can make the `reverse_pairs` function generic to accept any iterable collection (vectors, lists, maps, and so forth) that contains pairs of items. Instead of modifying the items in the collection, as in the previous example, you're going to implement this in a pure way. The function will apply the same transformation to all elements (swap the elements in a pair of values) and collect the results in a new collection (see example:knuth-problem/main.cpp). You've already seen that you can do this with `std::transform`.

```
template <
    typename C,
    typename P1 = typename std::remove_cv<
            typename C::value_type::first_type>::type,
    typename P2 = typename C::value_type::second_type
    >
std::vector<std::pair<P2, P1>> reverse_pairs(const C& items)
{
    std::vector<std::pair<P2, P1>> result(items.size());

    std::transform(
        std::begin(items), std::end(items),
        std::begin(result),
        [](const std::pair<const P1, P2>& p)
        {
            return std::make_pair(p.second, p.first);
        }
    );

    return result;
}
```

Initializes type C to be the type of the collection, P1 to be the type of the first item in a pair coming from the source collection (with const removed), and P2 to be the type of second item in the pair

Passes a lambda that reverses values in a single pair to std::transform, and lifts it to a new function that can perform the same task but on multiple items in a collection

You've lifted a function that takes a pair of values and returns a new pair with the same values, but in reverse order, to work on an arbitrary collection of pairs. When building more-complex structures and objects, you do so by composing simpler types. You can create structures that contain other types, vectors and other collections that contain multiple items of the same type, and so on. Because you need these objects to do something, you create functions that operate on them (whether non-member or member functions). Lifting allows you to easily implement these functions when they just need to pass the torch on to a function that operates on the underlying type.

For each of the more complex types, you need to create a lifting function, and you'll be able to call all the functions that work on the underlying type on your type as well. This is one of the places where the object-oriented and functional paradigms go hand in hand.

Most of what you've seen in this chapter is useful in the OOP world as well. You've seen that you can use partial application to bind a member function pointer to a specific instance of the object whose member it is (listing 4.11). It might be a nice exercise for you to investigate the relation between member functions and their implicit `this` argument and currying.

TIP For more information and resources about the topics covered in this chapter, see https://forums.manning.com/posts/list/41683.page.

Summary

- Higher-order functions such as `std::bind` can be used to transform existing functions into new ones. You can get a function of *n* arguments and easily turn it into a unary or a binary function that you can pass to algorithms such as `std::partition` or `std::sort` with `std::bind`.

- Placeholders give you a high level of expressiveness when defining which function arguments shouldn't be bound. They allow you to reorder the arguments in the original function, to pass the same argument multiple times, and so forth.

- Although `std::bind` provides a terse syntax to do partial function application, it might have performance penalties. You may want to consider using lambdas when writing performance-critical code that's often invoked. They're more verbose, but the compiler will be able to optimize them better than the function objects created by `std::bind`.

- Designing an API for your library is hard. Many use cases need to be covered. Consider creating an API that uses curried functions.

- One of the often-heard statements about functional programming is that it lets you write shorter code. If you create functions that are easily composed, you can solve complex problems with a fraction of the code the usual imperative programming approach would take.

Purity: Avoiding
mutable state

This chapter covers

- Problems of writing correct code with
  mutable state
- Understanding referential transparency and its
  relationship to purity
- Programming without changing values of
  variables
- Understanding situations in which mutable
  state isn't evil
- Using `const` to enforce immutability

We touched on the topics of immutability and pure functions in chapter 1. I said one of the main reasons for the existence of bugs is that it's hard to manage all the states a program can be in. In the object-oriented world, we tend to approach this issue by encapsulating parts of the program state into objects. We hide the data behind the class API and allow modification of that data only through that API.

This allows you to control which state changes are valid and should be performed, and which shouldn't. For example, when setting the birthdate of a person, we might want to verify the date isn't in the future, the person isn't older than her parents, and so on. This verification reduces the number of states the program can be in to only the states we consider valid. Although this improves the chances of writing correct programs, it still keeps you open to various problems.

5.1 Problems with the mutable state

Let's check out the following example. A `movie_t` class contains the movie name and a list of scores the users gave it. The class has a member function that calculates the average score for this movie:

```
class movie_t {
public:
    double average_score() const;

    ...

private:
    std::string name;
    std::list<int> scores;
};
```

You've already seen how to implement a function that calculates the average score for a movie (in chapter 2), so you can reuse that function here. The only difference is that you used to have the list of scores passed in as the parameter of the function, and now it's a member variable in the `movie_t` class.

> **Listing 5.1 Calculating the average score for a movie**

```
double movie_t::average_score() const
{
    return std::accumulate(scores.begin(),      ⟵┤ Calling begin and end on a const value
                           scores.end(), 0)        is the same as calling cbegin and cend.
        / (double)scores.size();
}
```

Now the question is whether this code is correct—whether it does what you want it to do. You have a sum of all items in a list, and you're dividing it by the number of scores. The code appears to be correct.

But what happens if someone adds a new score to the list *while* you're calculating the average score? Because you're using `std::list`, the iterators won't become invalid, and `std::accumulate` will finish without any errors. The code will return the sum of all items it processed. The problem is that the newly added score might be included in that sum, but also might not be, depending on where it was inserted (see figure 5.1). Also, `.size()` might return the old size, because C++ doesn't guarantee which argument of the division operator will be calculated first.

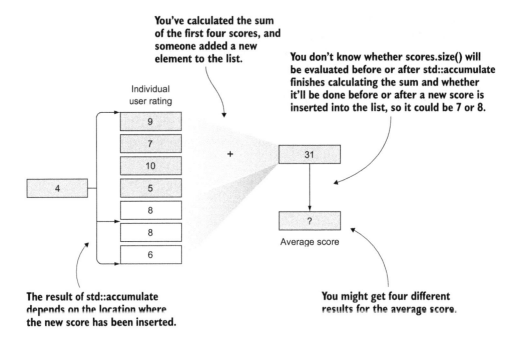

You've calculated the sum of the first four scores, and someone added a new element to the list.

You don't know whether scores.size() will be evaluated before or after std::accumulate finishes calculating the sum and whether it'll be done before or after a new score is inserted into the list, so it could be 7 or 8.

Individual user rating

Average score

The result of std::accumulate depends on the location where the new score has been inserted.

You might get four different results for the average score.

Figure 5.1   The result of the calculation depends on the order of evaluation of the division operands and on the place where the new item is inserted while you're calculating the average score.

You can't guarantee the result you calculate is correct in all possible cases. It would even be useful to know it's incorrect in all possible cases (so you could avoid using it, or fix it)—but you don't know that, either. Equally bad, the result of this function depends on the way other functions in the movie_t class are implemented (whether adding the score adds it to the beginning or to the end of the list), although it doesn't call any of those functions.

Although you need another function to run concurrently (at the same time) with average_score for it to fail, this isn't the only case where you might have problems because you allowed changes to the contents of the list of scores. It isn't rare after a few years of a project's existence to get a few variables whose values depend on each other.

For example, before C++11, std::list wasn't required to remember its size, and there was a possibility that the size member function would need to traverse the entire list in order to calculate the size. A perceptive developer may have seen this and decided to add a new member to your class that saves the number of scores in order to increase the performance of all parts of the code that need to know the number of scores you keep:

```
class movie_t {
public:
    double average_score() const;

    ...

private:
```

```
    std::string name;
    std::list<int> scores;
    size_t scores_size;
};
```

Now, `scores` and `scores_size` are tightly bound, and a change to one should be reflected on the other. Therefore, they aren't properly encapsulated. They aren't accessible from outside your class. The `movie_t` class is properly encapsulated, but inside your class, you can do whatever you want with `scores` and `scores_size` without the compiler ever complaining. It isn't hard to imagine that sometime in the future, a new developer will be working on the same code and will forget to update the size in a rarely executed corner case of this class.

In this case, the bug would probably be easy to catch, but bugs like these tend to be subtle and difficult to triage. During the evolution of a project, the number of intertwined sections of code usually tends to grow until someone decides to refactor the project.

Would you have these problems if the list of scores and the `scores_size` member variable were immutable—declared to be `const`? The first issue is based on the fact that someone could change the list while you're calculating the average score. If the list is immutable, no one can change it while you're using it, so this issue no longer exists.

What about the second issue? If these variables were immutable, they'd have to be initialized on the construction of `movie_t`. It would be possible to initialize `scores_size` to a wrong value, but that mistake would need to be explicit. It can't happen because somebody forgot to update its value—it would have to be because someone wrote incorrect code to calculate it. Another thing is that after the wrong value has been set, it'll persist being wrong; the error won't be some special case that's difficult to debug.

5.2   *Pure functions and referential transparency*

All these issues come from one simple design flaw: having several components in the software system be responsible for the same data, without knowing when another component is changing that data. The *simplest* way to fix this is to forbid changing any data. All the problems you saw will go away.

This is easier said than done. Any communication you have with the user changes a state. If one of your components reads a line of text from the standard input, you've changed the input stream for all other components—they'll never be able to read that exact same line of text. If one button reacts to a mouse click, other buttons will (by default) never be able to know the user clicked something.

Side effects sometimes aren't isolated to your program. When you create a new file, you're changing the data other programs in the system have access to—namely, the hard disk. You're changing the state of all other components in your software and all programs on the system as a side effect of wanting to store data to the disk. This is usually compartmentalized by having different programs access different directories on the file system. But still, you could easily fill up the free space on the disk, thus preventing other programs from saving anything.

Therefore, if you committed to never changing any state, you wouldn't be able to do anything useful. The only kind of programs you could write would be programs that calculated a result based on the arguments you passed in. You couldn't make interactive programs, you couldn't save any data to the disk or to a database, you couldn't send network requests, and so forth. Your programs would be useless.

Instead of saying you can't change any state, let's see how to design software in a way that keeps mutations and side effects to a minimum. But first, you need to better understand the difference between pure and nonpure functions. In chapter 1, I said pure functions use the values of the arguments passed to them only in order to return the result. They need to have no side effects that influence any other function in your program or any other program in your system. Pure functions also need to always return the same result when called with the same arguments.

We're going to define *purity* more precisely now, through a concept called *referential transparency*. Referential transparency is a characteristic of expressions, not just functions. Let's say an expression is anything that specifies a computation and returns a result. We'll say an expression is referentially transparent if the program wouldn't behave any differently if we replaced the entire expression with just its return value. If an expression is referentially transparent, it has no *observable side effects*, and therefore all functions used in that expression are pure.

Let's see what this means through an example. You're going to write a simple function with a vector of integers as its parameter. The function will return the largest value in that collection. In order to be able later to check that you calculated it correctly, you'll log the result to the standard output for errors (`std::cerr` is the character error stream). You'll call this function a couple of times from `main`.

Listing 5.2   Searching for and logging the maximum value

```
double max(const std::vector<double>& numbers)
{
    assert(!numbers.empty());
    auto result = std::max_element(numbers.cbegin(),
                                   numbers.cend());
    std::cerr << "Maximum is: " << *result << std::endl;
    return *result;
}

int main()
{
    auto sum_max =
        max({1}) +
        max({1, 2}) +
        max({1, 2, 3});

    std::cout << sum_max << std::endl; // writes out 6
}
```

Assume the numbers vector isn't empty, to have the std::max_element return a valid iterator.

Is the max function pure? Are all expressions you use it in referentially transparent—does the program change its behavior if you replace all calls to max with the return values?

Listing 5.3 Calls to max replaced by its return values

```
int main()
{
    auto sum_max =
        1 +          ┤ Result of max({I})
        2 +          ┤ Result of max({I, 2})
        3;           ┤ Result of max({I, 2, 3})
    std::cout << sum_max << std::endl;
}
```

The main program still calculates and writes out 6. But overall, the program doesn't behave the same. The original version of the program does more—it writes 6 to std::cout, but before that, it also writes the numbers 1, 2, and 3 (not necessarily in that order) to std::cerr. The max function isn't referentially transparent, and therefore it isn't pure.

I said earlier a pure function uses only its arguments to calculate the result. The max function does use its arguments to calculate the sum_max value. But max also uses std::cerr, which isn't passed in as the function parameter. And furthermore, it not only uses std::cerr, but also changes it by writing to it.

When you remove the part of max that writes to std::cerr, it becomes pure:

```
double max(const std::vector<double>& numbers)
{
    auto result = std::max_element(numbers.cbegin(),
                                   numbers.cend());
    return *result;
}
```

Now max uses the numbers argument only to calculate the result, and it uses std::max_element (which is a pure function) to do so.

We now have a more precise definition of a pure function. And we have the precise meaning for the phrase "has no observable side effects." As soon as a function call can't be completely replaced by its return value without changing the behavior of the program, it has *observable side effects.*

In order to stay on the pragmatic side of things and not become overly theoretical, we'll again use this definition in a more relaxed manner. It isn't useful to abandon logging debugging messages just to be able to call functions *pure.* If you don't think the output you're sending to std::cerr is of any real importance to the program's functionality, and you can write whatever you want to it without anyone noticing or caring about what was written, you can consider max to be pure even if it doesn't fit the preceding definition. When you replace the call to max with its return value, the only difference to the program execution is that it writes fewer things to std::cerr you don't care about; you can say the program behavior didn't change.

5.3 Programming without side effects

It isn't enough to say, "Don't use mutable state, and you'll live happily ever after," because the way to do so isn't obvious or intuitive. We've been taught to think about software (heck, we've been taught to think about real life) as if it were one big state machine that's changing all the time. The usual example is a car. Say you have a car that isn't running. Then you turn the key or press the Start button, and the car goes into a new state: it's *switching on*. When the *switching on* state finishes, the car goes into the *running* state.

In pure functional programming, instead of changing a value, you create a new one. Instead of changing a property of an object, you create a copy of that object, and just the value of that property is changed to the new value. When designing software like this, it isn't possible to have issues like those in the previous example, when someone changed the movie scores while you were processing them. This time, when you have a list of movie scores, nobody can change the list; they can only create new lists with the new scores added.

This approach sounds counterintuitive at first; it seems contrary to the way we usually think the world works. But strangely enough, the idea behind it has been part of the science-fiction scene for decades and even was discussed by some of the ancient Greek philosophers. There's a popular notion that we live in one of many parallel worlds—every time we make a choice, we create a new world in which we made *that* exact choice, and a few parallel worlds in which we made different choices.

When programming, we don't usually care about all possible worlds; we care about just one. And that's why we think we're changing a single world instead of creating new ones all the time and discarding the previous ones. It's an interesting notion, and regardless of whether that's how the world works, it does have its merits when developing software.

Let's demonstrate with a small example. Imagine a small game in which the user tries to get out of a maze, as illustrated in figure 5.2. The maze is defined with a square matrix, and each field can be `Hallway` if it's a hallway, `Wall` if it's a wall, `Start` if it's a starting point, and `Exit` if it's an exit from the maze. You want your game to look pretty, so you'll show different images depending on the direction in which the player is moving.

If you wanted to implement this in an imperative way, the program logic would look something like this (minus handling the pretty graphics—player orientation and transitions).

Listing 5.4 Moving around the maze

```
while (1) {
    - draw the maze and the player
    - read user input
    - if we should move (the user pressed one of the arrow keys)
      check whether the destination cell is a wall,
      and move the player to the destination cell if it isn't
```

```
                  - check whether we have found the exit,
                    show a message if we have,
                    and exit the loop
}
```

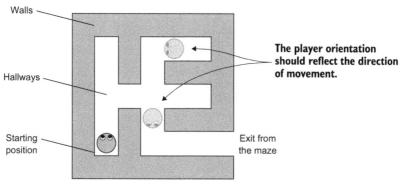

Figure 5.2   The maze is defined by a matrix in which each cell can be a wall or a hallway. The player can move around but can't go through the walls.

This is a perfect example of when mutable state is useful. You have a maze and a player, and you're moving the player around the maze, thus changing its state. Let's see how to model this in a world of immutable state.

First, notice the maze never changes, and the player is the only thing in the program that changes its state. You need to focus on the player, and the maze can easily be an immutable class.

In each step of the game, you need to *move* the player to a new position. What data is needed to calculate the new position?

- Which direction to move
- The previous position, to know where you're moving from
- Whether you can move to the desired position

You need to create a function that has these three parameters and returns the new position.

Listing 5.5   Function to calculate the player's next position

```
position_t next_position(
        direction_t direction,
        const position_t& previous_position,
        const maze_t& maze
    )
{
    const position_t desired_position{previous_position, direction};

    return maze.is_wall(desired_position) ? previous_position
                                          : desired_position;
}
```

Calculates the desired position even if it might be a wall

If the new position isn't a wall, returns it; otherwise, returns the old position

You've implemented the moving logic without a single mutable variable. You need to define the `position_t` constructor, which calculates the coordinates of the neighboring cell in the given direction.

Listing 5.6   Calculating the coordinates of the neighboring cell

```
position_t::position_t(const position_t& original,
                       direction_t direction)
    : x { direction == Left  ? original.x - 1 :
          direction == Right ? original.x + 1 :
                               original.x      }
    , y { direction == Up    ? original.y + 1 :
          direction == Down  ? original.y - 1 :
                               original.y      }
{
}
```

> Uses the ternary operator to match against the possible direction values and initialize the correct values of x and y. You could also use a switch statement in the body of the constructor.

Now that you have the logic nailed down, you need to know how to show the player. There is a choice: you can change the player orientation when you successfully move to another cell; or you can change the player orientation even if you haven't moved, to show the user that you did understand the command but are unable to comply because you encountered a wall. This is part of the presentation layer and isn't something you need to consider an integral part of the player. Both choices are equally valid.

In the presentation layer, you need to be able to draw the maze and the player inside it. Because the maze is immutable, showing it to the user won't change anything. The function that draws the player also doesn't need to change it. The function needs to know the position of the player and which direction the player should face:

```
void draw_player(const position_t& position,
                 direction_t direction)
```

I mentioned you have two choices when showing which way the player is facing. One is based on whether the player was moved; this can be easily calculated because you always create new instances of `position_t`, and the previous position is unchanged. The second option that changes the player orientation even if it didn't move can easily be implemented by orienting the player in the same direction you passed to the `next_position` function. You can also take this further; you could choose different images depending on the current time or the time since the player was last moved, and so forth.

Now you need to tie this logic together. Let's implement the event loop recursively for demonstration purposes. I said in chapter 2 that you shouldn't overuse recursion, because the compiler isn't guaranteed to optimize it when compiling your program. This example uses recursion only to demonstrate that the entire program can be implemented in a pure way—without ever changing any object after it's created.

Listing 5.7   Recursive event loop

```
void process_events(const maze_t& maze,
                    const position_t& current_position)
{
    if (maze.is_exit(current_position)) {
        // show message and exit
        return;
    }

    const direction_t direction = …;

    draw_maze();
    draw_player(current_position, direction);

    const auto new_position = next_position(
            direction,
            current_position,
            maze);

    process_events(maze, new_position);
}

int main()
{
    const maze_t maze("maze.data");
    process_events(
            maze,
            maze.start_position();
}
```

Calculates the direction based on user input

Shows the maze and the player

Gets the new position

Continues processing the events, but now with the player moved to the new cell

The main function only needs to load the maze and call process_events with the player's initial position.

This example shows a common way to model stateful programs while avoiding any state changes and keeping the functions pure. In real-world programs, things are usually much more complicated. Here, the only thing that needs to be changed is the position of the player. Everything else, including how the player is shown to the user, can be calculated from the way the position changes.

Larger systems have many movable parts. You could create a huge, all-encompassing *world* structure that you'd re-create every time you needed to change something in it. This would have a big performance overhead (even if you use data structures optimized for functional programming, as covered in chapter 8) and would significantly increase the complexity of your software.

Instead, you'll usually have *some* mutable state that you think would be inefficient to always have to copy and pass around, and you'll model your functions so they return statements about what should be changed in the world instead of always returning new copies of the world. What this approach brings to the table is a clear separation between mutable and pure parts of the system.

5.4   Mutable and immutable state in a concurrent environment

Most of today's software systems include some kind of concurrency—whether it's splitting complex calculations such as image processing into a few parallel threads so the entire job can be finished faster, or having various tasks performed at the same time so a web browser can download a file while the user browses a web page.

Mutable state can lead to problems because it allows shared responsibility (which is even against the best OOP practices). These problems are elevated in concurrent environments because the responsibility can be shared by multiple components at *the same time*.

A minimal example that shows the essence of this problem is creating two concurrent processes that try to change the value of a single integer variable. Imagine you want to count the number of clients currently connected to your server, so you can go into power-save mode when everyone disconnects. You start with two connected clients, and both of them disconnect at the same time:

```
void client_disconnected(const client_t& client)
{
    // Free the resources used by the client
    ...

    // Decrement the number of connected clients
    connected_clients--;

    if (connected_clients == 0) {
        // go to the power-save mode
    }
}
```

We'll focus on the `connected_clients--` line. It seems innocent. At the beginning, if all is well, `connected_clients == 2` because you have two clients. When one client disconnects, the `connected_clients` value will become 1; and when the second one disconnects, it'll become 0, and you'll go to power-save mode. The problem is that even if it looks like a simple statement to you, it isn't for the computer. The code needs to do the following:

1   Get the value from the memory to the processor.
2   Decrement the retrieved value.
3   Store the changed value back into memory.

As far as the processor is concerned, these steps are separate, and it doesn't care that the code is a single command from your point of view. If the `client_disconnected` function is called twice at the same time (from different threads), these three steps from one call can be interleaved in any way imaginable with the steps from the second call. One call might retrieve the value from the memory even before the other one has finished changing it. In that case, you'd end up with the value decremented only once (or, to be more precise, decremented from 2 to 1 two times), and the value will never go back to 0 (see figure 5.3).

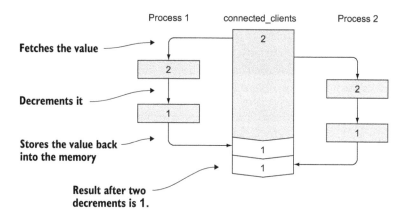

Figure 5.3   Two concurrent processes want to decrement a value. Each needs to retrieve the value from memory, decrement that value, and store it back into memory. Because the initial value is 2, you expect the result after decrementing it twice to be 0. But if the second process is allowed to read the value from memory before the first process has stored its result back into memory, you may end up with a wrong result.

If you have problems caused by concurrent access to a single integer, imagine what problems you'll have with more-complex data structures. Fortunately, this problem was solved a long time ago. People realized it's problematic to allow data to be changed when there's a possibility of concurrent access to that data. The solution was simple: let the programmer forbid concurrent access to the data via *mutexes*.

The problem with this approach is that you *want* to have things running in parallel—whether for efficiency or something else. And mutexes solve the problem with concurrency by removing concurrency:

> *I've often joked that instead of picking up Djikstra's cute acronym (mutex—which stands for mutual exclusion), we should have called the basic synchronization object "the bottleneck." Bottlenecks are useful at times, sometimes indispensable—but they're never good. At best, they're a necessary evil. Anything—anything—that encourages anyone to overuse them, to hold them too long, is bad. It's not just the straight-line performance impact of the extra recursion logic in the mutex lock and unlock that's the issue here—it's the far greater, wider, and much more difficult-to-characterize impact on the overall application concurrency.*

—David Butenhof on comp.programming.threads

Mutexes are necessary sometimes,[1] but they should be used rarely, and not as an excuse for bad software design. Mutexes, like `for` loops and recursion, are low-level constructs that are useful for implementing higher-level abstractions for concurrent

---

[1]   Check out *C++ Concurrency in Action* by Anthony Williams for more details about concurrency, mutexes, and how to write multithreaded code in the usual way. We'll cover functional programming techniques for writing concurrent and asynchronous software in chapters 10 and 12.

programming but aren't something that should appear too often in normal code. It might sound strange, but according to Amdahls's law, if you have only 5% of your code serialized (and 95% fully parallelized), the maximum speedup you can expect compared to not having anything parallelized is 20 times—no matter how many thousands of processors you throw at the problem (see figure 5.4).

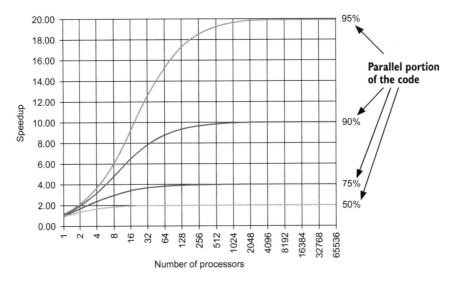

Figure 5.4   It would be ideal to have a tenfold speedup when increasing the number of processors 10 times. Unfortunately, the speedup doesn't increase linearly with the number of processors. According to Amdahl's law, if you have only 5% of your code serialized (through mutexes or other means), the most speedup you can achieve compared to running the code on a single processor is 20—even if you throw in 60,000 processors.

If lowering the level of parallelism your code can achieve isn't what you want, you need to find alternative solutions to mutexes for the concurrency problem. Remember that I said the problems appear only if you have mutable data shared across different concurrently running processes. Therefore, one solution is to not have concurrency, and another is not to use mutable data. But there's also a third option: to have mutable data, but not share it. If you don't share your data, you'll never have the problem that someone has changed it without you knowing.

You have four options: to have immutable data and not to share it, to have mutable data and not to share it, to have immutable data and to share it, and to have mutable data and to share it. Of all four, only the last situation is problematic (figure 5.5). And yet it seems as though 99% of all software somehow belongs to that one.

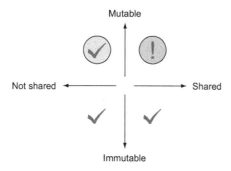

Figure 5.5 You can have both mutable and immutable states; you can share data or not. The only option that produces problems in the concurrent environment is when the data is both shared and mutable. The other three options are safe.

Chapters 10 and 12 cover this topic further. They present the FP abstractions that make concurrent and asynchronous programming, both with and without mutable data, almost as easy as ordinary functional programming.

5.5 *The importance of being const*

Now that you've seen some of the problems that arise from having mutable state, let's investigate the tools C++ provides to facilitate the development of code without mutable state. You have two ways of restricting mutation in C++: the const and constexpr keywords (with the latter being available since C++11).

The basic idea behind const is to prevent data mutation. This is done in C++ through its type system. When you declare an instance of a certain type T to be const, you're declaring the type to be const T. This is a simple concept with far-reaching consequences. Say you've declared a constant std::string variable called name and want to assign it to another variable:

```
const std::string name{"John Smith"};
```

```
std::string name_copy           = name;
std::string& name_ref           = name;  // error
const std::string& name_constref = name;
std::string* name_ptr           = &name;  // error
const std::string* name_constptr = &name;
```

The first assignment tries to assign the constant string name to a nonconstant string variable called name_copy. This will work—a new string will be constructed, and it'll hold a copy of the data name contains. This is OK, because if you later change the value of name_copy, the original string won't be changed.

The second assignment creates a reference to a std::string and tries to set it to refer to the name variable. When you try to compile it, you'll get an error because you're trying to create a reference to a std::string from a variable that has a different type: const std::string (and there's no inheritance here that would allow you to do so). You get a similar error when trying to assign the address of name to name_ptr, which is a pointer to a nonconstant string. This is the desired behavior, because if the compiler allowed you to do this, the name_ref variable would let you call functions on it that would change its value; and because it's only a reference to name, the changes would be performed on the name variable. The compiler stopped you even before you tried to change the value of name.

The third assignment creates a reference to const std::string from a variable whose type is exactly that. It'll pass without any errors. The assignment to a pointer to a constant string (name_constptr) will also work.

Constant references are special

Although the compiler allows you to create a reference to const T from a variable that has the same type is something that's to be expected, constant references (references to constant types) are special. In addition to being able to bind to a variable of type const T, a constant reference can also bind to a temporary value, in which case the constant reference prolongs the temporary variable's lifetime. For more information on the lifetime of temporary objects, check out http://mng.bz/o19v.

Next, what happens when you try to pass this constant string as an argument to a function? The print_name function accepts a string as its parameter, the print_name_ref function accepts a reference to a string, and the print_name_constref accepts a constant reference:

```
void print_name(std::string name_copy);
void print_name_ref(std::string& name_ref);   // error when called
void print_name_constref(const std::string& name_constref);
```

Similar to the previous case, it's OK to assign a value to a string variable from a constant string (a copy of the original string will be created), and to assign a string value to a constant reference to a string because you're preserving the const-ness of the name variable in both cases. The only thing that isn't allowed is assigning a const string to a non-const reference.

You've seen how const works with variable assignment and ordinary functions. Let's see how it relates to member functions. You'll use the person_t class and check out how C++ enforces const-ness.

Consider the following member functions:

```
class person_t {
public:
    std::string name_nonconst();
    std::string name_const() const;

    void print_nonconst(std::ostream& out);
    void print_const(std::ostream& out) const;

    ...

};
```

When you write member functions like these, C++ sees normal functions with an additional implicit argument: this. The const qualifier on a member function is nothing more than a qualifier for the type that this is pointing to. Therefore, the preceding member functions internally look something like this (in reality, this is a pointer, but let's pretend it's a reference for the sake of clarity):

```
std::string person_t_name_nonconst(
        person_t& this
    );
std::string person_t_name_const(
        const person_t& this
    );
void person_t_print_nonconst(
        person_t& this,
        std::ostream& out
    );
void person_t_print_const(
        const person_t& this,
        std::ostream& out
    );
```

When you start looking at member functions as if they were ordinary functions with an implicit parameter this, the meaning of calling member functions on constant and nonconstant objects becomes obvious—it's exactly the same as in the previous case, where you tried to pass constant and nonconstant objects to ordinary functions as arguments. Trying to call a nonconstant member function on a constant object results in an error because you're trying to assign a constant object to a nonconstant reference.

> ### Why is "this" a pointer?
>
> this is a constant pointer to an instance of the object the member function belongs to. According to the language rules, it can never be null (although, in reality, some compilers allow calling nonvirtual member functions on null pointers).
>
> The question is, then, if this can't be changed to point to another object, and it can't be null, why isn't it a reference instead of a pointer? The answer is simple: when this was introduced, C++ didn't have references yet. It was impossible to change this later because it would break backward compatibility with the previous language versions and break a lot of code.

As you've seen, the mechanism behind const is simple, but it works surprisingly well. By using const, you're telling the compiler you don't want a variable to be mutable, and the compiler will give you an error message any time you try to change that variable.

5.5.1 Logical and internal const-ness

I said you want to implement immutable types to avoid the problems of mutable state. Probably the simplest way to do this in C++ is to create classes in which all members are constant—similar to implementing the person_t class like this:

```
class person_t {
public:
    const std::string name;
    const std::string surname;

    …
};
```

You don't even need to create accessor member functions for these variables; you can just make them public. This approach has a downside: some compiler optimizations will stop working. As soon as you declare a constant member variable, you lose the move constructor and the move assignment operator (see http://mng.bz/JULm for more information about move semantics).

Let's choose a different approach. Instead of making all member variables constant, you'll make all (public) member functions constant:

```
class person_t {
public:
    std::string name() const;
    std::string surname() const;

private:
    std::string m_name;
    std::string m_surname;

    ...
};
```

This way, although the members aren't declared as const, the user of your class can't change them because this will point to an instance of const person_t in all member functions you implemented. This provides both *logical* const-*ness* (the user-visible data in the object never changes) and *internal* const-*ness* (no changes to the internal data of the object). At the same time, you won't lose any optimization opportunities because the compiler will generate all the necessary move operations for you.

The problem you're left with is that sometimes you need to be able to change your internal data but hide those changes from the user. As far as the user is concerned, you need to be immutable. This is necessary, for example, when you want to cache the result of a time-consuming operation.

Say you want to implement the employment_history function that returns the list of all previous jobs a person had. This function will need to contact the database in order to retrieve this data. Because all member functions are declared as const, the only place you can initialize all member variables is in the person_t constructor. Querying the database isn't a particularly fast operation, so you don't want to do it every time a new instance of person_t is created if it isn't useful for all users of this class. At the same time, for the users who do need to know the employment history, you don't want to query the database every time the employment_history function is called. This would be problematic not only because of performance, but also because this function might return different results when called multiple times (if the data in the database changes), which would ruin your promise that person_t is immutable.

This can be solved by creating a mutable member variable in your class—a member variable that can be changed even from const member functions. Because you want to guarantee that your class is immutable from the user's perspective, you have to ensure that two concurrent calls to `employment_history` can't return different values. You need to ensure that the second call isn't executed until the first one finishes loading the data.

Listing 5.8 Using `mutable` to implement caching

```
class person_t {
public:
    employment_history_t employment_history() const
    {
        std::unique_lock<std::mutex>
            lock{m_employment_history_mutex};

        if (!m_employment_history.loaded()) {
            load_employment_history();
        }

        return m_employment_history;
    }

}

private:
    mutable std::mutex m_employment_history_mutex;
    mutable employment_history_t m_employment_history;

    ...
};
```

Locks the mutex to guarantee that a concurrent invocation of employment_history can't be executed until you finish retrieving the data from the database

Gets the data if it isn't already loaded

The data is loaded; you're returning it to the caller.

When you exit this block, the lock variable will be destroyed and the mutex will be unlocked.

You want to be able to lock the mutex from a constant member function, so it needs to be mutable as well as the variable you're initializing.

This is the usual pattern of implementing classes that are immutable on the outside but that sometimes need to change internal data. It's required for constant member functions that either the class data is kept unchanged or all changes are synchronized (unnoticeable even in the case of concurrent invocations).

5.5.2 *Optimizing member functions for temporaries*

When you design your classes to be immutable, whenever you want to create a *setter* member function, you need to create a function that returns a copy of your object in which a specific member value is changed instead. Creating copies just to get a modified version of an object isn't efficient (although the compiler might be able to optimize the process in some cases). This is especially true when you no longer need the original object.

Imagine you have an instance of `person_t` and want to get an updated version with the name and surname changed. You'd have to write something like this:

```
person_t new_person {
    old_person.with_name("Joanne")
              .with_surname("Jones")
    };
```

The `.with_name` function returns a new instance of `person_t` with the name `Joanne`. Because you aren't assigning that instance to a variable, it'll be destroyed as soon as this entire expression is calculated. You're just calling `.with_surname` on it, which creates yet another instance of `person_t` that now has both the name Joanne and surname Jones.

You'll construct two separate instances of `person_t` and copy all the data that `person_t` holds twice, whereas you want to create only a single person—to assign to the `new_person` variable. It would be better if you could avoid this by detecting that `.with_surname` has been called on a temporary object, and that you don't need to create a copy of it, but you can move the data from it into the result. Fortunately, you can do this by creating two separate functions for each of `.with_name` and `.with_surname`—one that works on proper values, and one for temporaries.

Listing 5.9   Separating member functions for normal values and temporaries

```
class person_t {                                          │ This member function will
public:                                                   │ work on normal values
    person_t with_name(const std::string& name) const &   ◄─┘ and lvalue references.
    {
        person_t result(*this);          ◄─────┐ Creates a copy of the person

        result.m_name = name;            ◄─────┐ Sets the new name for that person. It's OK to
                                               │ change the name because this person_t instance
                                               │ still isn't visible from the outside world.

        return result;                   ◄─────┐ Returns the newly created person_t instance.
    }                                          │ From this point on, it's immutable.

    person_t with_name(const std::string& name) &&   ◄───┐ This one will be called on
    {                                                     │ temporaries and other
        person_t result(std::move(*this));   ◄───┐        │ rvalue references.
                                                 │ Calls the move constructor instead
                                                 │ of the copy constructor
        result.m_name = name;            ◄──┐ Sets the name

        return result;                   ◄──┐ Returns the newly created person
    }

};
```

You're declaring two overloads of the `.with_name` function. Just as you saw with the `const` qualifier, specifying the reference type qualifier on a member function affects only the type of the `this` pointer. The second overload will be called on objects from which you're allowed to steal the data—temporary objects and other rvalue references.

When the first overload is called, you create a new copy of the `person_t` object pointed to by `this`, set the new name, and return the newly created object. In the second overload, you create a new instance of `person_t` and move (instead of copy) all the data from the `person_t` object pointed to by `this` into the newly created instance.

Note that the second overload isn't declared to be `const`. If it was, you wouldn't be allowed to move the data from the current instance to the new one. You'd need to copy it as in the first overload.

Here you've seen one of the possible ways to optimize your code to avoid making copies of temporary objects. Like all optimizations, this one should be used only when it makes a measurable improvement; you should always avoid premature optimizations, and perform benchmarks whenever you decide to optimize something.

5.5.3 Pitfalls with const

The `const` keyword is one of the most useful things in C++, and you should design your classes to use it as much as possible, even when not programming in the functional style. Just like the rest of the type system, it makes a lot of common programming errors detectable during compilation.

But it isn't all fun and games. You may encounter a few pitfalls if you use `const` too much.

CONST DISABLES MOVING THE OBJECT

When writing a function that returns a value of some type (not a reference or a pointer to a value), you often define a local variable of that type, do something with it, and return it. That's what you did in both `.with_name` overloads. Let's extract the essence of this pattern:

```
person_t some_function()
{
    person_t result;

    // do something before returning the result

    return result;
}

...

person_t person = some_function();
```

If the compilers didn't perform any optimizations when compiling this code, `some_function` would create a new instance of `person_t` and return it to the caller. In this case, that instance would be passed to the copy (or move) constructor in order to initialize the `person` variable. When the copy (or move) is made, the instance that `some_function` returned is deleted. Just as in the previous case, where you had consecutive calls to `.with_name` and `.with_surname`, you create two new instances of `person_t`, one of which is temporary and is deleted immediately after `person` is constructed.

Fortunately, compilers tend to optimize this process to make `some_function` construct its local `result` variable directly in the space reserved by the caller for the `person` variable, thus avoiding any unnecessary copies or moves. This optimization is called *named return value optimization* (NRVO).

This is one of the rare cases in which using `const` may hurt you. When the compiler can't perform NRVO, returning a `const` object will incur a copy instead of being able to move the `const` into the result.

SHALLOW CONST

Another problem is that `const` can easily be subverted. Imagine the following situation: you have a `company_t` class that keeps a vector of pointers to all its employees.

You also have a constant member function that returns a vector containing the names of all employees:

```
class company_t {
public:
    std::vector<std::string> employees_names() const;

private:
    std::vector<person_t*> m_employees;
};
```

The compiler will forbid you to call any nonconstant member functions of `company_t` and `m_employees` from the `employees_names` member function because it's declared `const`. So, you're forbidden to change any data in this instance of `company_t`. But are the `person_t` instances that represent the employee data part of this instance of `company_t`? They aren't. Only the pointers to them are. You aren't allowed to change the pointers from the `employees_names` function, but you're allowed to change the objects those pointers point to.

This is a tricky situation that might lead you into trouble if you didn't design the `person_t` class to be immutable. If there were functions that mutated `person_t`, you'd be allowed to call them from `employees_names`; that would be nice if the compiler guarded you against it, because `const` should be a promise that you aren't changing anything.

The `const` keyword gives you the ability to declare your intent that an object shouldn't be modified, and it gets the compiler to enforce this constraint. Although writing it all the time is tedious, if you do, then every time you see a non-const variable, you'll *know* it's meant to be changed. In that case, every time you want to use the variable, you need to check all the places where it could have been modified. If a variable was declared as `const`, you'd be able to check its declaration and know its exact value when you decide to use it.

The propagate_const wrapper

A special wrapper for pointer-like objects, called `propagate_const`, can remedy this problem. Currently, it's published under the *Library Fundamentals Technical Specification* and should become part of a future C++ standard after C++17.

If your compiler and STL vendor provide experimental library features like these, you'll be able to find the `propagate_const` wrapper in the `<experimental/propagate_const>` header. As with all things that live in the `experimental::` namespace, the API and behavior of this wrapper may change in future revisions, so be warned.

If you're lucky enough to be able to use the `propagate_const` wrapper, it's as simple as wrapping types of all the pointer member variables (and other pointer-like types such as smart pointers) in your class with `std::experimental::propagate_const<T*>`. It'll detect when you use it from a constant member function, and in that case it'll behave like a pointer to const `T`.

TIP For more information and resources about the topics covered in this chapter, see https://forums.manning.com/posts/list/41684.page.

Summary

- Most computers have multiple processing units. When writing programs, you need to ensure that your code works correctly in multithreaded environments.
- If you overuse mutexes, you'll limit the level of parallelism your program can achieve. Because of the need for synchronization, program speed doesn't grow linearly with the number of processors you're using.
- Mutable state isn't necessarily bad; having it is safe as long as it isn't shared between multiple system components at the same time.
- When you make a member function const, you promise that the function won't change any data in the class (not a bit of the object will change), or that any changes to the object (to members declared as mutable) will be atomic as far as the users of the object are concerned.
- Copying the entire structure when you want to change only a single value isn't efficient. You can use special immutable data structures to remedy this (chapter 8 covers immutable data structures).

Lazy evaluation

Calculations take time. Say you have two matrices—A and B—and you're told you may need their product at some point. One thing you could do is to immediately calculate the product, and it'll be ready when you need it:

```
auto P = A * B;
```

The problem is that you may end up not needing the product at all—and you wasted your precious CPU cycles calculating it.

An alternative approach is to say if someone needs it, P should be calculated as A * B. Instead of doing the calculation, you're just defining it. When a part of your program needs the value of P, you'll calculate it. But not before.

You usually define calculations by creating functions. Instead of P being a value that holds the product of A and B, you can turn it into a lambda that captures A and B and returns their product when invoked:

```
auto P = [A, B] {
    return A * B;
};
```

If someone needs the value, they need to call it like a function P().

You've optimized your code for when you have a complex calculation whose result may not be needed. But you've created a new issue: what if the value is needed more than once? With this approach, you'd need to calculate the product every time it's needed. Instead, it would be better to remember the result the first time it's calculated.

This is what being lazy is all about: instead of doing the work in advance, you postpone it as much as possible. Because you're lazy, you also want to avoid doing the same thing multiple times, so after you get the result, you'll remember it.

6.1 Laziness in C++

Unfortunately, C++ doesn't support lazy evaluation out of the box like some other languages do, but it does provide tools you can use to simulate this behavior in your programs. You're going to create a template class called lazy_val that can store a computation and cache the result of that computation after it's executed (this is often called *memoization*). Therefore, this type needs to be able to hold the following:

- The computation
- A flag indicating whether you've already calculated the result
- The calculated result

I said in chapter 2 that the most efficient way to accept an arbitrary function object is as a template parameter. You'll follow that advice in this case as well; lazy_val will be templated on the type of the function object (the definition of the computation). You don't need to specify the resulting type as a template parameter because it can be easily deduced from the computation.

> **Listing 6.1 Member variables of the `lazy_val` class template**

You need to be able to tell whether you've already cached the computation result.

Stores the function object that defines the computation

Cache for the computed result. The type of the member variable is the return type of the computation.

```
template <typename F>
class lazy_val {
private:
    F m_computation;
    mutable bool m_cache_initialized;
    mutable decltype(m_computation()) m_cache;
    mutable std::mutex m_cache_mutex;

public:
    ...
};
```

You need the mutex in order to stop multiple threads from trying to initialize the cache at the same time.

You'll make the `lazy_val` template class immutable, at least when looked at from the outside world. You'll mark all member functions you create as `const`. Internally, you need to be able to change the cached value after you first calculate it, so all cache-related member variables must be declared as `mutable`.

Your choice to have the computation type as the template parameter for `lazy_val` has a downside, because automatic template deduction for types is supported only since C++17. Most of the time, you won't be able to specify the type explicitly because you'll be defining the computation through lambdas, and you can't write the type of a lambda. You'll need to create a `make_lazy_val` function, because automatic template argument deduction works for function templates, so you can use the `lazy_val` template with compilers that don't support C++17.

Listing 6.2 Constructor and a factory function

```
template <typename F>
class lazy_val {
private:
    ...

public:
    lazy_val(F computation)              Initializes the computation definition.
        : m_computation(computation)     Note the cache isn't initialized yet.
        , m_cache_initialized(false)
    {
    }
};

template <typename F>                                      Convenience function that
inline lazy_val<F> make_lazy_val(F&& computation)          creates a new lazy_val instance
{                                                          automatically deducing the
    return lazy_val<F>(std::forward<F>(computation));      type of the computation
}
```

The constructor doesn't need to do anything except store the computation and set to `false` the flag that indicates whether you've already calculated the result.

> **NOTE** In this implementation, you require that the result type of the computation is default constructible. You have the `m_cache` member variable, to which you don't assign an initial value, so the constructor of `lazy_val` implicitly calls the default constructor for it. This is a limitation of this particular implementation, not a requirement for the lazy value concept. The full implementation of this class template, which doesn't have this problem, can be found in the code example 06-lazy-val.

The last step is to create a member function that returns a value. If this is the first time the value is requested, the function will calculate and cache it. Otherwise, the function will return the cached value. You can define the call operator on `lazy_val`, thus making it a function object, or you can create a casting operator that would allow the lazy_val instance to look like a normal variable. Both approaches have their advantages, and choosing one over the other is mostly a matter of taste. Let's go for the latter.

The implementation is straightforward. You're locking the mutex so nobody can touch the cache until you're finished with it; and if the cache isn't initialized, you initialize it to whatever the stored computation returns.

Listing 6.3 Casting operator for the `lazy_val` class template

```
template <typename F>
class lazy_val {
private:
    ...

public:
    ...

    operator const decltype(m_computation())& () const
    {
        std::unique_lock<std::mutex>
            lock{m_cache_mutex};

        if (!m_cache_initialized) {
            m_cache = m_computation();
            m_cache_initialized = true;
        }

        return m_cache;
    }
};
```

Annotations:
- `operator const decltype(m_computation())& () const` — Allows implicit casting of an instance of lazy_val to the const-ref of the return type of the computation
- `std::unique_lock<std::mutex> lock{m_cache_mutex};` — Forbids concurrent access to the cache
- `if (!m_cache_initialized) { m_cache = m_computation(); m_cache_initialized = true; }` — Caches the result of the computation for later use

If you're well versed in writing multithreaded programs, you may have noticed this implementation is suboptimal. Every time the program needs the value, you lock and unlock a mutex. But you need to lock the m_cache variable only the first time the function is called—while you're calculating the value.

Instead of using a mutex, which is a general low-level synchronization primitive, you can use something that's tailored exactly for your use case. The casting operator does two things: it initializes the m_cache variable and returns the value stored in that variable, where the initialization needs to be performed only once per instance of lazy_val. So you have a part of the function that needs to be executed only the first time the function is called. The standard library provides a solution for this—the std::call_once function:

```
template <typename F>
class lazy_val {
private:
    F m_computation;
    mutable decltype(m_computation()) m_cache;
    mutable std::once_flag m_value_flag;

public:
    ...
```

```
operator const decltype(m_computation())& () const
{
    std::call_once(m_value_flag, [this] {
        m_cache = m_computation();
    });

    return m_cache;
}
};
```

You've replaced the mutex and the Boolean m_cache_initialized indicator from the previous implementation with an instance of std::once_flag. When the std::call_once function is invoked, it will check whether the flag is set; and if it isn't, it'll execute the function you've passed to it—the function that initializes the m_value member variable.

This solution guarantees the m_value will be initialized safely (no concurrent access by other threads while it's being initialized), and it'll be initialized only once. It's simpler than the first implementation—it clearly communicates what's being done, and it'll be more efficient because after the value is calculated, no further locking is needed.

6.2 Laziness as an optimization technique

Now that you've seen the most basic variant of laziness—calculating a single value the first time it's needed, and then caching it for later use—we can move on to more-advanced examples. You'll often encounter problems you can't solve by changing a type of a single variable to its lazy equivalent, as in the preceding example. It'll sometimes be necessary to develop alternative lazy versions of common algorithms that you're used to. Anytime you have an algorithm that processes an entire data structure, when you only need a few resulting items, you have the potential to optimize the code by being lazy.

6.2.1 Sorting collections lazily

Say you have a collection of a few hundred employees stored in a vector. You have a window that can show 10 employees at a time; the user has the option to sort the employees based on various criteria such as name, age, number of years working for the company, and so forth. When the user chooses to sort the list by the age of the employees, the program should show the 10 oldest employees and allow the user to scroll down to see the rest of the sorted list.

You can do this easily by sorting the entire collection and displaying 10 employees at a time. Although this may be a good approach if you're expecting the user to be interested in the entire sorted list, it will be overkill if that isn't the case. The user may be interested only in the *top 10* lists, and every time the criteria for sorting changes, you're sorting the entire collection.

To make this as efficient as possible, you need to think of a lazy way to sort the collection. You can base the algorithm on quicksort because it's the most commonly used in-memory sorting algorithm.

What the basic variant of quicksort does is simple: it takes an element from the collection, moves all elements that are greater than that element to the beginning of the collection, and moves the rest toward the end of collection (you could even use `std::partition` for this step). This is then repeated for both newly created partitions.

What should you change in order for the algorithm to be lazy—to sort only the part of the collection that needs to be shown to the user, while leaving the rest unsorted? You can't avoid doing the partitioning step, but you can delay the recursive calls on the parts of the collection you don't need sorted yet (see figure 6.1).

You'll sort elements only when (or if) the need arises. This way, you avoid all the recursive invocations of the algorithm on the section of the array that doesn't need to be sorted. You can find a simple implementation of this algorithm in the lazy-sorting example that accompanies this book.

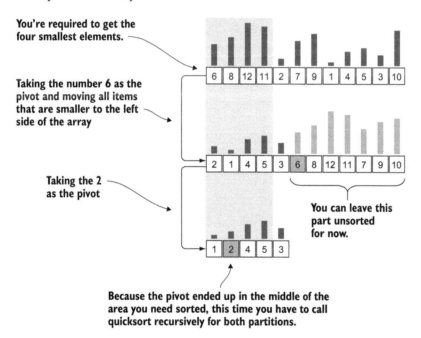

Figure 6.1 When sorting just a part of the collection, you can optimize the quicksort algorithm not to recursively call itself for the partitions that don't need to be sorted.

The complexity of the lazy quicksort algorithm

Because the C++ standard specifies the required complexity for all algorithms it defines, someone may be interested in the complexity of the lazy quicksort algorithm you just defined. Let the size of the collection be n, and assume you want to get the top k items.

For the first partitioning step, you need $O(n)$ operations; for the second, $O(n/2)$; and so on, until you reach the partition size you need to fully sort. In total, for partitioning, you have $O(2n)$ in the common case, which is the same as $O(n)$.

To fully sort the partition of size k, you need $O(k \log k)$ operations, because you need to perform the regular quicksort. Therefore, the total complexity will be $O(n + k \log k)$, which is pretty neat: it means if you're searching for the maximum element in the collection, you'll be in the same ballpark as the `std::max_element` algorithm: $O(n)$. And if you're sorting the entire collection, it'll be $O(n \log n)$, like the normal quicksort algorithm.

6.2.2 *Item views in the user interfaces*

Although the focus of the previous example was to show how to modify a particular algorithm to be lazier, the reason you needed laziness is common. Every time you have a large amount of data but a limited amount of screen space to show that data to the user, you have the opportunity to optimize by being lazy. A common situation is that your data is stored in a database somewhere, and you need to show it to the user one way or another.

To reuse the idea from the previous example, imagine you have a database containing data about your employees. When showing the employees, you want to display their names along with their photos. In the previous example, the reason you needed laziness was that sorting the entire collection when you needed to show only 10 items at a time was superfluous.

Now you have a database, and it's going to do the sorting for you. Does this mean you should load everything at once? Of course not. You're not doing the sorting, but the database is—just like a lazy sort, databases tend to sort the data when it's requested. If you get all the employees at once, the database will have to sort all of them. But sorting isn't the only problem. On your side, you need to display the picture of each employee—and loading a picture takes time and memory. If you loaded everything at once, you'd slow your program to a crawl and use too much memory.

Instead, the common approach is to load the data lazily—to load it only when you need to show it to the user (see figure 6.2). This way, you use less processor time and less memory. The only problem is that you can't be completely lazy. You won't be able to save all the previously loaded employee photos because doing so would, again, require too much memory. You'd need to start forgetting previously loaded data and reload it after it was needed again.

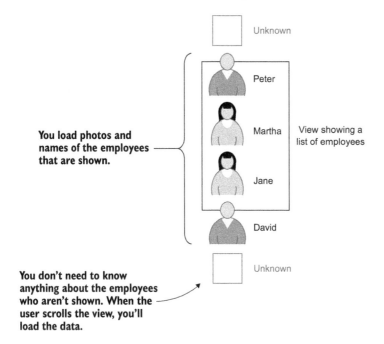

You load photos and
names of the employees
that are shown.

Unknown

Peter

Martha

Jane

David

Unknown

View showing a
list of employees

You don't need to know
anything about the employees
who aren't shown. When the
user scrolls the view, you'll
load the data.

Figure 6.2 You don't need to get the data that's not shown to the user. You
can fetch the required information when it's needed.

6.2.3 *Pruning recursion trees by caching function results*

The good thing about C++ not directly supporting laziness is that you can implement
it as you wish; you're in control of how lazy you want to be on a case-by-case basis. Let's
use a common example: calculating Fibonacci numbers. Following the definition, you
could implement it like this:

```
unsigned int fib(unsigned int n)
{
    return n == 0 ? 0 :
           n == 1 ? 1 :
                    fib(n - 1) + fib(n - 2);
}
```

This implementation is inefficient. You have two recursive calls in the common case,
and each performs duplicate work because both `fib(n)` and `fib(n - 1)` need to calculate `fib(n - 2)`. Both `fib(n - 1)` and `fib(n - 2)` need to calculate `fib(n - 3)`, and
so on. The number of recursive calls will grow exponentially with the number n (see
figure 6.3).

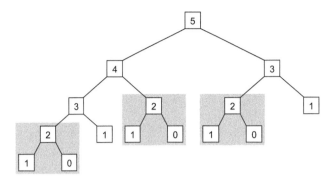

Figure 6.3   With `fib` **implemented recursively, you calculate the same value more than once. The recursion tree that calculates** `fib(5)` **contains three identical subtrees calculating** `fib(2)` **and two identical subtrees calculating** `fib(3)`. **The multiplication of work grows exponentially with n.**

This function is pure, so it'll always return the same result when given a specific value as the input. After you calculate `fib(n)`, you can store the result somewhere and reuse that value anytime someone needs `fib(n)`. If you cache all the previously calculated results, you can remove all the duplicate subtrees. This way, your evaluation tree will look like figure 6.4. (The exact order of evaluation may be different, because C++ doesn't guarantee `fib(n - 1)` will be called before `fib(n - 2)`, but all possible trees will essentially be the same—there will be no repeated subtrees.)

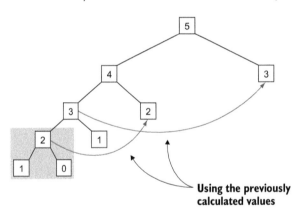

Using the previously calculated values

Figure 6.4   With `fib` **implemented lazily, you can avoid evaluating the same trees over and over. If one branch calculates** `fib(2)`, **other branches will use the previously calculated value. Now, the number of nodes this tree has grows linearly with n.**

Listing 6.4   Fibonacci implementation with caching

```
std::vector<unsigned int> cache{0, 1};

unsigned int fib(unsigned int n)
{
    if (cache.size() > n) {
        return cache[n];
    } else {
        const auto result = fib(n - 1) + fib(n - 2);
        cache.push_back(result);
        return result;
    }
}
```

You can use a vector as the cache because in order to out fib(n), you need to know fib(k) for all k < n.

Returns the value if it's already in the cache

Gets the result and adds it to the cache. You can use push_back to add the nth element, because you know all the previous values are filled.

The good thing about this approach is that you don't need to invent new algorithms to calculate the Fibonacci numbers. You don't even need to understand how the algorithm works. You just need to recognize that it calculates the same thing multiple times and that the result is always the same because the `fib` function is pure.

The only downside is, you're taking much more memory to store the cached values. If you want to optimize this, investigate how your algorithm works and when the cached values are being used.

If you analyzed the code, you'd see that you never use any values in the cache except the two last inserted ones. You can replace the entire vector with a cache that stores just two values. To match the `std::vector` API, you're going to create a class that looks like a vector but remembers only the last two inserted values (see example:fibonacci/main.cpp).

Listing 6.5   Efficient cache for calculating Fibonacci numbers

```
class fib_cache {
public:
    fib_cache()
        : m_previous{0}
        , m_last{1}
        , m_size{2}
    {
    }

    size_t size() const
    {
        return m_size;
    }

    unsigned int operator[] (unsigned int n) const
    {
        return n == m_size - 1 ? m_last :
               n == m_size - 2 ? m_previous :
                                 0;
    }

    void push_back(unsigned int value)
    {
        m_size++;
        m_previous = m_last;
        m_last = value;
    }
};
```

Start of the Fibonacci series: {0, 1}

Size of the cache (not excluding the forgotten values)

Returns the requested numbers if they're still in the cache. Otherwise, returns 0. Alternatively, you could throw an exception.

Adds a new value to the cache, and increases the size

6.2.4 *Dynamic programming as a form of laziness*

Dynamic programming is a technique of solving complex problems by splitting them into many smaller ones. When you solve the smaller ones, you store their solutions so you can reuse them later. This technique is used in many real-world algorithms, including finding the shortest path and calculating a string distance.

In a sense, the optimization you did for the function that calculates the *n*th Fibonacci number is also based on dynamic programming. You had a problem `fib(n)`, and you split it into two smaller problems: fib(n - 1) and fib(n - 2). (It was helpful that this is the definition of Fibonacci numbers.) By storing the results of all the *smaller* problems, you significantly optimized the initial algorithm.

Although this was an obvious optimization for the fib function, that's not always the case. Let's consider the problem of calculating the similarity between two strings. One of the possible measures for this is the Levenshtein distance[1] (or *edit distance*), which is the minimal number of deletions, insertions, and substitutions needed to transform one string to another. For example:

- *example* and *example*—The distance is 0, because these are the same strings.
- *example* and *exam*—The distance is 3, because you need to delete three characters from the end of the first string.
- *exam* and *eram*—The distance is 1, because you only need to replace *x* with *r*.

This problem can easily be solved. If you've already calculated the distance between two strings a and b, you can easily calculate the following distances:

- Between a, and b with one character appended (representing the operation of adding a character to the source string).
- Between a with one character appended, and b (representing the operation of removing a character from the source string).
- Between a and b, with a character appended to both of them. (If the characters are the same, the distance is the same; otherwise, you have the operation of replacing one character with another.)

You have many solutions for transforming the source string a into the destination string b, as shown in figure 6.5. You want to use the solution that requires the minimum number of operations.

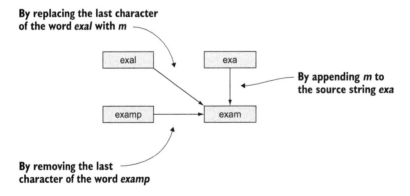

By replacing the last character of the word exal with *m*

By appending *m* to the source string *exa*

By removing the last character of the word *examp*

Figure 6.5 Each invocation of lev(m, n) calculates the minimum distance for all paths whose last operation is addition, for all paths whose last operation is removal, and for all paths whose last operation is replacing a character.

---

[1] For more information on Levenshtein distance, check out https://en.wikipedia.org/wiki/Levenshtein_distance.

You'll denote the distance between the first m characters of the string a and the first n characters of the string b as lev(m, n). The distance function can be implemented recursively.

Listing 6.6 Recursively calculating the Levenshtein distance

If either string is empty, the distance is the length of the other one.

Skips passing the strings a and b as parameters, for clarity

Counts the operation of adding a character

Counts the operation of replacing a character, but only if you haven't replaced a character with the same one

Counts the operation of removing a character

```
unsigned int lev(unsigned int m, unsigned int n)
{
    return m == 0 ? n
        : n == 0 ? m
        : std::min({
            lev(m - 1, n) + 1,
            lev(m, n - 1) + 1,
            lev(m - 1, n - 1) + (a[m - 1] != b[n - 1])
        });
}
```

Implemented like this, the function lev searches the space of all possible transformations that convert string a to b (at least, paths that don't generate unnecessary operations such as adding and consequently removing the same character). Just as in the case of fib(n), the number of function invocations will grow exponentially with m and n.

Although we all know how to implement fib(n) with a single loop, and nobody would write the implementation we started with, this time it's not obvious from the definition of the problem how it could be optimized. What *is* obvious is that just like fib(n), lev(m, n) is a pure function; the result always depends only on its arguments, and it has no side effects. You can't have more than m * n different results. And the only way the implementation can have exponential complexity is if it calculates the same thing multiple times.

What's the immediate solution that comes to mind? Cache all previously calculated results. Because you have two unsigned integers as arguments for the function, it's natural to use a matrix as the cache.

6.3 *Generalized memoization*

Although it's usually better to write custom caches for each problem separately so you can control how long a specific value stays in the cache (as in the case of the *forgetful* cache for the memoized version of fib(n)) and determine the best possible structure to keep the cache in (for example, using a matrix for lev(m, n)), it's sometimes useful to be able to put a function into a wrapper and automatically get the memoized version of the function out.

The general structure for caching, when you can't predict what arguments the function will be invoked with, is a map. Any pure function is a mapping from its arguments to its value, so the cache will be able to cover any pure function without problems.

Listing 6.7   Creating a memoized wrapper from a function pointer

```
template <typename Result, typename... Args>
auto make_memoized(Result (*f)(Args...))
{
    std::map<std::tuple<Args...>, Result> cache;

    return [f, cache](Args... args) mutable -> Result
    {
        const auto args_tuple =
            std::make_tuple(args...);
        const auto cached = cache.find(args_tuple);

        if (cached == cache.end()) {
            auto result = f(args...);
            cache[args_tuple] = result;
            return result;

        } else {
            return cached->second;
        }
    };
}
```

> Creates a cache that maps tuples of arguments to the calculated results. If you wanted to use this in a multithreaded environment, you'd need to synchronize the changes to it with a mutex, as in listing 6.1.

> Lambda that gets the arguments and checks whether the result is already cached

> In case of a cache miss, calls the function and stores the result to the cache

> If the result is found in the cache, returns it to the caller

Now that you have a way to turn any function into its memoized counterpart, let's try doing so with the function that generates Fibonacci numbers.

Listing 6.8   Using the `make_memoized` function

```
auto fibmemo = make_memoized(fib);

std::cout << "fib(15) = " << fibmemo(15)
          << std::endl;
std::cout << "fib(15) = " << fibmemo(15)
          << std::endl;
```

> Calculates fibmemo(15) and caches the result

> The next time fibmemo(15) is called, loads the result from the cache instead of calculating it again

If you try to benchmark this program, you'll see you've optimized the second call to `fibmemo(15)`. But the first call is slower, and it gets exponentially slower when the argument to `fibmemo` is increased. The problem is that you still don't have the fully memoized version of the `fib` function. The `fibmemo` function is caching the result, but `fib` isn't using that cache. It calls itself directly. The `make_memoized` function works well for ordinary functions, but it doesn't optimize the recursive ones.

If you want to memoize the recursive calls as well, you have to modify `fib` not to call itself directly, but to allow you to pass it another function to call, instead:

```
template <typename F>
unsigned int fib(F&& fibmemo, unsigned int n)
{
    return n == 0 ? 0
         : n == 1 ? 1
         : fibmemo(n - 1) + fibmemo(n - 2);
}
```

This way, when you invoke `fib`, you can pass it your memoized version for its recursive calls. Unfortunately, the memoization function will have to be more complex, because you need to inject the memoized version into the recursion. If you tried to memoize a recursive function, you'd be caching just its last result, not the results of the recursive invocations, because the recursive calls would call the function itself instead of the memoized wrapper.

You need to create a function object that can store the function you need to memoize along with the cached results of previous invocations (see example:recursive -memoization/main.cpp).

Listing 6.9 Memoization wrapper for recursive functions

```
class null_param {};

template <class Sig, class F>
class memoize_helper;

template <class Result, class... Args, class F>
class memoize_helper<Result(Args...), F> {
private:
    using function_type = F;
    using args_tuple_type
        = std::tuple<std::decay_t<Args>...>;

    function_type f;
    mutable std::map<args_tuple_type, Result> m_cache;
    mutable std::recursive_mutex m_cache_mutex;

public:
    template <typename Function>
    memoize_helper(Function&& f, null_param)
        : f(f)
    {
    }

    memoize_helper(const memoize_helper& other)
        : f(other.f)
    {
    }

    template <class... InnerArgs>
    Result operator()(InnerArgs&&... args) const
    {
        std::unique_lock<std::recursive_mutex>
            lock{m_cache_mutex};

        const auto args_tuple =
            std::make_tuple(args...);
        const auto cached = m_cache.find(args_tuple);

        if (cached != m_cache.end()) {
            return cached->second;
```

Dummy class used in the constructor to avoid overload collision with copy-constructor

Defines the cache, and, because it's mutable, synchronizes all the changes

The constructors need to initialize the wrapped function. You could made copy-constructor copy the cached values as well, but that's not necessary.

Searches for the cached value

If the cached value is found, returns it without calling f

```
        } else {
            auto&& result = f(
                    *this,
                    std::forward<InnerArgs>(args)...);
            m_cache[args_tuple] = result;
            return result;
        }
    }
};
```

> If the cached value isn't found, calls f and stores the result. Passes *this as the first argument: the function to be used for the recursive call.

```
template <class Sig, class F>
memoize_helper<Sig, std::decay_t<F>>
make_memoized_r(F&& f)
{
    return {std::forward<F>(f), detail::null_param()};
}
```

Now, when you want to create the memoized version of f ib, you can write this:

```
auto fibmemo = make_memoized_r<
            unsigned int(unsigned int)>(
    [](auto& fib, unsigned int n) {
        std::cout << "Calculating " << n << "!\n";
        return n == 0 ? 0
            : n == 1 ? 1
            : fib(n - 1) + fib(n - 2);
    });
```

All invocations will now be memoized. The lambda will indirectly call itself through a reference to the memoize_helper class, which will be passed to it as its first argument fib. One benefit with this implementation, compared to make_memoized, is that it accepts any type of function object, whereas previously you had to pass a function pointer.

6.4   *Expression templates and lazy string concatenation*

The previous examples focused mostly on runtime optimizations—situations when your program may take different code paths—but you want to be able to optimize for all of them. Lazy evaluation can be beneficial even if you know in advance every step of your program.

Consider one of the most common program operations—string concatenation:

```
std::string fullname = title + " " + surname + ", " + name;
```

You want to concatenate a few strings. This implementation is perfectly valid and does just what you want. But it isn't as fast as it could be. Let's look at this from the compiler's perspective. operator+ is a left-associative binary operator, so the preceding expression is equivalent to this:

```
std::string fullname = (((title + " ") + surname) + ", ") + name;
```

When evaluating the title + " " subexpression, a new temporary string is created. For each of the following concatenations, the append function is called on that temporary string (see figure 6.6). For each of the appends, the string needs to grow to be able to fit the new data. Sometimes the currently allocated buffer inside this temporary string won't be able to hold all the data it needs to; in that case, a new buffer will need to be allocated and the data from the old one copied into it.

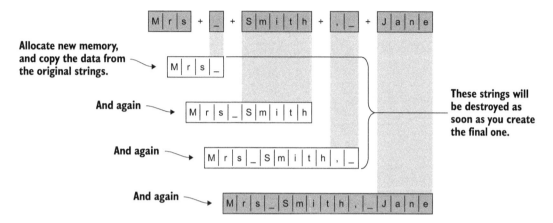

Figure 6.6 When you concatenate strings eagerly, you may need to allocate new memory if the previous buffer isn't large enough to store the concatenated string.

This process is inefficient. You're generating (and destroying) buffers you don't need. When you have a few strings to concatenate, it would be much more efficient to delay calculating the result until you know all the strings you need to concatenate. Then you can create a buffer that's large enough to store the final result, and copy the data from the source strings just once.

This is where expression templates come in: they allow you to generate expression definitions instead of calculating the value of an expression. Rather than implement operator+ to return a concatenated string, you can make it return a definition of the expression it represents so you can evaluate it later. In this case, the source of the problem is that operator+ is a binary operator, whereas you need to concatenate more strings. So, let's create a structure that represents an expression that concatenates multiple strings (see example:string-concatenation/main.cpp). Because you have to store an arbitrary number of strings, you'll create a recursive structure template; each node will keep a single string (the data member) and a node that keeps the rest (the tail member).

Listing 6.10   Structure that holds an arbitrary number of strings

```
template <typename... Strings>
class lazy_string_concat_helper;

template <typename LastString, typename... Strings>
class lazy_string_concat_helper<LastString,
                                 Strings...> {
private:
    LastString data;        ◄─────┐ Stores the copy of the original string
```

```
        lazy_string_concat_helper<Strings...> tail;
public:
    lazy_string_concat_helper(
            LastString data,
            lazy_string_concat_helper<Strings...> tail)
        : data(data)
        , tail(tail)
    {
    }

    int size() const
    {
        return data.size() + tail.size();
    }

    template <typename It>
    void save(It end) const
    {
        const auto begin = end - data.size();
        std::copy(data.cbegin(), data.cend(),
                begin);
        tail.save(begin);
    }

    operator std::string() const
    {
        std::string result(size(), '\0');
        save(result.end());
        return result;
    }

    lazy_string_concat_helper<std::string,
                              LastString,
                              Strings...>
    operator+(const std::string& other) const
    {
        return lazy_string_concat_helper
            <std::string, LastString, Strings...>(
                other,
                *this
            );
    }
    }
};
```

Stores the structure that contains other strings

Calculates the size of all strings combined

The structure stores strings in reverse order: the data member variable contains the string that comes last, so it needs to go to the end of the buffer.

When you want to convert the expression definition into a real string, allocate enough memory and start copying the strings into it.

Creates a new instance of the structure with one string added to it

Because this is a recursive structure, you need to create the base case so you don't end up with an infinite recursion:

```
template <>
class lazy_string_concat_helper<> {
public:
    lazy_string_concat_helper()
    {
    }

    int size() const
    {
```

```
        return 0;
    }

    template <typename It>
    void save(It) const
    {
    }

    lazy_string_concat_helper<std::string>
    operator+(const std::string& other) const
    {
        return lazy_string_concat_helper<std::string>(
                other,
                *this
            );
    }
};
```

This structure can hold as many strings as you want. It performs no concatenations until you ask for the result by casting it to std::string. The casting operator will create a new string and copy the data from the stored strings into it (see figure 6.7).

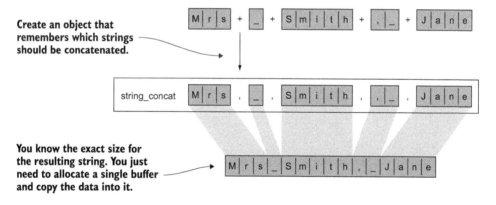

Figure 6.7 Instead of generating a string, operator+ generates an object that remembers which strings should be concatenated. When you need to create the resulting string, you'll know the exact size of the buffer you need to generate.

Listing 6.11 Using your structure for efficient string concatenation

```
lazy_string_concat_helper<> lazy_concat;

int main(int argc, char* argv[])
{
    std::string name = "Jane";
    std::string surname = "Smith";

    const std::string fullname =
        lazy_concat + surname + ", " + name;

    std::cout << fullname << std::endl;
}
```

You can't overload the operator+ on std::string, so use a small trick to force the use of the concatenation structure by appending to an instance of it.

This behaves similarly to the `lazy_val` structure at the beginning of this chapter. But this time you're not defining the computation that should be lazily executed through a lambda, but generating the computation from the expression the user wrote.

6.4.1 *Purity and expression templates*

You may have noticed that you're storing copies of original strings in the `lazy_string_concat_helper` class. It would be much more efficient to use references to them, instead. We started with the idea of optimizing string concatenation as much as possible. Let's optimize this as well:

```
template <typename LastString, typename... Strings>
class lazy_string_concat_helper<LastString,
                                Strings...> {
private:
    const LastString& data;
    lazy_string_concat_helper<Strings...> tail;

public:
    lazy_string_concat_helper(
            const LastString& data,
            lazy_string_concat_helper<Strings...> tail)
        : data(data)
        , tail(tail)
    {
    }

    ...
};
```

Two potential pitfalls exist. First, you can't use this expression outside the scope in which the strings were defined. As soon as you exit the scope, the strings will be destroyed, and the references you keep in the `lazy_string_concat_helper` object will become invalid.

Second, the user will expect the result of string concatenation to be a string, not some other intermediary type. This may lead to unexpected behavior if your optimized concatenation is used with the automatic type deduction.

Consider the following example:

```
std::string name = "Jane";
std::string surname = "Smith";

const auto fullname =
        lazy_concat + surname + ", " + name;

name = "John";

std::cout << fullname << std::endl;
```

You think you've created a string "Smith, Jane"...

...but the output is "Smith, John".

The problem is that you're now storing references to the strings you need to concatenate. If the strings change between the point where you created the expression (the declaration of the `fullname` variable) and the point where you're required to compute the result (writing `fullname` to the standard output), you'll get an unexpected result. Changes to the strings made *after* you think you concatenated them will be reflected in the result string.

This is an important thing to keep in mind: in order to work as expected, laziness requires purity. Pure functions give you the same result whenever you call them with the same arguments. And that's why you can delay executing them without any consequences. As soon as you allow side effects such as changing a value of a variable to influence the result of your operation, you'll get undesired results when trying to make it execute lazily.

Expression templates let you generate structures that represent a computation instead of immediately calculating that expression. This way, you can choose when the computation will take place; you can change the normal order in which C++ evaluates expressions and transform the expressions any way you want.[2]

> **TIP** For more information and resources about the topics covered in this chapter, see https://forums.manning.com/posts/list/41685.page.

Summary

- Executing code lazily and caching results can significantly improve the speed of your programs.
- It's not often easy (and sometimes not even possible) to construct lazy variants of algorithms you use in your programs, but if you manage to do it, you can make your programs much more responsive.
- A big class of algorithms has exponential complexity that can be optimized to be linear or quadratic just by caching intermediary results.
- Levenshtein distance has many applications (in sound processing, DNA analysis, and spell checking, for instance) but can also find its place in regular programs. When you need to notify the UI of changes in a data model, it's useful to be able to minimize the number of operations the UI needs to perform.
- Although you should write the caching mechanisms for each problem separately, it's sometimes useful to have functions such as `make_memoized` to benchmark the speed gain you could achieve by caching function results.
- Expression templates are a powerful mechanism for delaying computation. They're often used in libraries that operate on matrices, and other places where you need to optimize expressions before handing them to the compiler.

---

[2] If you need to build and transform more-complex expression trees, check out the Boost.Proto library at http://mng.bz/pEqP.

Ranges 7

This chapter covers

- The problems of passing iterator pairs to algorithms

- What ranges are and how to use them

- Creating chained range transformations using the pipe syntax

- Understanding range views and actions

- Writing succulent code without `for` loops

In chapter 2, you saw why you should avoid writing raw `for` loops and that you should instead rely on using generic algorithms provided to you by the STL. Although this approach has significant benefits, you've also seen its downsides. The algorithms in the standard library were not designed to be easily composed with each other. Instead, they're mostly focused on providing a way to allow implementation of a more advanced version of an algorithm by applying one algorithm multiple times.

A perfect example is `std::partition`, which moves all items in a collection that satisfy a predicate to the beginning of the collection, and returns an iterator to the first element in the resulting collection that doesn't satisfy the predicate. This allows you to create a function that does multigroup partitioning—not limited to predicates that return `true` or `false`—by invoking `std::partition` multiple times.

As an example, you're going to implement a function that groups people in a collection based on the team they belong to. It receives the collection of persons, a function that gets the team name for a person, and a list of teams. You can perform `std::partition` multiple times—once for each team name—and you'll get a list of people grouped by the team they belong to.

Listing 7.1   Grouping people by the team they belong to

```
template <typename Persons, typename F>
void group_by_team(Persons& persons,
                   F team_for_person,
                   const std::vector<std::string>& teams)
{
    auto begin = std::begin(persons);
    const auto end = std::end(persons);

    for (const auto& team : teams) {
        begin = std::partition(begin, end,
                [&](const auto& person) {
                    return team == team_for_person(person);
                });
    }
}
```

Although this way to compose algorithms is useful, a more common use case is to have a resulting collection of one operation passed to another. Recall the example from chapter 2: you had a collection of people, and you wanted to extract the names of female employees only. Writing a `for` loop that does this is trivial:

```
std::vector<std::string> names;

for (const auto& person : people) {
    if (is_female(person)) {
        names.push_back(name(person));
    }
}
```

If you wanted to solve the same problem by using the STL algorithms, you'd need to create an intermediary collection to copy the persons that satisfy the predicate (`is_female`) and then use `std::transform` to extract the names for all persons in that collection. This would be suboptimal in terms of both performance and memory.

The main issue is that STL algorithms take iterators to the beginning and end of a collection as separate arguments instead of taking the collection itself. This has a few implications:

- The algorithms can't return a collection as a result.
- Even if you had a function that returned a collection, you wouldn't be able to pass it directly to the algorithm: you'd need to create a temporary variable so you could call `begin` and `end` on it.
- For the previous reasons, most algorithms mutate their arguments instead of leaving them immutable and just returning the modified collection as the result.

These factors make it difficult to implement program logic without having at least local mutable variables.

7.1   *Introducing ranges*

There have been a few attempts to fix these problems, but the concept that proved to be most versatile was ranges. For the time being, let's think of ranges as a simple structure that contains two iterators—one pointing to the first element in a collection, and one pointing to the element after the last one.

> **NOTE** Ranges haven't become part of the standard library yet, but an ongoing effort exists for their inclusion into the standard, currently planned for C++20. The proposal to add ranges into C++ standard is based on the range-v3 library by Eric Niebler, which we'll use for the code examples in this chapter. An older but more battle-tested library is Boost.Range. It's not as full of features as range-v3, but it's still useful, and it supports older compilers. The syntax is mostly the same, and the concepts we'll cover apply to it as well.

What are the benefits of keeping two iterators in the same structure instead of having them as two separate values? The main benefit is that you can return a complete range as a result of a function and pass it directly to another function without creating local variables to hold the intermediary results.

Passing pairs of iterators is also error prone. It's possible to pass iterators belonging to two separate collections to an algorithm that operates on a single collection, or to pass the iterators in in incorrect order—to have the first iterator point to an element that comes after the second iterator. In both cases, the algorithm would try to iterate through all elements from the starting iterator until it reached the end iterator, which would produce undefined behavior.

By using ranges, the previous example becomes a simple composition of `filter` and `transform` functions:

```
std::vector<std::string> names =
    transform(
        filter(people, is_female),
        name
    );
```

The `filter` function will return a range containing elements from the `people` collection that satisfy the `is_female` predicate. The `transform` function will then take this result and return the range of names of everybody in the filtered range.

You can nest as many range transformations such as `filter` and `transform` as you want. The problem is that the syntax becomes cumbersome to reason about when you have more than a few composed transformations.

For this reason, the range libraries usually provide a special *pipe* syntax that overloads the | operator, inspired by the UNIX shell pipe operator. So, instead of nesting the function calls, you can pipe the original collection through a series of transformations like this:

```
std::vector<std::string> names = people | filter(is_female)
                                         | transform(name);
```

As in the previous example, you're filtering the collection of persons on the `is_female` predicate and then extracting the names from the result. The main difference here is, after you get accustomed to seeing the operator `|` as meaning *pass through a transformation* instead of *bitwise or*, this becomes easier to write and reason about than the original example.

7.2   Creating read-only views over data

A question that comes to mind when seeing code like that in the previous section is how efficient it is, compared to writing a `for` loop that does the same thing. You saw in chapter 2 that using STL algorithms incurs performance penalties because you need to create a new vector of persons to hold the copies of all females from the `people` collection in order to be able to call `std::transform` on it. From reading the solution that uses ranges, you may get the impression that nothing has changed but the syntax. This section explains why that's not the case.

7.2.1   Filter function for ranges

The `filter` transformation still needs to return a collection of people so you can call `transform` on it. This is where the magic of ranges comes into play. A range is an abstraction that represents a collection of items, but nobody said it's a collection—it just needs to behave like one. It needs to have a start, to know its end, and to allow you to get to each of its elements.

Instead of having `filter` return a collection like `std::vector`, it'll return a range structure whose `begin` iterator will be a smart proxy iterator that points to the first element in the source collection that satisfies the given predicate. And the `end` iterator will be a proxy for the original collection's `end` iterator. The only thing the proxy iterator needs to do differently than the iterator from the original collection is to point only at the elements that satisfy the filtering predicate (see figure 7.1).

In a nutshell, every time the proxy iterator is incremented, it needs to find the next element in the original collection that satisfies the predicate.

Listing 7.2   Increment operator for the filtering proxy iterator

```
auto& operator++()                        Iterator to the collection you're filtering. When the proxy
{                                         iterator is to be incremented, find the first element after
    ++m_current_position;                 the current one that satisfies the predicate.
    m_current_position =
        std::find_if(m_current_position,       Starts the search from the next element
                     m_end,
                     m_predicate);         If no more elements satisfy the
                                           predicate, returns an iterator pointing to
                                           the end of the source collection, which is
    return *this;                         also the end of the filtered range
}
```

With a proxy iterator for filtering, you don't need to create a temporary collection containing copies of the values in the source collection that satisfy the predicate. You've created a new *view* of existing data.

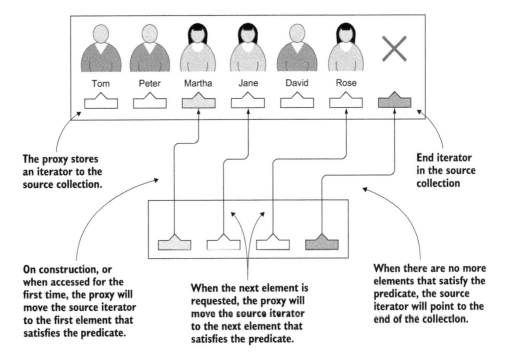

The proxy stores an iterator to the source collection.

End iterator in the source collection

On construction, or when accessed for the first time, the proxy will move the source iterator to the first element that satisfies the predicate.

When the next element is requested, the proxy will move the source iterator to the next element that satisfies the predicate.

When there are no more elements that satisfy the predicate, the source iterator will point to the end of the collection.

Figure 7.1 The view created by `filter` stores an iterator to the source collection. The iterator points to only the elements that satisfy the filtering predicate. The user of this view will be able to use it as if it were a normal collection of people with only three elements in it: Martha, Jane, and Rose.

You can pass this view to the `transform` algorithm, and it'll work just as well as it would on a real collection. Every time it requires a new value, it requests the proxy iterator to be moved one place to the right, and it moves to the next element that satisfies the predicate in the source collection. The `transform` algorithm goes through the original collection of people but can't *see* any person who isn't female.

7.2.2 *Transform function for ranges*

In a manner similar to `filter`, the `transform` function doesn't need to return a new collection. It also can return a view over the existing data. Unlike `filter` (which returns a new view that contains the same items as the original collection, just not all of them), `transform` needs to return the same number of elements found in the source collection, but it doesn't give access to the elements directly. It returns each element from the source collection, but transformed.

The increment operator doesn't need to be special; it just needs to increment the iterator to the source collection. This time, the operator to dereference the iterator will be different. Instead of returning the value in the source collection, you first apply the transformation function to it (see figure 7.2).

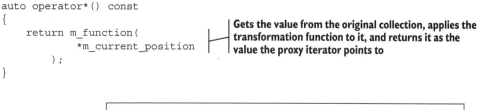

```
auto operator*() const
{
    return m_function(
            *m_current_position
        );
}
```

Gets the value from the original collection, applies the transformation function to it, and returns it as the value the proxy iterator points to

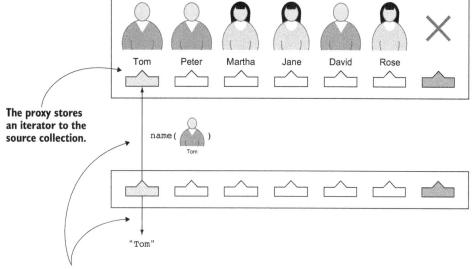

The proxy stores an iterator to the source collection.

When an element is requested from the proxy, it returns the result of the transformation function applied to the element from the source collection.

Figure 7.2   The view created by `transform` stores an iterator to the source collection. The iterator accesses all the elements in the source collection, but the view doesn't return them directly; it first applies the transformation function to the element and returns its result.

This way, just as with `filter`, you avoid creating a new collection that holds the transformed elements. You're creating a view that instead of showing original elements as they are, shows them transformed. Now you can pass the resulting range to another transformation, or you can assign it to a proper collection as in the example.

7.2.3   *Lazy evaluation of range values*

Even if you have two range transformations in the example—one `filter` and one `transform`—the calculation of the resulting collection takes only a single pass through the source collection, just as in the case of a handwritten `for` loop. Range views are evaluated lazily: when you call `filter` or `transform` on a collection, it defines a view; it doesn't evaluate a single element in that range.

Let's modify the example to fetch the names of the first three females in the collection. You can use the `take(n)` range transformation, which creates a new view over the source range that shows only the first *n* items in that range (or fewer if the source range has fewer than n elements):

```
std::vector<std::string> names = people | filter(is_female)
                                        | transform(name)
                                        | take(3);
```

Let's analyze this snippet part by part:

1 When `people | filter(is_female)` is evaluated, nothing happens other than a new view being created. You haven't accessed a single person from the `people` collection, except potentially to initialize the iterator to the source collection to point to the first item that satisfies the `is_female` predicate.

2 You pass that view to `| transform(name)`. The only thing that happens is that a new view is created. You still haven't accessed a single person or called the `name` function on any of them.

3 You apply `| take(3)` to that result. Again, is creates a new view and nothing else.

4 You need to construct a vector of strings from the view you got as the result of the `| take(3)` transformation.

To create a vector, you must know the values you want to put in it. This step goes through the view and accesses each of its elements.

When you try to construct the vector of names from the range, all the values in the range have to be evaluated. For each element added to the vector, the following things happen (see figure 7.3):

1 You call the dereference operator on the proxy iterator that belongs to the range view returned by `take`.

2 The proxy iterator created by `take` passes the request to the proxy iterator created by `transform`. This iterator passes on the request.

3 You try to dereference the proxy iterator defined by the `filter` transformation. It goes through the source collection and finds and returns the first person that satisfies the `is_female` predicate. This is the first time you access any of the persons in the collection, and the first time the `is_female` function is called.

4 The person retrieved by dereferencing the `filter` proxy iterator is passed to the `name` function, and the result is returned to the `take` proxy iterator, which passes it on to be inserted into the `names` vector.

When an element is inserted, you go to the next one, and then the next one, until you reach the end. Now, because you've limited your view to three elements, you don't need to access a single person in the `people` collection after you find the third female.

This is lazy evaluation at work. Even though the code is shorter and more generic than the equivalent handwritten `for` loop, it does exactly the same thing and has no performance penalties.

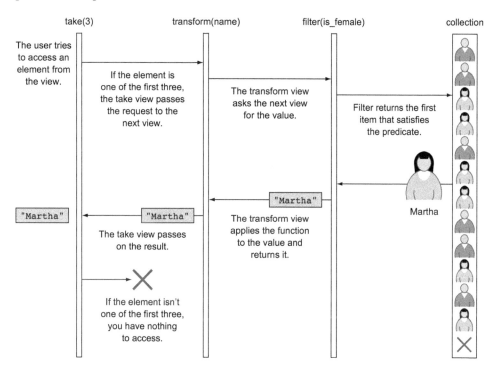

Figure 7.3 When accessing an element from the view, the view proxies the request to the next view in the composite transformation, or to the collection. Depending on the type of the view, it may transform the result, skip elements, traverse them in a different order, and so on.

7.3 Mutating values through ranges

Although many useful transformations can be implemented as simple views, some require changing the original collection. We'll call these transformations *actions* as opposed to *views*.

One common example for the action transformation is sorting. To be able to sort a collection, you need to access all of its elements and reorder them. You need to change the original collection, or create and keep a sorted copy of the whole collection. The latter is especially important when the original collection isn't randomly accessible (a linked list, for example) and can't be sorted efficiently; you need to copy its elements into a new collection that's randomly accessible and sort that one instead.

> ## Views and actions in the range-v3 library
>
> As mentioned earlier, because the range-v3 library is used as the base for the proposal for extending the STL with ranges, we'll use it in the code examples, and we'll use its nomenclature. The range transformations that create views such as `filter`, `transform`, and `take` live in the `ranges::v3::view` namespace, whereas the actions live in `ranges::v3::action`. It's important to differentiate between these two, so we'll specify the namespaces `view` and `action` from now on.

Imagine you have a function `read_text` that returns text represented as a vector of words, and you want to collect all the words in it. The easiest way to do this is to sort the words and then remove consecutive duplicates. (We'll consider all words to be lowercase in this example, for the sake of simplicity.)

You can get the list of all words that appear in given text by piping the result of the `read_text` function through `sort` and `unique` actions, as illustrated in figure 7.4 and shown here:

```
std::vector<std::string> words =
          read_text() | action::sort
                      | action::unique;
```

Because you're passing a temporary to the `sort` action, it doesn't need to create a copy to work on; it can reuse the vector returned by the `read_text` function and do the sorting in place. The same goes for `unique`—it can operate directly on the result of the `sort` action. If you wanted to keep the intermediary result, you would use `view::unique` instead, which doesn't operate on a real collection, but creates a view that skips all repeated consecutive occurrences of a value.

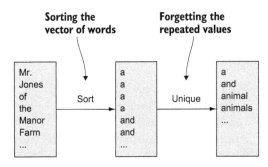

Figure 7.4   To get a list of words that appear in text, it's sufficient to sort them and then remove the consecutive repeated values.

This is an important distinction between views and actions. A view transformation creates a lazy view over the original data, whereas an action works on an existing collection and performs its transformation eagerly.

Actions don't have to be performed on temporaries. You can also act on lvalues by using the operator `|=`, like so:

```
std::vector<std::string> words = read_text();
words |= action::sort | action::unique;
```

This combination of views and actions gives you the power to choose when you want something to be done lazily and when you want it to be done eagerly. The benefits of having this choice are that you can be lazy when you don't expect all items in the source collection to need processing, and when items don't need to be processed more than once; and you can be eager to calculate all elements of the resulting collection if you know they'll be accessed often.

7.4 Using delimited and infinite ranges

We started this chapter with the premise that a range is a structure that holds one iterator to the beginning and one to the end—exactly what STL algorithms take, but in a single structure. The end iterator is a strange thing. You can never dereference it, because it points to an element after the last element in the collection. You usually don't even move it. It's mainly used to test whether you've reached the end of a collection:

```
auto i = std::begin(collection);
const auto end = std::end(collection);
for (; i != end; i++) {
    // ...
}
```

It doesn't really need to be an iterator—it just needs to be something you can use to test whether you're at the end. This special value is called a *sentinel,* and it gives you more freedom when implementing a test for whether you've reached the end of a range. Although this functionality doesn't add much when you're working with ordinary collections, it allows you to create delimited and infinite ranges.

7.4.1 Using delimited ranges to optimize handling input ranges

A *delimited range* is one whose end you don't know in advance—but you have a predicate function that can tell you when you've reached the end. Examples are null-terminated strings: you need to traverse the string until you reach the '\0' character, or traverse the input streams and read one token at a time until the stream becomes invalid—until you fail to extract a new token. In both cases, you know the beginning of the range, but in order to know where the end is, you must traverse the range item by item until the end test returns true.

Let's consider the input streams and analyze the code that calculates the sum of the numbers it reads from the standard input:

```
std::accumulate(std::istream_iterator<double>(std::cin),
                std::istream_iterator<double>(),
                0);
```

You're creating two iterators in this snippet: one proper iterator, which represents the start of the collection of doubles read from std::cin, and one special iterator that doesn't belong to any input stream. This iterator is a special value that the std::accumulate algorithm will use to test whether you've reached the end of the collection; it's an iterator that behaves like a sentinel.

The std::accumulate algorithm will read values until its traversal iterator becomes equal to the end iterator. You need to implement operator== and operator!= for

std::istream_iterator. The equality operator must work with both the proper iterators and special sentinel values. The implementation has a form like this:

```
template <typename T>
bool operator==(const std::istream_iterator<T>& left,
                const std::istream_iterator<T>& right)
{
    if (left.is_sentinel() && right.is_sentinel()) {
        return true;

    } else if (left.is_sentinel()) {
        // Test whether sentinel predicate is
        // true for the right iterator

    } else if (right.is_sentinel()) {
        // Test whether sentinel predicate is
        // true for the left iterator

    } else {
        // Both iterators are normal iterators,
        // test whether they are pointing to the
        // same location in the collection
    }
}
```

You need to cover all the cases—whether the left iterator is a sentinel, and the same for
the right iterator. These are checked in each step of an algorithm.

This approach is inefficient. It would be much easier if the compiler knew something
was a sentinel at compile time. This is possible if you lift the requirement that the end of
a collection has to be an iterator—if you allow it to be anything that can be equally compared to a proper iterator. This way, the four cases in the previous code become separate
functions, and the compiler will know which one to call based on the involved types. If it
gets two iterators, it'll call operator== for two iterators; if it gets an iterator and a sentinel,
it'll call operator== for an iterator and a sentinel; and so on.

Range-based for loops and sentinels

The range-based for loop, as defined in C++11 and C++14, requires both the begin
and end to have the same type; they need to be iterators. The sentinel-based ranges
can't be used with the range-based for loop in C++11 and C++14. This requirement was
removed in C++17. You can now have different types for the begin and end, which effectively means the end can be a sentinel.

7.4.2   *Creating infinite ranges with sentinels*

The sentinel approach gives you optimizations for delimited ranges. But there's more:
you're now able to easily create infinite ranges as well. Infinite ranges don't have an
end, like the range of all positive integers. You have a start—the number 0—but no end.

Although it's not obvious why you'd need infinite data structures, they come in handy
from time to time. One of the most common examples for using a range of integers is

enumerating items in another range. Imagine you have a range of movies sorted by their scores, and you want to write out the first 10 to the standard output along with their positions as shown in listing 7.4 (see example:top-movies).

To do this, you can use the view::zip function. It takes two ranges[1] and pairs the items from those ranges. The first element in the resulting range will be a pair of items: the first item from the first range and the first item from the second range. The second element will be a pair containing the second item from the first range and the second item from the second range, and so on. The resulting range will end as soon as any of the source ranges ends (see figure 7.5).

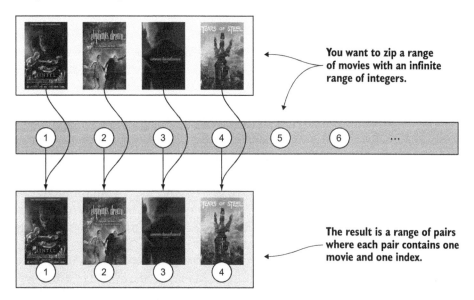

You want to zip a range of movies with an infinite range of integers.

The result is a range of pairs where each pair contains one movie and one index.

Figure 7.5 The range doesn't have a notion of an item index. If you want to have the indices for the elements in a range, you can zip the range with the range of integers. You'll get a range of pairs, and each pair will contain an item from the original range along with its index.

Listing 7.4 Writing out the top 10 movies along with their positions

```
template <typename Range>
void write_top_10(const Range& xs)
{
    auto items =
        view::zip(xs, view::ints(1))
            | view::transform([](const auto& pair) {
                return std::to_string(pair.second) +
                    " " + pair.first;
            })
            | view::take(10);
```

Zips the range of movies with the range of integers, starting with I. This gives a range of pairs: a movie name and the index.

The transform function takes a pair and generates a string containing the rank of the movie and the movie name.

You're interested in the first I0 movies.

[1] view::zip can also zip more than two ranges. The result will be a range of n-tuples instead of a range of pairs.

```
    for (const auto& item : items) {
        std::cout << item << std::endl;
    }
}
```

Instead of the infinite range of integers, you could use integers from 1 to xs.length() to enumerate the items in xs. But that wouldn't work as well. As you've seen, you could have a range and not know its end, you probably couldn't tell its size without traversing it. You'd need to traverse it twice: once to get its size, and once for view::zip and view::transform to do their magic. This is not only inefficient, but also impossible to do with some range types. Ranges such as the input stream range can't be traversed more than once; after you read a value, you can't read it again.

Another benefit of infinite ranges isn't in using them, but in designing your code to be able to work on them. This makes your code more generic. If you write an algorithm that works on infinite ranges, it'll work on a range of any size, including a range whose size you don't know.

7.5   *Using ranges to calculate word frequencies*

Let's move on to a more complicated example to see how programs can be more elegant if you use ranges instead of writing the code in the old style. You'll reimplement the example from chapter 4: calculating the frequencies of the words in a text file. To recap, you're given a text, and you want to write out the *n* most frequently occurring words in it. We'll break the problem into a composition of smaller transformations as before, but we're going to change a few things to better demonstrate how range views and actions interact with each other.

The first thing you need to do is get a list of lowercase words without any special characters in them. The data source is the input stream. You'll use std::cin in this example.

The range-v3 library provides a class template called istream_range that creates a stream of tokens from the input stream you pass to it:

```
std::vector<std::string> words =
        istream_range<std::string>(std::cin);
```

In this case, because the tokens you want are of std::string type, the range will read word by word from the standard input stream. This isn't enough, because you want all the words to be lowercase and you don't want punctuation characters included. You need to transform each word to lowercase and remove any nonalphanumeric characters (see figure 7.6).

Listing 7.5   Getting a list of lowercase words that contain only letters or digits

```
std::vector<std::string> words =
        istream_range<std::string>(std::cin)
        | view::transform(string_to_lower)      ◀── Makes all words lowercase
        | view::transform(string_only_alnum)    ◀── Keeps only letters and digits
        | view::remove_if(&std::string::empty);  ◀┐
```

You may get empty strings as the result when a token doesn't contain a single letter or a digit, so you need to skip those.

You're creating an input stream range that will return a range of words.

You're transforming each word to lowercase— view::transform(tolower).

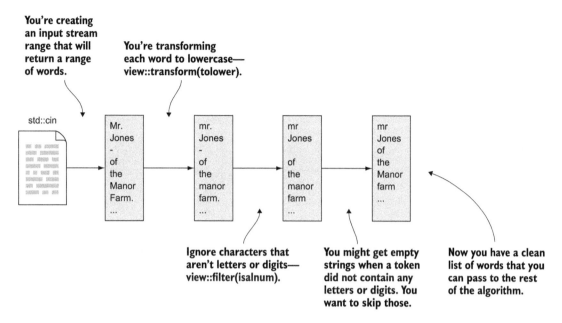

std::cin

Ignore characters that aren't letters or digits— view::filter(isalnum).

You might get empty strings when a token did not contain any letters or digits. You want to skip those.

Now you have a clean list of words that you can pass to the rest of the algorithm.

Figure 7.6   You have an input stream from which to read words. Before you can calculate the word frequencies, you need a list of words converted to lowercase with all punctuation removed.

For the sake of completeness, you also need to implement `string_to_lower` and `string_only_alnum` functions. The former is a transformation that converts each character in a string to lowercase, and the latter is a filter that skips characters that aren't alphanumeric. A `std::string` is a collection of characters, so you can manipulate it like any other range:

```
std::string string_to_lower(const std::string& s)
{
    return s | view::transform(tolower);
}

std::string string_only_alnum(const std::string& s)
{
    return s | view::filter(isalnum);
}
```

You have all the words to process, and you need to sort them (see figure 7.7). The `action::sort` transformation requires a randomly accessible collection, so it's lucky you declared `words` to be a `std::vector` of strings. You can request it to be sorted:

```
words |= action::sort;
```

Now that you have a sorted list, you can easily group the same words by using `view::group_by`. It'll create a range of word groups (the groups are, incidentally, also ranges). Each group will contain the same word multiple times—as many times as it appeared in the original text.

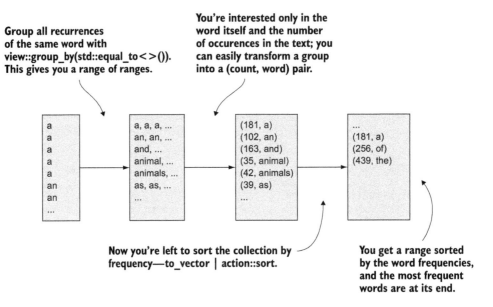

Group all recurrences of the same word with view::group_by(std::equal_to < >()). This gives you a range of ranges.

You're interested only in the word itself and the number of occurences in the text; you can easily transform a group into a (count, word) pair.

Now you're left to sort the collection by frequency—to_vector | action::sort.

You get a range sorted by the word frequencies, and the most frequent words are at its end.

Figure 7.7   You get a range of sorted words. You need to group the same words, count how many words you have in each group, and then sort them all by the number of occurrences.

You can transform the range into pairs; the first item in the pair is the number of items in a group, and the second is the word. This will give you a range containing all the words in the original text along with the number of occurrences for each.

Because the frequency is the first item in a pair, you can pass this range through action::sort. You can do so as in the previous code snippet, by using operator|=, or you can do it inline by first converting the range to a vector, as shown next (see example:word-frequency). This will allow you to declare the results variable as const.

Listing 7.6   Getting a sorted list of frequency-word pairs from a sorted list

```
const auto results =
    words | view::group_by(std::equal_to<>())          Groups multiple occurrences of
          | view::transform([](const auto& group) {    words from the words range
                const auto begin = std::begin(group);      Gets the size of each
                const auto end   = std::end(group);         group, and returns a
                const auto count = distance(begin, end);    pair consisting of the
                const auto word  = *begin;                  word frequency and
                                                            the word
                return std::make_pair(count, word);
          })
          | to_vector | action::sort;       To sort the words by frequency, you first
                                            need to convert the range into a vector.
```

The last step is to write the *n* most frequent words to the standard output. Because the results have been sorted in ascending order, and you need the most frequent words, not the least frequent ones, you must first reverse the range and then take the first *n* elements:

```
for (auto value: results | view::reverse
                          | view::take(n)) {
    std::cout << value.first << " " << value.second << std::endl;
}
```

That's it. In fewer than 30 lines, you've implemented the program that originally took a dozen pages. You've created a set of easily composable, highly reusable components; and, not counting the output, you haven't used any `for` loops.

Range-based for loop and ranges

As previously mentioned, the range-based `for` loop started supporting sentinels in C++17. The preceding code won't compile on older compilers. If you're using an older compiler, the range-v3 library provides a convenient `RANGES_FOR` macro that can be used as a replacement for the range-based `for`:

```
RANGES_FOR (auto value, results | view::reverse
                                | view::take(n)) {
    std::cout << value.first << " " << value.second << std::endl;
}
```

Additionally, if you sorted the range of words the same way you sorted the list of results (without `operator|=`), you'd have no mutable variables in your program.

TIP   For more information and resources about the topics covered in this chapter, see https://forums.manning.com/posts/list/43776.page.

Summary

- One frequent source of errors when using STL algorithms is passing incorrect iterators to them—sometimes even iterators belonging to separate collections.
- Some collection-like structures don't know where they end. For those, it's customary to provide sentinel-like iterators; these work but have unnecessary performance overhead.
- The ranges concept is an abstraction over any type of iterable data. It can model normal collections, input and output streams, database query result sets, and more.
- The ranges proposal is planned for inclusion in C++20, but libraries provide the same functionality today.
- Range views don't own the data, and they can't change it. If you want to operate on and change existing data, use actions instead.
- Infinite ranges are a nice measure of algorithm generality. If something works for infinite ranges, it'll work for finite ones as well.
- By using ranges and thinking of program logic in terms of range transformations, you can decompose the program into highly reusable components.

Functional
data structures

So far, I've talked mostly about higher-level functional programming concepts, and we spent quite a while examining the benefits of programming without mutable state. The problem is that programs tend to have many moving parts. While discussing purity in chapter 5, I said one of the options is to have only the main component with mutable state. All other components are pure and calculate a series of changes that should be performed on the main component, but without actually changing anything. Then the main component can perform those changes on itself.

This approach creates a clear separation between the pure parts of the program and those that deal with the mutable state. The problem is that it's often not easy to design software like this, because you need to pay attention to the order in which the calculated changes to the state should be applied. If you don't do that properly, you may encounter data races similar to those you have when working with mutable state in a concurrent environment.

Therefore, it's sometimes necessary to avoid all mutations—to not even have the central mutable state. If you used the standard data structures, you'd have to copy the data each time you needed a new version of it. Whenever you wanted to change an element in a collection, you'd need to create a new collection that was the same as the old one, but with the desired element changed. This is inefficient when using the data structures provided by the standard library. In this chapter, we'll cover data structures that are efficient to copy. Creating a modified copy of a data structure will also be an efficient operation.

8.1 *Immutable linked lists*

One of the oldest data structures optimized for this type of usage is a singly linked list, which was the basis for the oldest FP language: Lisp (short for List Processing). Linked lists are inefficient for most tasks because they have bad memory locality that doesn't play well with the caching facilities of modern hardware. But they're the simplest example of how an immutable structure can be implemented, so they're the perfect structure for introducing this topic.

A *list* is a collection of nodes; each node contains a single value and a pointer to the next node in the list (`nullptr` if it's the last element of the list), as shown in figure 8.1. The basic operations on a list are adding and removing elements to the start or the end of the list, inserting or removing elements from the middle, or changing the stored value in a specific node.

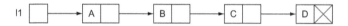

Figure 8.1   A singly linked list. Each node contains a value and a pointer to the next item.

We'll focus on modifying the start and the end because all other operations can be expressed through them. Keep in mind that when I say *modifying*, I mean *creating a new modified list from the old one, while the old one remains unchanged.*

8.1.1 *Adding elements to and removing them from the start of a list*

Let's first talk about modifying the start of the list. If an existing list can never change, creating a new list with a specified value prepended is trivial. You can create a new node with the value that points to the head of the previously created list (see figure 8.2). This gives you two lists: the old one that hasn't changed, and the new one that has the same elements as the old one, plus an element prepended.

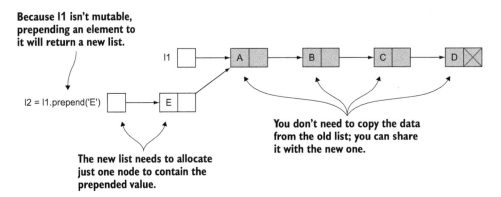

Because l1 isn't mutable, prepending an element to it will return a new list.

l2 = l1.prepend('E')

The new list needs to allocate just one node to contain the prepended value.

You don't need to copy the data from the old list; you can share it with the new one.

Figure 8.2   Prepending an element to an immutable list returns a new list. It doesn't need to copy any of the existing nodes from the original list; it can reuse them. This approach isn't viable in the mutable version of the list because changing one list would have the side effect of changing all other lists that share data with it.

Removing an element from the start of the list is similar. You create a new head for the list that points to the second element in the original list. Again, you get two lists: one with the old data, and one with the new data (see figure 8.3).

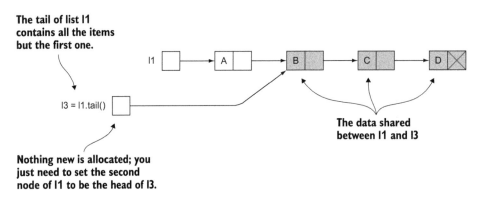

The tail of list l1 contains all the items but the first one.

l3 = l1.tail()

Nothing new is allocated; you just need to set the second node of l1 to be the head of l3.

The data shared between l1 and l3

Figure 8.3   Getting the tail of a list creates a new list from the original one that will contain the same elements modulo the head. The resulting list can share all the nodes with the original one, and still nothing needs to be copied.

These operations are efficient ($O(1)$), concerning both execution time and memory. You don't need to copy any data, because both lists share the same data.

One important thing to note is that if you have the guarantee that the old list can never be changed, and you don't provide a function to change the newly added element, you can guarantee that the new list is also immutable.

8.1.2 Adding elements to and removing them from the end of a list

Although changing the beginning of a list is trivial, the end is more problematic. The usual approach of appending to the end of a list is to find the last element and make it point to a new node. The problem is, this can't work for the immutable list (see figure 8.4).

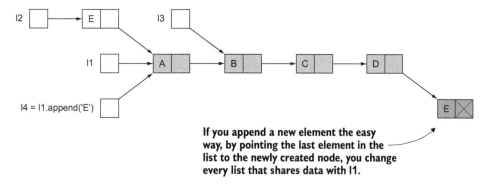

If you append a new element the easy way, by pointing the last element in the list to the newly created node, you change every list that shares data with l1.

Figure 8.4 If you tried the same trick of avoiding copying the data when appending to a list, and made the last element in the old list point to the newly created node, you'd change every list that shared its data with the list you were modifying. It's interesting to note that if two lists share any nodes, they share the end as well.

If you were to create the new node and make the last node in the old list point to it, you'd change the old list. And not only the old list, but all lists that share data with it—all of them would have a new element appended.

You can't efficiently append an element to an immutable list. You need to copy the original list and then append a new element to the copy (see figure 8.5).

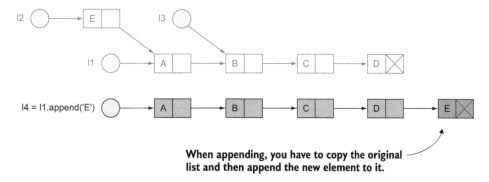

When appending, you have to copy the original list and then append the new element to it.

Figure 8.5 If you want to create a list that's the same as the original but has an extra element at its end, you need to copy all nodes from the original list and only then point the last node to the newly created node that contains the appended value.

The same goes for removing an element from the end. If you removed it in place, you'd change all existing lists that shared the same data as the current one.

8.1.3   Adding elements to and removing them from the middle of a list

To add an element to or remove it from the middle of a list, you need to create a copy of all elements that come before it in the original list—just as when changing the end of the list (see figure 8.6). More specifically, you need to remove all the elements that come before the location you want changed. This will give you the part of the original list that you can reuse in the resulting list. Than you insert the desired element and re-add all the elements from the old list that should go in front of it.

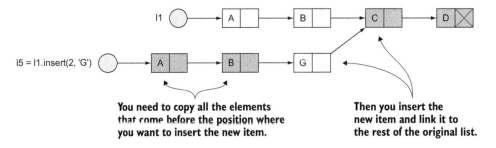

Figure 8.6   Inserting an element into the middle of a list is equivalent to removing all the items from the original list that should come before the element you're inserting and then prepending that element and all the previously removed items. The only nodes you share with the original list are nodes that come after the item you've inserted.

These inefficiencies make the singly linked list efficient only for implementing stack-like structures that only add items to and remove them from the beginning of a list (see table 8.1).

Table 8.1   Complexity of the singly linked list functions

O(1)	O(n)
Getting the first element	Appending
Prepending an element	Concatenating
Removing the first element	Inserting at some position
	Getting the last element
	Getting the nth element

8.1.4   Memory management

One of the requirements for implementing a list is that the nodes must be dynamically allocated. If you define a list only to be a structure that holds a value and a pointer to another list, you may get into trouble when one of the lists goes out of scope and is deleted. All the lists that depend on that list will then become invalid.

Because you have to dynamically allocate the nodes, you need a way to get rid of them when they're no longer needed. When a list goes out of the scope, you need to free all the nodes that belong only to this list, and none of the nodes that are shared. For example, when l5 from figure 8.7 goes out of scope, you need to delete all nodes up to C, and nothing else.

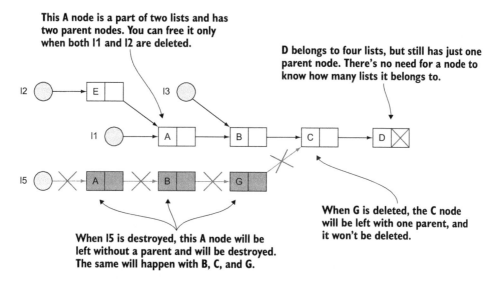

This A node is a part of two lists and has two parent nodes. You can free it only when both l1 and l2 are deleted.

D belongs to four lists, but still has just one parent node. There's no need for a node to know how many lists it belongs to.

When G is deleted, the C node will be left with one parent, and it won't be deleted.

When l5 is destroyed, this A node will be left without a parent and will be destroyed. The same will happen with B, C, and G.

Figure 8.7   When a list is deleted, you need to destroy the nodes that no other list uses. The nodes don't know how many lists they belong to, but they need to know how many immediate parents they have. When all parents of a node are destroyed, you can destroy that node as well; there's no list that it's the head of, or any node that points to it.

Ideally, you'd like to use smart pointers to implement automatic memory cleanup. For regular linked lists, you might go for `std::unique_ptr` because the head of the list owns its tail, and the tail should be destroyed if the head is.

But that's not the case here. As you can see in the figure, each node can have multiple owners because it can belong to multiple lists. Therefore, you need to use `std::shared_ptr`. It keeps a reference count and automatically destroys the object instance it points to when the count reaches zero. In this case, that will happen when you want to destroy a node that doesn't belong to any other list.

Garbage collection

Most functional programming languages rely on garbage collection to free up the memory that's no longer used. In C++, you can achieve the same by using smart pointers.

In the case of most data structures, the ownership model is clear. For example, for lists, the list head is the owner of the rest of the list (not necessarily the only owner, because multiple lists can share the same data).

The simplest structure for `list` and its internal node class could look like this:

```
template <typename T>
class list {
public:
    ...

private:
    struct node {
        T value;
        std::shared_ptr<node> tail;
    };

    std::shared_ptr<node> m_head;
};
```

This correctly frees all nodes that are no longer needed when an instance of `list` is destroyed. `list` checks whether it's the sole owner of the node that represents it head, and destroys it if it's true. Then the destructor of the node checks whether it's the only owner of the node representing its tail, and destroys it if it is. This continues until a node with another owner is found, or until you reach the end of the list.

The problem is that all these destructors are invoked recursively, and if you had a large enough list, you might end up overflowing the stack. To avoid this, you need to provide a custom destructor that will flatten out the recursion into a single loop.

Listing 8.1   Flattening the recursive structure destruction

```
~node()
{
    auto next_node = std::move(tail);        ← std::move is necessary here. Otherwise,
    while (next_node) {                         next_node.unique() will never return true.
        if (!next_node.unique()) break;      ← If you're not the only owner of
                                                the node, don't do anything.

        std::shared_ptr<node> tail;          ┐ Steals the tail of the node you're
        swap(tail, next_node->tail);         ├ processing, to stop the node's destructor
        next_node.reset();                   ┘ from destroying it recursively

        next_node = std::move(tail);         ← std::move isn't necessary here but could
    }                                          improve performance.
}
```

Freely destroys the node; no recursive calls because you've set its tail to be nullptr

If you wanted to make this code thread-safe, you'd need to do so manually. Although the reference counting in `std::shared_ptr` is thread-safe, you have multiple separate calls that might modify it in this implementation.

8.2 Immutable vector-like data structures

Because of their inefficiencies, lists are unsuitable for most use cases. You need a structure that will have efficient operations and fast lookup.

`std::vector` has a few things going for it, mainly because it stores all its elements in one chunk of memory:

- Fast index-based access, because given the index, it can directly calculate the location in memory of the corresponding element—by adding the index to the address of the first element in the vector.
- When the CPU needs a value from memory, modern hardware architectures don't fetch only that value, but instead fetch a chunk of surrounding memory and cache it for faster access. When iterating over values in `std::vector`, this comes in handy: accessing the first element will fetch a few elements at the same time, which makes subsequent access faster.
- Even in problematic cases, when the vector needs to reallocate memory and copy or move the previous data to the new location, the vector will benefit from everything being in the same block of memory, because modern systems are optimized to move blocks of memory.

The problem with `std::vector` is that if you wanted to use it as an immutable structure, you'd need to copy all the data every time you wanted to create a modified version of it. You need an alternative that will behave as similarly as possible to `std::vector`.

One of the popular alternatives is the *bitmapped vector trie* (prefix tree), a data structure invented by Rick Hickey for the Clojure programming language (which is, in turn, heavily inspired by a paper by Phil Bagwell[1]).

> **Copy-on-write**
>
> We often pass objects to functions that use them without modifying them. Always copying an entire object when passing it is superfluous when the invoked function doesn't change it.
>
> Copy-on-write (COW), or *lazy copying*, is an optimization that delays creating a copy of the data until somebody tries to modify it. When the copy constructor or the assignment operator is called, the object saves the reference to the original data and nothing else.
>
> When the user invokes any member function that's supposed to change the object, you can't allow it to change the original data, so you need to create a proper copy and then change it. You can change the original data in place only if no other object has access to it.
>
> You can find more information about COW in Herb Sutter's *More Exceptional C++* (Addison-Wesley Professional, 2001).

---

[1] Phil Bagwell, "Ideal Hash Trees," 2001, https://lampwww.epfl.ch/papers/idealhashtrees.pdf.

The structure starts with a COW vector, but with its maximum size limited to a pre-defined number *m*. In order for operations on this structure to be as efficient as possible, the number *m* needs to be a power of 2 (you'll see why later). Most of the implementations set the limit to 32, but to keep the figures simpler, we'll draw the vectors as if the limit was 4.

Until you reach that limit, the structure behaves like an ordinary COW vector (see figure 8.8). When you try to insert the next element, a new vector with the same limit is created, and that new element is its first element. Now you have two vectors: one that's full, and one containing a single item. When a new element is appended, it'll go into the second vector until it gets full, at which point a new vector will be created.

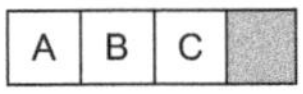

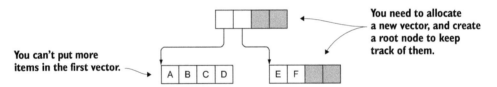

Figure 8.8 If you have at most *m* elements, the bitmapped vector trie will contain just one COW vector.

To keep the vectors *together* (they're still, logically, a part of the same structure), you create a vector of vectors: a vector that contains pointers to at most *m* subvectors that contain the data (see figure 8.9). When the top-level vector gets full, you create a new level. If you have at most *m* items, you'll have just one level. If you have at most *m* × *m* items, you'll have two levels. If you have at most *m* × *m* × *m* items, you'll have three levels (see figure 8.10), and so on.

Figure 8.9 When you add an item that can't fit into a vector of capacity *m*, you create another vector and place the new element inside it. To track all the vectors you create, you need an index: a new vector of capacity *m* that holds the pointer to the vectors you created to hold the data. You get a trie with two levels.

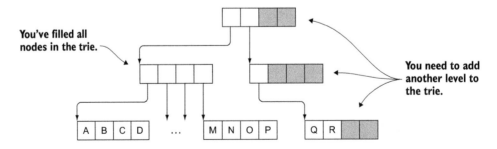

Figure 8.10 When you fill up the root vector and can't add more items to it, you create another trie in which you can store more elements. To keep track of all these tries, you create a new root node.

8.2.1 Element lookup in bitmapped vector tries

This structure is a special kind of trie in which the values are stored in the leaf nodes. The non-leaf nodes hold no data; they keep the pointers to the nodes in the lower level. All the leaf nodes are sorted by index. The leftmost leaf always contains the values from 0 to $m - 1$; the next leaf contains the items from m to $2m - 1$, and so forth.

I said you want a fast index-based lookup. If you're given the index i of an element, how do you find the element?

The idea is simple. If you have only one level—a single vector—then i is the index of the element in the vector. If you have two levels, the upper level contains m elements for each of its indices (it contains a pointer to a vector of m elements). The first leaf vector contains items up to $m - 1$; the second contains items from m up to $2m - 1$; the third from $2m$ to $3m - 1$, and so on. You can easily find which leaf the ith element is in: the leaf whose index is $i \ / \ m$ (and this is analogous for the higher levels).

When you're given an index of an element, you can look at it as if it's an array of bits, not a number. You can split that array into chunks. This gives you the path from the root node to the element you're searching for: each chunk is the index of the child node you need to visit next, and the last chunk is the index of the element in the leaf vector (see figure 8.11).

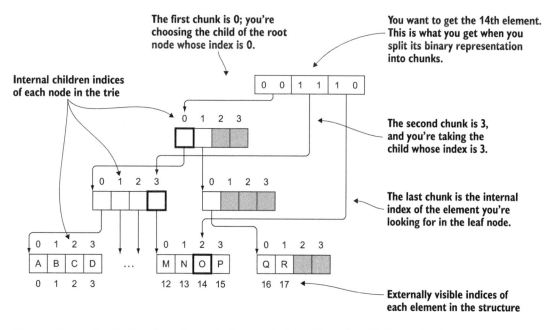

Figure 8.11 Finding the item for a given index is easy. Each level has internal indices going from 0 to m, and m should be a power of 2 (in this figure, $m = 4$, although in reality it's usually 32). The internal indices of each node, if looked at as arrays of bits, go from 00 to 11. You can look at the index of the requested element as an array of bits that you split into two-by-two chunks. Each chunk is the internal index in the corresponding trie node.

This approach gives you a logarithmic lookup, with *m* being the logarithm base. Usually you'll choose for *m* to be 32, which will make the trie shallow in most cases. For example, a trie of depth 5 can contain 33 million items. Because of this shallowness and the system's limited memory, in practice, the lookup is done in constant time ($O(1)$) for tries where *m* is 32 or greater. Even if you fill the whole addressable memory with one collection, you still won't go above 13 levels. (The exact number isn't that important, but the fact that it's a fixed number is.)

8.2.2   *Appending elements to bitmapped vector tries*

Now that you've seen how to perform lookups on the bitmapped vector trie, let's move to the next topic: how to update it. This would be trivial if you were implementing a mutable version of the structure; you'd find the first free space and place the new element there. If all the leaf nodes were filled, you'd create a new leaf.

The problem is that you want to keep the old versions untouched. You can do this in a way similar to that for the linked lists: create a new trie that shares as much data as possible with the previous one.

If you compare the three tries in figure 8.12, you can see that the differences aren't big. The main variance is that the leaves differ. You need to copy the leaf that's affected by the append. Then, because the leaf is changed, the new trie also needs a new parent for that leaf, a new parent of that parent, and so on.

To append an element, you need to copy not only the leaf node, but also the entire path down to the inserted element (see figure 8.13).

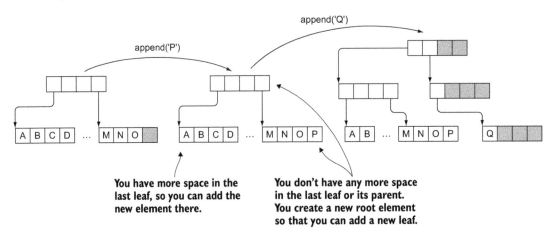

You have more space in the last leaf, so you can add the new element there.

You don't have any more space in the last leaf *or* its parent. You create a new root element so that you can add a new leaf.

Figure 8.12   In a mutable binary vector trie, appending a new element is simple. If an empty space is left in the last leaf node, you can store the value there. If all leaves are full, you create a new one. You need to create a pointer to the new leaf in the level above it. Recursively, if the parent node has room, you store the pointer there. If not, you create a new node, and you store a pointer to it in the level above it. This is repeated until you reach the root. If the root node has no room, you create a new node and make it a parent of the previous one.

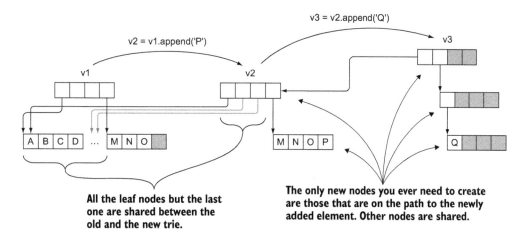

Figure 8.13 In the immutable binary vector trie, the principle of adding a new element is the same. The difference is that, because you want the previous collection to be untouched, you need to create a new trie to hold the new data. Fortunately, as was the case with linked lists, you can share most of the data between the old and the new tries. The only nodes you need to create are those on the path to the element you're adding. All other nodes can be shared.

We have a few cases to cover here:

- The last leaf has room for a new element.
- Any of the non-leaf nodes have room for a new element.
- All nodes are full.

The first case is the simplest. You copy the path to the leaf node, duplicate the leaf node, and insert the new element into the newly created leaf (see figure 8.14).

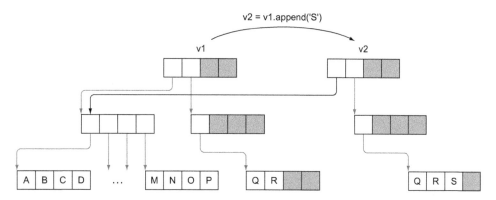

Figure 8.14 When appending a new element to a trie that has a leaf with room for it, you have to duplicate that leaf and all its parents. You can then add the new value into the newly copied leaf.

In the second case, you have to find the lowest node that's not full. You create all the levels below it until you create the leaf to which you add the new element (see figure 8.15).

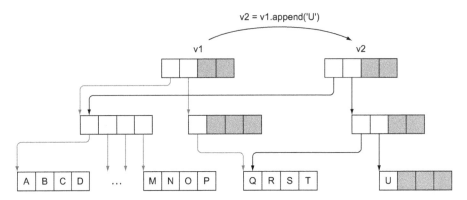

Figure 8.15   When you don't have any room in the last leaf, you need to create a new one that contains just the element you're appending to the trie. The newly created leaf should be inserted into the layer above it.

The third case is the most complex. If you don't have a node with free space, you can't store any more elements under the current root node. You need to create a new root node and make the previous root its first element. After that, you come to the same situation as in the second case: you have room on a non-leaf node (see figure 8.16).

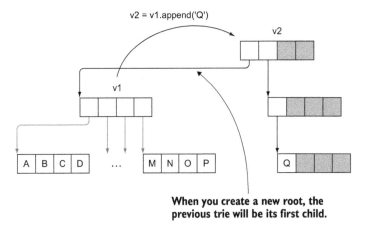

When you create a new root, the previous trie will be its first child.

Figure 8.16   This is a corner case where none of the leaves have space, and none of the other nodes, including the root, have space. In this case, you can't create a new path inside this trie, so you need to create a new root item that will link to the previous trie, and a new trie with the same depth that contains just the newly added item.

What's the efficiency of appending? You're either copying the path nodes or allocating new ones, and sometimes you need to create a new root node. All of these operations, by themselves, are constant time (each node has at most a constant number of elements). If you use the same reasoning behind the claim that the lookup is constant time, you can consider that you have a constant number of nodes to copy or allocate. Appending to this structure is also O(1).

8.2.3 *Updating elements in bitmapped vector tries*

Now that you've seen how to append an element, let's analyze what you need to do to update one. Again, let's think of what would be changed in the structure if you made it mutable and changed an element at a predefined position.

You need to find the leaf that contains the element and then modify the element. You don't need to create any new nodes; you get the same trie structure, but with a single value changed.

Updating is similar to the first case you had when appending: when the last leaf has space to store the new element. The new trie can share everything with the old one, apart from the path you used to reach the element you're updating.

8.2.4 *Removing elements from the end of the bitmapped vector trie*

Removing an element from the end is similar to appending, just in reverse. You have three separate cases:

- The last leaf contains more than one element.
- The last leaf contains only one element.
- The root contains one element after removing an element.

In the first case, you need to copy the path to the leaf node that contains the element you want removed, and remove the element from the newly created leaf node.

In the second case, you have a leaf with only one element. In the newly created trie, that leaf node shouldn't exist. Again, you copy the whole path and trim the empty nodes from its end. You remove the leaf, but you also remove its parent if it no longer has any children, and its parent, and so on.

If you get a root node with a single child after trimming the empty nodes, you need to set that child to be the new root to reduce the number of levels for your trie.

8.2.5 *Other operations and the overall efficiency of bitmapped vector tries*

You've seen how to update elements, or how to append them to or remove them from the end. You've also seen that these operations on the bitmapped vector trie are efficient.What about other operations such as prepending or inserting elements at a specified position? And what about concatenation?

Unfortunately, with these operations, you can't do anything smart (see table 8.2). Prepending and inserting needs to shift all other elements one step to the right. And concatenation needs to allocate enough leaf nodes and copy them from the collection you're concatenating.

Table 8.2   Complexity of the bitmapped vector trie functions

O(1)	O(n)
Accessing element by index	Prepending
Appending an element	Concatenating
	Inserting at a position

These are the same complexities you have with `std::vector`. Changing the existing elements, and adding elements to and removing elements from the end of the collection, are constant time; and inserting elements at or removing elements from the beginning or the middle of the collection is linear.

Even if the algorithm complexity is the same, the bitmapped vector trie can't be exactly as fast as `std::vector`. When you access an element, it has to go through several layers of indirection, and it'll have cache misses slightly more often because it keeps its elements not in a contiguous block of memory, but rather in several contiguous chunks.

One case where bitmapped vector trie beats the ordinary vector is copying, which is what you needed in the first place. You have a structure that has a comparable speed to `std::vector` while being optimized for immutable usage; instead of modifying existing values, you're always creating slightly modified copies of the original data.

I talked about immutability in the previous chapters, and how to use the features of C++ such as `const` to implement safer, more concise code. The standard collection classes in the STL aren't optimized for this use case. They're meant to be used in the mutable manner. They can't be safely shared among different components unless you copy them, which is inefficient.

The structures in this chapter, especially the bitmapped vector trie, live on the other side of the spectrum. They're designed to be as efficient as possible when you want to use them in the pure functional style: to never change any data you set once. Although they have somewhat lower performance, they make copying blazingly fast.

> **TIP**   For more information and resources about the topics covered in this chapter, see https://forums.manning.com/posts/list/43777.page. For more information on immutable data structures, the book that's usually recommended is Chris Okasaki's *Purely Functional Data Structures* (Cambridge University Press, 1999).

Summary

- The main optimization in all immutable data structures, which are also called *persistent,* is data sharing. It allows you to keep many slightly modified versions of the same data without the memory overhead you'd have if you used the classes from the standard library.
- Having an efficient way to store past values of a variable allows you to travel through the history of your program. If you store all the previous states of your program, you can jump back to any of them whenever you want.
- Similar modifications exist for other structures as well. For example, if you needed an immutable associative container, you could use red-black trees, modified to share the data between different instances, similar to what you did for the bitmapped vector trie.
- Immutable data structures have always been an active area of research. Many contributions came from academia (as is often the case with functional programming), as well as from developers.
- It's always worth checking which structures would be suited best for any particular case. Unlike the go-to collection in C++ (`std::vector`), all immutable data structures have downsides (even if they're as magical as bitmapped vector tries). Some of them might not be well suited for a given case.

Algebraic data types
and pattern matching

During the course of this book, we've tackled a few problems the program state introduces. You've seen how to design software without mutable state and how to implement data structures that are efficient to copy. But we still haven't dealt with all the problems of program state: we haven't covered unexpected or invalid states.

Consider the following situation. Suppose you have an application that counts the total number of words on a web page. The program can start counting as soon as it retrieves part of the web page. It has three basic states:

- *Initial state*—The counting process hasn't started yet.
- *Counting state*—The web page is being retrieved, and counting is in progress.
- *Final state*—The web page is fully retrieved, and all the words have been counted.

When you implement something like this, you usually create a class to contain all the data you need. You end up with a class that contains the handler through which the web page is accessed (a socket or a data stream), the counter to contain the number of words, and flags that indicate whether the process has started and whether it has finished.

You could have a structure like this:

```
struct state_t {
    bool started = false;
    bool finished = false;
    unsigned count = 0;
    socket_t web_page;
};
```

The first thing that comes to mind is, `started` and `finished` don't need to be separate `bool` flags: you could replace them with an enum containing the three values `init`, `running`, and `finished`. If you keep them as separate values, you open yourself to having invalid states such as `started` being `false` while `finished` is `true`.

You'll have the same problems with other variables. For example, `count` should never be greater than zero if `started` is `false`, and it should never be updated after `finished` becomes `true`; the `web_page` socket should be open only if `started` is `true` and `finished` is `false`; and so forth.

When you replace the `bool` values with an enum that can have three values, you reduce the number of states your program can be in. Therefore, you remove some of the invalid states. Doing the same for other variables would also be useful.

9.1 Algebraic data types

In the functional world, building new types from old ones is usually done through two operations: sum and product (these new types are thus called *algebraic*). A product of two types A and B is a new type that contains an instance of A and an instance of B (it'll be a Cartesian product of the set of all values of type A and the set of all values of B). In the example of counting words on a web page, `state_t` is a product of two `bool`s: one `unsigned` and one `socket_t`. Similarly, the product of more than two types is a new type that contains an instance of each of the types involved in the product.

This is something we're accustomed to in C++. Every time we want to combine multiple types into one, we either create a new class or use `std::pair` or `std::tuple` when we don't need the member values to be named.

Pairs and tuples

The `std::pair` and `std::tuple` types are useful generic types for creating quick-and-dirty product types. `std::pair` is a product of two types, whereas `std::tuple` can have as many types as you want.

One of the most useful features of pairs and tuples is that when you create product types with them, you get lexicographical comparison operators for free. It isn't rare to see people implement comparison operators for their classes through tuples. For example, if you have a class that holds a person's name and surname, and you want to

(continued)

implement a less-than operator for it to compare the surname first and then the name, you can do this:

```
bool operator<(const person_t& left, const person_t& right)
{
    return std::tie(left.m_surname, left.m_name) <
           std::tie(right.m_surname, right.m_name);
}
```

The `std::tie` function creates a tuple of references to the values passed to it. No copies of the original data are created when creating the tuple; the original strings are compared.

The problem with pairs and tuples is, the values stored in them aren't named. If you see a function that returns `std::pair<std::string, int>`, you can't tell what those values mean from the type. If the return type was a structure with member variables called `full_name` and `age`, you wouldn't have that problem.

For this reason, pairs and tuples should be used rarely, and their usage should always be localized. It's a bad idea to ever make them a part of a public API (even if some parts of the STL do so).

The sum types aren't as prominent in C++ as product types. The sum type of types `A` and `B` is a type that can hold an instance of `A` or an instance of `B`, but not both at the same time.

Enums as sum types

Enums are a special kind of sum type. You define an enum by specifying the different values it can hold. An instance of that enum type can hold exactly one of those values. If you treat these values as one-element sets, the enum is a sum type of those sets.

You can think of sum types as a generalization of an enum. Instead of providing one-element sets when defining the sum type, you specify sets with an arbitrary number of elements.

In the example scenario, you have three main states: the initial state, the counting state, and the finished state. The initial state doesn't need to contain any additional information, the counting state contains a counter and the handler for accessing the web page, and the finished state needs to contain only the final word count. Because these states are mutually exclusive, when you write the program for this scenario, you can model the state by creating a sum type of three types—one type for each state.

9.1.1   *Sum types through inheritance*

C++ provides multiple ways to implement sum types. One way is to create a class hierarchy; you have a superclass representing the sum type and derived classes to represent summed types.

To represent the three states for the example program, you can create a superclass `state_t` and three subclasses—one for each of the main states—`init_t`, `running_t`, and `finished_t`. The `state_t` class can be empty because you need it only as a placeholder; you'll have only a pointer to its subclasses. To check which state you're in, you can use `dynamic_cast`. Alternatively, because dynamic casting is slow, you can add an integer tag to the superclass, to differentiate between the subclasses.

Listing 9.1 Tagged superclass for creating sum types through inheritance

```
class state_t {
protected:
    state_t(int type)
        : type(type)
    {
    }
public:
    virtual ~state_t() {};
    int type;

};
```

It shouldn't be possible to create instances of this class, so make the constructor protected. It can be called only by classes that inherit from state_t.

Each subclass should pass a different value for the type argument. You can use it as an efficient replacement for dynamic_cast.

You've created a class that you can't instantiate directly. You can use it only as a handler to instances of its subclasses. Next, create a subclass for each state that you want to represent.

Listing 9.2 Types to denote different states

```
class init_t : public state_t {
public:
    enum { id = 0 };
    init_t()
        : state_t(id)
    {
    }
};
```

The class representing the initial state doesn't need to hold any data; you still don't have the handler to the web page or the counter. It only needs to set the type to its ID (zero).

```
class running_t : public state_t {
public:
    enum { id = 1 };
    running_t()
        : state_t(id)
    {
    }

    unsigned count() const
    {
        return m_count;
    }

    ...
```

```
private:
    unsigned m_count = 0;
    socket_t m_web_page;
};
```

> For the running state, you need a counter and the handler to the web page whose words you want to count.

```
class finished_t : public state_t {
public:
    enum { id = 2 };
    finished_t(unsigned count)
        : state_t(id)
        , m_count(count)
    {
    }

    unsigned count() const
    {
        return m_count;
    }

private:
    unsigned m_count;
};
```

> When the counting is finished, you no longer need the handler to the web page. You only need the calculated value.

The main program now needs a pointer to state_t (an ordinary pointer or a unique_ptr). Initially, it should point to an instance of init_t; when the state changes, that instance should be destroyed and replaced with an instance of another state subtype (see figure 9.1).

> All the state classes inherit from a common state_t type.

> The class that handles the program state contains just a pointer to the state_t subclass that represents the current state.

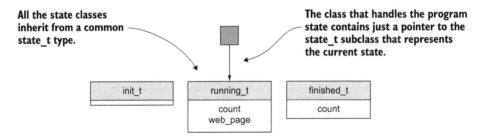

init_t   running_t   finished_t
                count   count
                web_page

Figure 9.1   Implementing sum types with inheritance is simple. You can create multiple classes that inherit a common state_t class, and the current state is denoted by a pointer pointing to an instance of one of these classes.

Listing 9.3   The main program

```
class program_t {
public:
    program_t()
        : m_state(std::make_unique<init_t>())
    {
    }

    ...
```

> The initial state should be an instance of init_t. m_state should never be null.

```
    void counting_finished()
    {
        assert(m_state->type == running_t::id);

        auto state = static_cast<running_t*>(
            m_state.get());

        m_state = std::make_unique<finished_t>(
            state->count());
    }
private:
    std::unique_ptr<state_t> m_state;
};
```

> If counting is finished, it should mean you were in the counting state. If you can't guarantee this assumption holds, you can use if-else instead of assert.

> You know the exact type of the class m_state points to, so you can statically cast to it.

> Switches to the new state that holds the end result. The previous state is destroyed.

With this approach, you can no longer have invalid states. The count can't be greater than zero if you haven't started counting yet (the count doesn't even exist, in that case). The count can't accidentally change after the counting process is finished, and you know exactly which state the program is in at all times.

What's more, you don't need to pay attention to the lifetimes of resources you acquire for specific states. Focus on the web_page socket for a moment. In the original approach of putting all variables you'll need in the state_t structure, you could forget to close the socket after you finish reading from it. The socket instance continues to live for as long as the instance of state_t lives. By using the sum type, all the resources needed for a specific state will automatically be released as soon as you switch to another state. In this case, the destructor of running_t will close the web_page socket.

When you use inheritance to implement sum types, you get open sum types. The state can be any class that inherits from state_t, which makes it easily extendable. Although this is sometimes useful, you usually know exactly which possible states the program should have, and you don't need to allow other components to extend the set of states dynamically.

The inheritance approach also has a few downsides. If you want to keep its openness, you need to use virtual functions and dynamic dispatch (at least for the destructors), you have to use type tags in order not to rely on slow dynamic casts, and you must allocate the state objects dynamically on the heap. You also need to take care never to make the m_state pointer invalid (nullptr).

9.1.2 *Sum types through unions and std::variant*

The alternative approach to inheritance-based sum types is std::variant, which provides a type-safe implementation of unions. With std::variant, you can define closed sum types—sum types that can hold exactly the types you specify and nothing else.

When using inheritance to implement sum types, the type of the m_state member variable is a (smart) pointer to state_t. The type doesn't communicate anything about the possible states; m_state can point to any object that inherits from state_t.

With std::variant, all the types you want to use to handle the program state need to be explicitly specified when defining the m_state variable; they'll be encoded in the type of `m_state`. In order to extend the sum type, you need to change the type definition, which wasn't the case with the solution based on inheritance (see figure 9.2).

> **TIP** `std::variant` was introduced in C++17. If you have an older compiler and an older STL implementation that doesn't support C++17 features, you can use `boost::variant` instead.

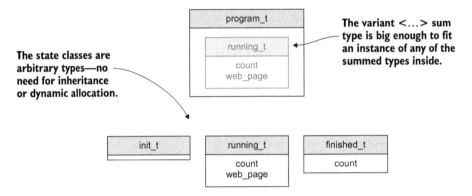

Figure 9.2 **Variants can be used to define proper sum types. You get a value type that can contain a value of any of the summed types in its own memory space. The variant instance will be at least the size of the biggest type you're summing, regardless of the value it currently holds.**

To implement the program state by using `std::variant`, you can reuse the definitions of the `init_t`, `running_t`, and `finished_t` classes, with the exception that you don't need them to be subclasses of some common type, and you don't need to create integer tags for them:

```
class init_t {
};

class running_t {
public:
    unsigned count() const
    {
        return m_count;
    }

    ...

private:
    unsigned m_count = 0;
    socket_t m_web_page;
};

class finished_t {
public:
    finished_t(unsigned count)
        : m_count(count)
```

```
    {
    }

    unsigned count() const
    {
        return m_count;
    }

private:
    unsigned m_count;
};
```

All the boilerplate you had to add in order for inheritance (dynamic polymorphism, to be exact) to work properly has gone away. The init_t class is now empty because it doesn't have any state to remember. The running_t and finished_t classes define only their state and nothing else. Now the main program can have a std::variant value that can hold any of these three types (see figure 9.3).

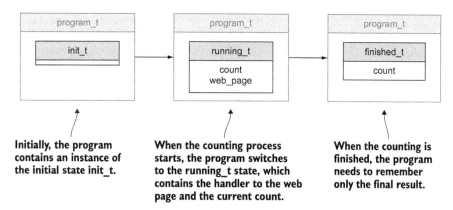

Figure 9.3 When counting the number of words on a web page, you have three main states. Before you have the web page, you can't do anything. When you get the web page, you can start counting. While counting, you need to store the current count and the handler to the web page. When the counting is finished, you no longer need the handle to the web page; you can just store the final count.

Listing 9.4   The main program using std::variant

```
class program_t {
public:
    program_t()
        : m_state(init_t())
    {
    }

    ...

    void counting_finished()
    {
```

Initially, the state is an instance of init_t.

```
        auto* state = std::get_if<running_t>(&m_state);

        assert(state != nullptr);

        m_state = finished_t(state->count());
    }
private:
    std::variant<init_t, running_t, state_t> m_state;
};
```

Uses std::get_if to check whether there's a value of a specified type in std::variant. Returns nullptr if the variant doesn't hold the value of the specified type.

assert (state != nullptr);

Changing the current state is as easy as assigning the new value to the variable.

You initialized m_state from a value of type init_t. You didn't pass it a pointer (new init_t()) as you did in the implementation that used inheritance. std::variant isn't based on dynamic polymorphism; it doesn't store pointers to objects allocated on the heap. It stores the actual object in its own memory space, just as with ordinary unions. The difference is, it automatically handles construction and destruction of the objects stored within, and it knows exactly the type of the object it contains at any given time.

When accessing the value stored in std::variant, you can use std::get or std::get_if. Both can access the elements of variant either by type or by index of the type in the variant's declaration:

```
std::get<running_t>(m_state);
std::get_if<1>(&m_state);
```

The difference is that std::get either returns a value or throws an exception if the variant doesn't hold a value of the specified type, whereas std::get_if returns a pointer to the contained value, or a null pointer on error.

The benefits of std::variant compared to the first solution are numerous. It requires almost no boilerplate, because the type tags are handled by std::variant. You also don't need to create an inheritance hierarchy in which all the summed types must inherit from a supertype; you can sum existing types such as strings and vectors. Also, std::variant doesn't perform any dynamic memory allocations. The variant instance will, like a regular union, have the size of the largest type you want to store (plus a few bytes for bookkeeping).

The only drawback is that std::variant can't be easily extended. If you want to add a new type to the sum, you need to change the type of the variant. In the rare cases in which extensibility is necessary, you have to go back to the inheritance-based sum types.

> **NOTE**   An alternative to the inheritance-based open sum types is the std::any class. It's a type-safe container for values of any type. Although it's useful in some circumstances, it isn't as efficient as std::variant, and shouldn't be used as a simple-to-type replacement for std::variant.

9.1.3   *Implementing specific states*

Now that you have the program_t class and classes to represent the potential states, you can proceed to implement the logic. The question is, where should the logic be implemented? You could make the obvious choice and implement everything in `program_t`, but then, in each function you made, you'd need to check whether you were in the correct state. For example, if to implement the function that starts the counting process in the `program_t` class, you'd first need to check whether the current state was `init_t` and then change the state to `running_t`.

You can check this by using the `index` member function of `std::variant`. It returns the index of the current type that occupies the variant instance. Because `init_t` is the first type you specified when defining the type of the `m_state` member variable, its index will be zero:

```
void count_words(const std::string& web_page)
{
    assert(m_state.index() == 0);

    m_state = running_t(web_page);

    … // count the number of words

    counting_finished();
}
```

After you check for the current state, you switch to `running_t` and start the counting process. The process is synchronous (we'll deal with concurrency and asynchronous execution in chapters 10 and 12), and when it finishes, you can process the result.

As you can see in the preceding snippet, you'll call the `counting_finished` function, which should switch to the `finished_t` state. You need to check for the current state in this function as well. The `counting_finished` function should be called only when you're in the `running_t` process. You need the result of the process, so instead of using `index`, you use `std::get_if` and assert on its result:

```
void counting_finished()
{
    const auto* state = std::get_if<running_t>(&m_state);

    assert(state != nullptr);

    m_state = finished_t(state->count());
}
```

The state you end up in is `finished_t`, which needs to remember only the calculated word count.

Both of these functions deal with state changes, so it might not be a bad idea to have them in `program_t` even if you need to perform the checks that you're in the correct state. What if a function needs to handle a part of program logic that's relevant only to a particular state?

For example, the `running_t` state needs to open a stream through which to fetch the contents of a web page. It needs to read that stream word by word and count the number of words in it. It doesn't change the main program states. It doesn't even care about the other states in the program; it can do its work with only the data it contains.

For this reason, there's no point in having any part of this logic in the `program_t` class. The logic can be in `running_t`:

```
class running_t {
public:
    running_t(const std::string& url)
        : m_web_page(url)
    {
    }

    void count_words()
    {
        m_count = std::distance(
                std::istream_iterator<std::string>(m_web_page),
                std::istream_iterator<std::string>());
    }

    unsigned count() const
    {
        return m_count;
    }

private:
    unsigned m_count = 0;
    std::istream m_web_page;
};
```

This is the recommended approach to designing programs with state based on sum types: put the logic that deals with one state inside the object that defines that state, and put the logic that performs state transitions into the main program. A full implementation of this program that works with files instead of web pages is available in the word-counting-states example.

An alternative approach is to keep the logic out of the `program_t` class and put everything in the state classes. This approach removes the need for checks with `get_if` and `index`, because a member function of a class representing a particular state will be called only if you're in that state. The downside is that now the state classes need to perform program state changes, which implies that they need to know about each other, thus breaking encapsulation.

9.1.4   *Special sum type: Optional values*

I've already mentioned `std::get_if`, which returns a pointer to a value if the value exists, or a null pointer otherwise. A pointer is used to allow this special case—denoting the missing value.

Pointers can have a lot of different meanings in different situations, and they're bad at communicating what they're used for. When you see a function that returns a pointer, you have a few options:

- It's a factory function that returns an object you'll become the owner of.
- It's a function that returns a pointer to an existing object you don't own.
- It's a function that can fail, and it communicates the failure by returning the null pointer as the result.

To tell which of these is the case with a function you want to call, such as `std::get_if`, you need to check its documentation.

Instead, it's often better to use types that clearly communicate the function result. In the first case, it would be better to replace the pointer with `std::unique_ptr`. In the second case, `std::shared_ptr` (or `std::weak_ptr`) will do.

The third case is special. There's no reason the function result needs to be a pointer. The only reason it's a pointer instead of an ordinary value is to *extend* the original type with a "no value present" state: to denote that the value is optional—it can exist, but it can be undefined.

You can say that an optional value of some type T is either a value of type T or empty. So, the value is a sum of all values T can have, and a single value to denote that the value doesn't exist. This sum type can be easily implemented with `std::variant`:

```
struct nothing_t {};

template <typename T>
using optional = std::variant<nothing_t, T>;
```

Now, when you see a function that returns `optional<T>`, you immediately know you're getting either a value of type T or *nothing*. You don't have to think about the lifetime of the result or whether you should destroy it. You can't forget to check whether it's null, as is the case with pointers.

Optional values are useful enough that the standard library provides `std::optional`—a more convenient implementation than the one you created by aliasing `std::variant`.

> **TIP**   `std::optional`, like `std::variant`, was introduced with C++17. If you have an older compiler, you can use `boost::optional` instead.

Because `std::optional` is a more specific sum type than `std::variant`, it also comes with a more convenient API. It provides member functions to check whether it contains a value, `operator->` to access the value if it exists, and so forth.

You can implement your own `get_if` function. You'll use `std::get_if` and check whether the result is valid or a null pointer. If the function points to a value, you'll return that value wrapped inside `std::optional`, and you'll return an empty optional object if it's null:

```
template <typename T, template Variant>
std::optional<T> get_if(const Variant& variant)
{
    T* ptr = std::get_if<T>(&variant);

    if (ptr) {
        return *ptr;
    } else {
        return std::optional<T>();
    }
}
```

You can use the same approach to wrap any function that uses pointers to denote the missing values. Now that you have a variant of get_if that returns an optional, you can easily reimplement the counting_finished function:

```
void counting_finished()
{
    auto state = get_if<running_t>(m_state);

    assert(state.has_value());

    m_state = finished_t(state->count());
}
```

The code looks mostly the same as the code that used pointers. The most obvious difference is that you had state != nullptr in the assert statement, and now you have state.has_value(). You could make both assert on state, because both pointers and optionals can be converted to bool: true if they have a valid value, or false if they're empty.

The main difference between these two approaches is more subtle. The std::optional instance is a proper value and owns its data. In the example that used a pointer, you'd get an undefined behavior if m_state was destroyed or changed to contain another state type between the call to std::get_if and state->count(). In this example, the optional object contains the copy of the value, so you can't have that problem. In this example, you don't need to think about the lifetime of any variable; you can rely on the default behavior the C++ language provides.

9.1.5   *Sum types for error handling*

The optional values can be useful for denoting whether an error has occurred. For example, you implemented the get_if function that either returns a value if all is well or returns nothing—an empty optional—if you try to get the instance of a type that's not currently stored in the variant. The problem in this use case is that optional values only focus on the value and its presence, and give you no information about the error when the value isn't present.

If you want to track the errors as well, you can create a sum type that will contain either a value or an error. The error can be an integer error code or a more intricate structure—even a pointer to an exception (std::exception_ptr).

You need a sum type of T and E, where T is the type of the value you want to return and E is the error type. As with optional, you can define the type as std::variant<T, E>, but that won't give you a nice API. You'd need to use a functions such as index, std::get or std::get_if to reach the value or the error, which isn't convenient. It will be nicer to have a class dedicated to this use case, which will have better named member functions such as value and error.

For this, you'll roll your own implementation called expected<T, E>. When a function returns a value of this type, it will clearly communicate that you expect a value of type T, but that you can also get an error of type E.

Internally, the class will be a simple tagged union. A flag denotes whether you currently hold a value or an error, and you'll have a union of T and E types.

Listing 9.5   Internal structure of expected<T, E>

```
template<typename T, typename E>
class expected {
private:
    union {
        T m_value;
        E m_error;
    };

    bool m_valid;
};
```

The easy part of the implementation is the getter functions. If you need to return a value, but there's an error, you can throw an exception, and vice versa.

Listing 9.6   Getter functions for expected<T, E>

```
template<typename T, typename E>
class expected {
    ...

    T& get()
    {
        if (!m_valid) {
            throw std::logic_error("Missing a value");
        }

        return m_value;
    }

    E& error()
    {
        if (m_valid) {
            throw std::logic_error("There is no error");
        }

        return m_error;
    }
};
```

The const variants of the getter functions would be the same. They would just return values or const-references instead of normal references.

The complex part is handling the values inside the union. Because it's a union of potentially complex types, you need to manually call constructors and destructors when you want to initialize or deinitialize them.

Constructing a new value of expected<T, E> can be done from a value of type T or from an error of type E. Because these two types can be the same, you'll make dedicated functions for each of them instead of using ordinary constructors. This isn't mandatory, but it makes the code cleaner.

Listing 9.7   Constructing values of expected<T, E>

```
template<typename T, typename E>
class expected {
    ...

    template <typename... Args>
    static expected success(Args&&... params)
    {
        expected result;
        result.m_valid = true;
        new (&result.m_value)
            T(std::forward<Args>(params)...);
        return result;
    }

    template <typename... Args>
    static expected error(Args&&... params)
    {
        expected result;
        result.m_valid = false;
        new (&result.m_error)
            E(std::forward<Args>(params)...);
        return result;
    }
};
```

Default constructor that creates an uninitialized union

Initializes the union tag. You'll have a valid value inside.

Calls placement new to initialize the value of type T in the memory location of m_value

Creating the error instance is the same, apart from calling the constructor for type E instead of the constructor of T.

Now, if you have a function that can fail, you can call success or error when returning the result.

Placement new

Unlike the regular new syntax, which allocates memory for a value and initializes that value (calls the constructor), the *placement new* syntax allows you to use already-allocated memory and construct the object inside it. In the case of expected<T, E>, the memory is preallocated by the union member variable you define. Although this isn't a technique you should use often, it's necessary if you want to implement sum types that don't perform dynamic memory allocation at runtime.

To properly handle the lifetime of an expected<T, E> instance and the values stored in it, you need to create the destructor and the copy and move constructors, along with the assignment operator. The destructor for expected<T, E> needs to call the destructor for m_value or for m_error, depending on which of those you're currently holding:

```
~expected() {
    if (m_valid) {
        m_value.~T();
    } else {
        m_error.~E();
    }
}
```

The copy and move constructors are similar. You need to check whether the instance that you're copying or moving from is valid and then initialize the proper member of the union.

Listing 9.8 The copy and move constructors for expected<T, E>

If the original instance contained an
error, copy that error into this instance.

The copy constructor initializes the flag that
denotes whether you have a value or an error.

```
expected(const expected& other)
      : m_valid(other.m_valid)
   {
       if (m_valid) {
           new (&m_value) T(other.m_value);
       } else {
           new (&m_error) E(other.m_error);
       }
   }
```

If the instance being copied from
contains a value, you call the copy
constructor on that value to initialize
the other m_value member variable
using the placement new syntax.

```
expected(expected&& other)
      : m_valid(other.m_valid)
   {
       if (m_valid) {
           new (&m_value) T(std::move(other.m_value));
       } else {
           new (&m_error) E(std::move(other.m_error));
       }
   }
```

The move constructor behaves
like the copy constructor, but
you can steal the data from
the original instance.

Instead of calling the
copy constructor for
m_value or m_error,
you can call the move
constructor.

These are straightforward. The biggest problem is implementing the assignment operator. It needs to work for four cases:

- Both the instance you're copying to and the instance you're copying from contain valid values.
- Both instances contain errors.
- `this` contains an error, and `other` contains a value.
- `this` contains a value, and `other` contains an error.

As is customary, you're going to implement the assignment operator by using the copy-and-swap idiom, which means you need to create a `swap` function for the `expected<T, E>` class; see listing 9.9.

Copy-and-swap idiom

To ensure a strongly exception-safe class that can't leak any resources when an exception occurs and that can guarantee an operation either is successfully completed or isn't completed at all, you usually use the copy-and-swap idiom when implementing the assignment operator. In a nutshell, you create a temporary copy of the original object and then swap the internal data with it. If all goes well, when the temporary object is destroyed, it'll destroy the previous data with it.

If an exception is thrown, you never take the data from the temporary object, which leaves your instance unchanged. For more information, check out the Herb Sutter's post "Exception-Safe Class Design, Part 1: Copy Assignment" (www.gotw.ca/gotw/059.htm) and "What Is the Copy-and-Swap Idiom?" on Stack Overflow (http://mng.bz/ayHD).

Listing 9.9 Swap function for expected<T, E>

```
void swap(expected& other)
{
    using std::swap;
    if (m_valid) {
        if (other.m_valid) {
            swap(m_value, other.m_value);

        } else {
            auto temp = std::move(other.m_error);
            other.m_error.~E();
            new (&other.m_value) T(std::move(m_value));
            m_value.~T();
            new (&m_error) E(std::move(temp));
            std::swap(m_valid, other.m_valid);
        }
    } else {
        if (other.m_valid) {
            other.swap(*this);

        } else {
            swap(m_error, other.m_error);
        }
    }
}

expected& operator=(expected other)
{
    swap(other);
    return *this;
}
```

If "other" contains a value and so does the this instance, swap them.

If the this instance is valid but "other" contains an error, store the error in a temporary variable so you can move your value into "other." Then you can safely set the error for your instance.

If "this" contains an error and "other" is valid, you can base the implementation on the previous case.

If both instances contain an error, swap the error values.

The assignment operator is trivial. The "other" argument contains a copy of the value you want assigned to your instance. (You get "other" by value, not as a const reference.) You swap it with your instance.

Having implemented this, the rest is easy. You can create a casting operator to bool that will return true if you have a valid value or false otherwise. Also, you'll create a casting operator to convert the instance to std::optional so you can use expected<T, E> with the code that uses std::optional:

```
operator bool() const
{
    return m_valid;
}

operator std::optional<T>() const
{
    if (m_valid) {
        return m_value;
    } else {
        return std::optional<T>();
    }
}
```

Now you can use the expected type as a drop-in replacement of std::optional. Redefine the get_if function yet again; for the sake of simplicity, use std::string as the error type:

```
template <typename T, template Variant,
        template Expected = expected<T, std::string>>
Expected get_if(const Variant& variant)
{
    T* ptr = std::get_if<T>(variant);

    if (ptr) {
        return Expected::success(*ptr);
    } else {
        return Expected::error("Variant doesn't contain the desired type");
    }
}
```

You get a function that returns either a value or a detailed error message. This is useful for debugging purposes or when you need to show the error to the user. Embedding errors in the type is also useful in asynchronous systems because you can easily transfer the errors between different asynchronous processes.

9.2   *Domain modeling with algebraic data types*

The main idea when designing data types is to make illegal states impossible to represent. That's why the size member function of std::vector returns an unsigned value (even if some people don't like unsigned types[1])—so the type reinforces your intuition that the size can't be negative—and why algorithms like std::reduce (which we talked about in chapter 2) take proper types to denote the execution policy instead of ordinary integer flags.

You should do the same with the types and functions you create. Instead of thinking about which data you need in order to cover all the possible states your program can be in, and placing them in a class, consider how to define the data to cover *only* the states your program can be in.

I'm going to demonstrate this by using a new scenario: the *Tennis kata* (http://codingdojo.org/kata/Tennis). The aim is to implement a simple tennis game. In tennis, two players (pretending doubles don't exist) play against each other. Whenever a player isn't able to return the ball to the other player's court, the player loses the ball and the score is updated.

The scoring system in tennis is unique but simple:

- Possible scores are 0, 15, 30, and 40.
- If a player has 40 points and wins the ball, they win the game.
- If both players have 40, the rules become a bit different: the game is then in *deuce*.

---

[1] See David Crocker, "Danger—Unsigned Types Used Here," *David Crocker's Verification Blog,* April 7, 2010, http://mng.bz/sq4z.

- When in deuce, the player who wins the ball has the *advantage*.
- If the player wins the ball while having the advantage, they win the game. If the player loses the ball, the game returns to deuce.

In this section, we'll check out several implementations of the program state for a game of tennis. We'll discuss the problems of each until we reach a solution that will allow the implementation to have no invalid states.

9.2.1   *The naive approach, and where it falls short*

The naive approach to solving this problem is to create two integer scores to track the number of points each player has. You can use a special value to denote when a player has the advantage:

```
class tennis_t {
private:
    int player_1_points;
    int player_2_points;
};
```

This approach covers all the possible states, but the problem is, it allows you to set an invalid number of points for a player. Usually, you solve this by verifying the data you get in the setter, but it would be more useful if you didn't need to verify anything—if the types forced you to have the correct code.

The next step would be to replace the number of points with an enum value that only allows you to set a valid number of points:

```
class tennis_t {
    enum class points {
        love, // zero points
        fifteen,
        thirty,
        forty
    };

    points player_1_points;
    points player_2_points;
};
```

This significantly lowers the number of states the program can be in, but it still has problems. First, it allows both players to have 40 points (which technically isn't allowed—that state has a special name), and you have no way to represent advantage. You could add deuce and advantage to the enum, but that would create new invalid states (one player could be in deuce, while the other had zero points).

This isn't a good approach for solving this problem. Instead, let's go top-down, try to split the original game into disjunctive states, and then define those states.

9.2.2   *A more sophisticated approach: Top-down design*

From the rules, you see the game has two main states: the state in which the scoring is numeric, and the state in which the players are in the deuce or advantage. The state with normal scoring keeps the scores of both players at the same time. Unfortunately, things aren't that simple. If you used the previously defined `points` enum, you'd have the possibility of both players having 40 points, which isn't allowed: it should be represented as the deuce state.

You could try to solve this by removing the `forty` enum value, but you'd lose the ability to have a 40-something score. Back to the drawing board. The *normal scoring state* isn't a single state—two players can have scores up to 30, or one player can have 40 points and the other player up to 30:

```
class tennis_t {
    enum class points {
        love,
        fifteen,
        thirty
    };

    enum class player {
        player_1,
        player_2
    };

    struct normal_scoring {
        points player_1_points;
        points player_2_points;
    };

    struct forty_scoring {
        player leading_player;
        points other_player_scores;
    };
};
```

That's all the *regular* scoring states. You're left with the deuce and advantage states. Again, let's consider these as clearly different states, not a single state. The deuce state doesn't need to hold any values, whereas the advantage state should indicate which player has the advantage:

```
class tennis_t {
    ...

    struct deuce {};

    struct advantage {
        player player_with_advantage;
    };
};
```

Now you need to define the sum type of all the states:

```
class tennis_t {
    ...

    std::variant
        < normal_scoring
```

```
      , forty_scoring
      , deuce
      , advantage
      > m_state;
};
```

You've covered all the possible states the tennis game can be in, and you can't have a single illegal state.

> **NOTE** One state is potentially missing: the game-over state, which should denote which player won. If you want to print out the winner and terminate the program, you don't need to add that state. But if you want the program to continue running, you need to implement that state as well. It would be trivial to do; you'd just need to create another structure with a single member variable to store the winner, and expand the m_state variant.

As usual, it isn't always worth it to go this far in removing the invalid states (you might decide to deal with the 40–40 case manually), but the main point of this example is to demonstrate the process of designing algebraic data types that match the domain you want to model. You start by splitting the original state space into smaller independent subparts, and then describe those independent parts individually.

9.3   *Better handling of algebraic data types with pattern matching*

The main issue when implementing programs with optional values, variants, and other algebraic data types is that every time you need a value, you have to check whether it's present and then extract it from its wrapper type. You'd need the equivalent checks even if you created the state class without sum types, but only when you set the values, not every time you wanted to access them.

Because this process can be tedious, many functional programming languages provide a special syntax that makes it easier. Usually, this syntax looks like a switch-case statement on steroids that can match not only against specific values, but also on types and more-complex patterns.

Imagine you created an enum in the tennis scenario to denote the state of the program. It would be common to see a switch statement like this somewhere in the code:

```
switch (state) {
    case normal_score_state:
        ...
        break;

    case forty_scoring_state:
        ...
        break;

    ...
};
```

Depending on the value of the `state` variable, the code will execute a specific case label. But sadly, this code works only on integer-based types.

Now imagine a world in which this code could also test strings, and could work with variants and execute different cases based on the type of the variable contained in the variant. And what if each case could be a combination of a type check, a value check, and a custom predicate you could define? This is what pattern matching in most functional programming languages looks like.

C++ provides ways to do pattern matching for template metaprogramming (as you'll see in chapter 11), but not for normal programs, so we need another approach. The standard library provides a `std::visit` function that takes an instance of `std::variant` and a function that should be executed on the value stored inside. For example, to print out the current state in the tennis game (given that you implemented the operator `<<` to write the state types to the standard output), you could do this:

```
std::visit([] (const auto& value) {
        std::cout << value << std::endl;
    },
    m_state);
```

You're passing a generic lambda (a lambda with an argument type specified as `auto`) so that it can work on values of different types, because the variant can have four completely different types, and all of this is still statically typed.

Using a generic lambda with `std::visit` is often useful, but it isn't sufficient in most cases. You want to be able to execute different code based on which value is stored in the variant—just as you can do with the `case` statement.

One way you can do this is by creating an overloaded function object that will separate implementations for different types; the correct one will be called based on the type of the value stored in the variant instance. To make this as short as possible, let's use the language features available in C++17. The implementation compatible with older compilers is available in the accompanying code examples:

```
template <typename... Ts>
struct overloaded : Ts... { using Ts::operator()...; };

template <typename... Ts> overloaded(Ts...) -> overloaded<Ts...>;
```

The `overloaded` template takes a list of function objects and creates a new function object that presents the call operators of all provided function objects as its own (the using `Ts::operator()...` part).

> **NOTE** The code snippet that implements the overloaded structure uses the template argument deduction for classes that were introduced in C++17. The template argument deduction relies on the constructor of the class to figure out the template parameters. You can either provide a constructor or provide a deduction guideline as in the preceding example.

You can now use this in the tennis example. Every time a player wins the ball, the `point_for` member function is called and updates the game state accordingly:

```
void point_for(player which_player)
{
    std::visit(
        overloaded {
            [&](const normal_scoring& state) {
                // Increment the score, or switch the state
            },
            [&](const forty_scoring& state) {
                // Player wins, or we switch to deuce
            },
            [&](const deuce& state) {
                // We switch to advantage state
            },
            [&](const advantage& state) {
                // Player wins, or we go back to deuce
            }
        },
        m_state);
}
```

`std::visit` calls the overloaded function object, and the object matches the given type against all its overloads and executes the one that's the best match (type-wise). Although the syntax isn't as pretty, this code provides an efficient equivalent of the `switch` statement that works on the type of the object stored in a variant.

You can easily create a `visit` function for `std::optional`, for the expected class, and even for inheritance-based sum types that will give you a unified syntax to handle all the sum types you create.

9.4 *Powerful pattern matching with the Mach7 library*

So far, you've seen simple pattern matching on types. You could easily create matching on specific values by hiding the `if`-`else` chains behind a structure similar to `overloaded`.

But it would be much more useful to be able to match on more-advanced patterns. For example, you might want separate handlers for `normal_scoring` when the player has fewer than 30 points and when they have 30 points, because in that case you need to change the game state to `forty_scoring`.

Unfortunately, C++ doesn't have a syntax that allows this. But a library called Mach7 lets you write more-advanced patterns, although with a bit of awkward syntax.

> ### The Mach7 library for efficient pattern matching
>
> The Mach7 library (https://github.com/solodon4/Mach7) was created by Yuriy Solodkyy, Gabriel Dos Reis, and Bjarne Stroustrup, and serves as an experiment that will eventually be used as the base for extending C++ to support pattern matching. Although the library started as an experiment, it's considered stable enough for general use. It's generally more efficient than the visitor pattern (not to be confused with `std::visit` for variants). The main downside of Mach7 is its syntax.

With the Mach7 library, you can specify the object you want to match against and then list all the patterns to use for matching and actions to perform if the pattern is matched. In the tennis game scenario, the implementation of the `point_for` member function would look like this:

```
void point_for(player which_player)
{
    Match(m_state)
    {
        Case(C<normal_scoring>())          ◄─── Increments the score, or
                                                 switches the state

        Case(C<forty_scoring>())           ◄─── Player wins, or switches
                                                 to deuce

        Case(C<deuce>())       ◄─── Switches to advantage state

        Case(C<advantage>())   ◄─── Player wins, or goes back
    }                                  to deuce
    EndMatch
}
```

You might want to split the second pattern into several separate ones. If the player who won the ball had 40 points before, you know they've won the game. Otherwise, you need to see whether you can increase the points of the second player, or you need to switch to the `deuce` state.

If the program is currently in `forty_scoring` state, and the player who has 40 points has won the ball, they win the game regardless of how many points the other player has. You can denote this with the `C<forty_scoring>(which_player, _)` pattern. The underscore means you don't care about a value when matching—in this case, you don't care about the number of points the other player has.

If the ball wasn't won by the player who had 40 points, you want to check whether the other player had 30 points so you can switch to the `deuce` state. You can match this with the `C<forty_scoring>(_, 30)` pattern. You don't need to match against a particular player because you know if the player who previously had 40 points won the ball, you'll match it with the previous pattern.

If neither of these two patterns matches, you need to increase the number of points for the second player. You can check that the program is in `forty_scoring` state.

Listing 9.10 Matching on deconstructed types

```
void point_for(player which_player)
{
    Match(m_state)
    {
        ...

        Case(C<forty_scoring>(which_player, _))   ◄─── If the player who had 40 points
                                                         won the ball, they win the game;
                                                         no need to consider the number
                                                         of points the other player has.

        Case(C<forty_scoring>(_, 30))   ◄─── If the ball was won by the player who didn't
                                               have 40 points (the previous case wasn't a
                                               match), and the current number of points for
                                               the other player is 30, the game is in deuce.
```

```
        Case(C<forty_scoring>())
                                                    If neither of the previous cases was a match,
                                                    increase the number of points for the player.
        ...
    }
    EndMatch
}
```

No matter which path you take when handling programs with algebraic types—std::visit with overloaded function objects, or full pattern matching with a library like Mach7—you have to write more-correct programs. The compiler will force you to write exhaustive patterns, or the program won't compile, and the space of possible states will be kept as minimal as possible.

> **TIP** For more information and resources about the topics covered in this chapter, see https://forums.manning.com/posts/list/43778.page.

Summary

- Implementing program state through algebraic data types requires some thinking and produces longer code, but it allows you to minimize the number of states your program can be in and removes the possibility of having invalid states.
- Inheritance, dynamic dispatch, and the visitor pattern are often used in OO programming languages to implement sum types. The main problem with using inheritance to implement sum types is that it incurs runtime performance penalties.
- If you know exactly which types you want to sum, variants are a better choice for implementing sum types than inheritance. The main downside of std::variant is that it incurs a lot of boilerplate because of the std::visit function.
- Unlike exceptions—which should denote, as their name indicates, exceptional situations a program can find itself in—optional values and the expected class are perfect for explicitly stating the possibility of failures. They also travel across multiple threads and multiple processes more easily.
- The idea of having a type that contains either a value or an error has been popular in the functional programming world for a long time. This concept became popular in the C++ community after Andrei Alexandrescu gave a talk called "Systematic Error Handling in C++" at a 2012 C++ and Beyond conference (http://mng.bz/q5XF), where he presented his version of the expected type. That version of expected was similar to ours, but it supported only std::exception_ptr as the error type.

Monads

10

This chapter covers

- Understanding functors
- Going one step further from `transform` with monads
- Composing functions that return wrapper types
- Handling asynchronous operations in FP style

The functional programming world isn't big on design patterns, but common abstractions pop up everywhere. These abstractions allow you to handle different types of problems from significantly different domains in the same way.

In C++, we already have one abstraction like this: iterators. With ordinary arrays, we can use pointers to move around and access data. We can use the operators ++ and - - to go to the next and previous elements, respectively, and we can dereference them with the * operator. The problem is, this works only for arrays and structures that keep their data in a contiguous chunk of memory. It doesn't work for data structures such as linked lists, sets, and maps implemented using trees.

For this purpose, iterators were created. They use operator overloading to create an abstraction that has the same API as pointers, which can work not only for arrays but for various different data structures. Iterators also work for things such as input and output streams that aren't traditionally considered *data structures*.

Chapter 7 introduced another abstraction that builds on top of iterators: ranges. Ranges go one step further than iterators by abstracting over different data structures instead of abstracting only the data access in those structures. You'll see ranges pop up in this chapter as well.

10.1 *Not your father's functors*

I'm going to break a bit from the usual form of this book: instead of starting with an example, I'll start by defining a concept and then explore the examples. We're going to begin with a *functor*. As I mentioned in chapter 3, many C++ developers use this word to mean *a class with the call operator*, but this is a misnomer. When we talk about functors in FP, we're talking about something quite different.

A functor is a concept from an abstract branch of mathematics called *category theory*, and its formal definition sounds as abstract as the theory it comes from. We'll define it in a way that should be more intuitive to C++ developers.

A class template F is a functor if it has a `transform` (or `map`) function defined on it (see figure 10.1). The `transform` function takes an instance f of a type F<T1> and a function t: T1 → T2, and it returns a value of type F<T2>. This function can have multiple forms, so we'll use the pipe notation from chapter 7 for clarity.

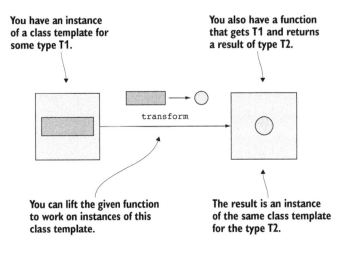

You have an instance of a class template for some type T1.

You also have a function that gets T1 and returns a result of type T2.

transform

You can lift the given function to work on instances of this class template.

The result is an instance of the same class template for the type T2.

Figure 10.1   A functor is a class template over a type T. You can lift any function operating on T to work on instances of that class template.

The transform function needs to obey the following two rules:

- Transforming a functor instance with an identity function returns the same (*equal to*) functor instance:

  ```
  f | transform([](auto value) { return value; }) == f
  ```

- Transforming a functor with one function and then with another is the same as transforming the functor with the composition of those two functions (see figure 10.2):

  ```
  f | transform(t1) | transform(t2) ==
  f | transform([=](auto value) { return t2(t1(value)); })
  ```

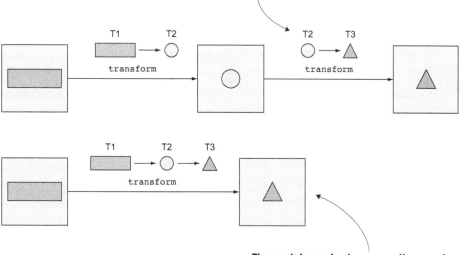

The result of a transformation is an instance of the same functor, and you can pass it to another transformation.

The result has to be the same as if you performed a single transformation on the functor by using the composition of transformation functions.

Figure 10.2 The main rule the `transform` function needs to obey is that composing two transforms—one that lifts function `f` and another that lifts function `g`—needs to have the same effect as having a single transformation with the composition of `f` and `g`.

This looks much like the `std::transform` algorithm and `view::transform` from the ranges library. That's not accidental: generic collections from the STL and ranges *are* functors. They're all wrapper types that have a well-behaved `transform` function defined on them. It's important to note that the other direction doesn't hold: not all functors are collections or ranges.

10.1.1 Handling optional values

One of the basic functors is the `std::optional` type from chapter 9. It just needs a transform function defined on it.

Listing 10.1 Defining the transform function for `std::optional`

```
template <typename T1, typename F>
auto transform(const std::optional<T1>& opt, F f)
    -> decltype(std::make_optional(f(opt.value())))
{
    if (opt) {
        return std::make_optional(f(opt.value()));
    } else {
        return {};
    }
}
```

Specify the return type, because you're returning just {} when there's no value.

If opt contains a value, transforms it using f and returns the transformed value in a new instance of std::optional

If no value, returns an empty instance of std::optional

Alternatively, you can create a range view that will give a range of one element when `std::optional` contains a value and an empty range otherwise (see figure 10.3). This will allow you to use the pipe syntax. (Check out the `functors-optional` code example, which defines the `as_range` function that converts `std::optional` to a range of at most one element.)

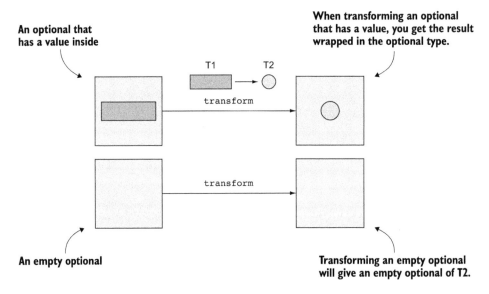

An optional that has a value inside

T1   T2

transform

When transforming an optional that has a value, you get the result wrapped in the optional type.

transform

An empty optional

Transforming an empty optional will give an empty optional of T2.

Figure 10.3   An *optional* is a wrapper type that can contain a single value or can contain nothing. If you transform an optional that contains a value, you get an optional containing the transformed value. If the optional didn't contain anything, you get an empty optional as the result.

What's the benefit of using the `transform` function compared to handling the missing values manually with an `if-else` statement? Consider the following scenario. You have a system that manages user logins. It can have two states: the user is either logged in or not. It's natural to represent this with a `current_login` variable of the `std::optional<std::string>` type. The `current_login` optional value will be empty if the user isn't logged in; it will contain the username otherwise. We'll make the `current_login` variable a global one to simplify the code examples.

Now imagine you have a function that retrieves the full name of the user and a function that creates an HTML-formatted string of anything you pass to it:

```
std::string user_full_name(const std::string& login);
std::string to_html(const std::string& text);
```

To get the HTML-formatted string of the current user (see figure 10.4), you could always check whether there's a current user, or you can create a function that returns `std::optional<std::string>`. The function returns an empty value if no user is logged in, and it returns the formatted full name if a user is logged in. This function is trivial to implement now that you have a `transform` function that works on optional values:

```
transform(
    transform(
        current_login,
        user_full_name),
    to_html);
```

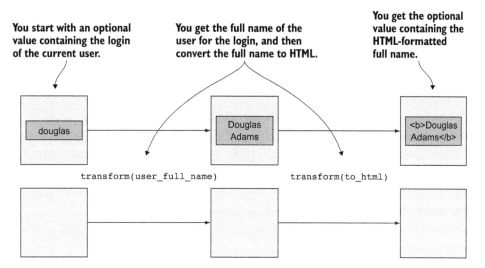

You start with an optional value containing the login of the current user.

You get the full name of the user for the login, and then convert the full name to HTML.

You get the optional value containing the HTML-formatted full name.

Figure 10.4 You can apply a chain of lifted functions to an optional value. In the end, you get an optional object containing the result of all transformations composed.

Alternatively, to return a range, you can perform the transformations by using the pipe syntax:

```
auto login_as_range = as_range(current_login);
login_as_range | view::transform(user_full_name)
               | view::transform(to_html);
```

Looking at these two implementations, one thing pops out: nothing says this code works on optional values. It can work for arrays, vectors, lists, or anything else for which a `transform` function is defined. You won't need to change the code if you decide to replace `std::optional` with any other functor.

Peculiarity of ranges

It's important to note that there's no automatic conversion from `std::optional` to a range and vice versa, so you need to perform the conversion manually. Strictly speaking, the `view::transform` function isn't properly defined to make something a functor. This function always returns a range, and not the same type you passed to it.

This behavior can be problematic because you're forced to convert the types manually. But it's a minor nuisance when you consider the benefits ranges provide.

Imagine you want to create a function that takes a list of usernames and gives you a list of formatted full names. The implementation of that function would be identical to the one that works on optional values. The same goes for a function that uses `expected<T, E>` instead of `std::optional<T>`. This is the power that widely applicable abstractions such as functors bring you: you can write generic code that works unchanged in various scenarios.

10.2 *Monads: More power to the functors*

Functors allow you to easily handle transformations of wrapped values, but they have a serious limitation. Imagine the functions `user_full_name` and `to_html` can fail. And instead of returning strings, they return `std::optional<std::string>`:

```
std::optional<std::string> user_full_name(const std::string& login);
std::optional<std::string> to_html(const std::string& text);
```

The `transform` function won't help much in this case. If you tried to use it and wrote the same code as in the previous example, you'd get a complicated result. As a reminder, `transform` received an instance of a functor `F<T1>` and a function from `T1` to `T2`, and it returned an instance of `F<T2>`.

Look at the following code snippet:

```
transform(current_login, user_full_name);
```

What's its return type? It's not `std::optional<std::string>`. The `user_full_name` function takes a string and returns an optional value that makes `T2 = std::optional<std::string>`. That, in turn, makes the result of `transform` a nested optional value `std::optional<std::optional<std::string>>` (see figure 10.5). The more transformations you perform, the more nesting you get—and this is unpleasant to work with.

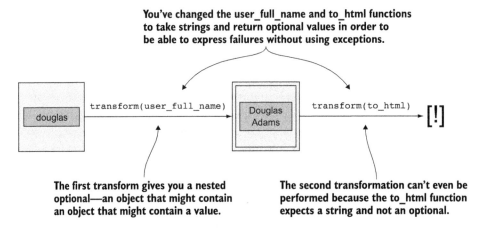

You've changed the user_full_name and to_html functions to take strings and return optional values in order to be able to express failures without using exceptions.

The first transform gives you a nested optional—an object that might contain an object that might contain a value.

The second transformation can't even be performed because the to_html function expects a string and not an optional.

Figure 10.5 If you try to compose multiple functions that take a value and return an instance of a functor, you'll start getting nested functors. In this case, you get an optional of an optional of some type, which is mostly useless. What's more, in order to chain two transformations, you'd need to lift the second one twice.

This is where monads come into play. A monad M<T> is a functor that has an additional function defined on it—a function that removes one level of nesting:

```
join: M<M<T>> → M<T>
```

With `join` (see figures 10.6 and 10.7), you no longer have a problem of using functions that don't return ordinary values but instead return monad (functor) instances.

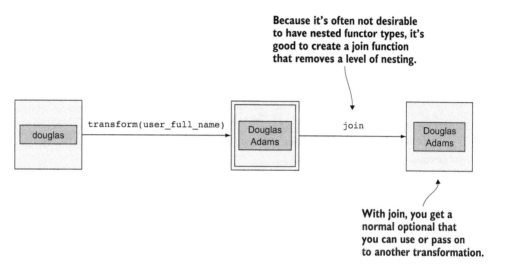

Because it's often not desirable to have nested functor types, it's good to create a join function that removes a level of nesting.

With join, you get a normal optional that you can use or pass on to another transformation.

Figure 10.6 Transforming a functor with a function that doesn't return a value, but rather a new instance of that functor, results in nested functor types. You can create a function that will remove nesting.

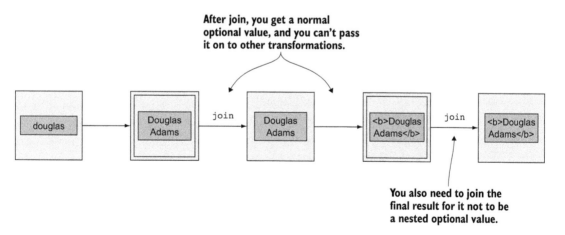

After join, you get a normal optional value, and you can't pass it on to other transformations.

You also need to join the final result for it not to be a nested optional value.

Figure 10.7 You can use optional values to denote errors in computations. With `join`, you can easily chain multiple transformations that can fail.

You can now write the code like this:

```
join(transform(
    join(transform(
        current_login,
        user_full_name)),
    to_html));
```

Or like this, if you prefer the range notation:

```
auto login_as_range = as_range(current_login);
login_as_range | view::transform(user_full_name)
               | view::join
               | view::transform(to_html)
               | view::join;
```

When you changed the return type of the functions, you made an intrusive change. If you implemented everything by using if-else checks, you'd have to make significant changes to the code. Here, you needed to avoid wrapping a value multiple times.

It's obvious that you can simplify this even more. In all of the preceding transformations, you perform join on the result. Can you merge those into a single function?

You can—and this is a more common way to define monads. You can say that a monad M is a wrapper type that has a constructor (a function that constructs an instance of M<T> from a value of type T) and an mbind function (it's usually called just bind, but we'll use this name so it doesn't get confused with std::bind), which is a composition of transform and join:

```
construct : T → M<T>
mbind     : (M<T1>, T1 → M<T2>) → M<T2>
```

It's easy to show that all monads are functors. It's trivial to implement transform by using mbind and construct.

As was the case with functors, there are a few rules. They aren't required in order to use monads in your programs:

- If you have a function f: T1 → M<T2> and a value a of type T1, wrapping that value into the monad M and then binding it with a function f is the same as calling the function f on it:

```
mbind(construct(a), f)) == f(a)
```

- This rule is the same, just turned around. If you bind a wrapped value to the construction function, you get the same wrapped value:

```
mbind(m, construct) == m
```

- This rule is less intuitive. It defines the associativity of the mbind operation:

```
mbind(mbind(m, f), g) == mbind(m, [] (auto x) {
    return mbind(f(x), g) })
```

Although these rules may look off-putting, they exist to precisely define a well-behaving monad. You'll rely on your intuition from now on: a monad is something that you can construct and `mbind` to a function.

10.3 Basic examples

Let's begin with a few simple examples. When learning C++ the right way, you first learn about basic types, and the first *wrapper type* is `std::vector`. So, let's see how to create a functor from it. You need to check two things:

- A functor is a class template with one template parameter.
- You need a `transform` function that can take one vector, and a function that can transform its elements. `transform` will return a vector of transformed elements (see figure 10.8).

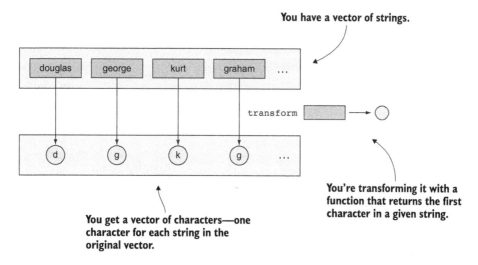

Figure 10.8 Transforming a vector gives you a new vector with the same number of elements. For each element in the original collection, you get an element in the result.

`std::vector` is a class template, so you're good there. And with ranges, implementing the proper `transform` function is a breeze:

```
template <typename T, typename F>
auto transform(const std::vector<T>& xs, F f)
{
    return xs | view::transform(f) | to_vector;
}
```

You're treating the given vector as a range and transforming each of its elements with f. In order for the function to return a vector, as required by the functor definition, you need to convert the result back to the vector. If you wanted to be more lenient, you could return a range.

Now that you have a functor, let's turn it into a monad. Here you need the `construct` and `mbind` functions. `construct` should take a value and create a vector out of it. The natural thing is to use the actual constructor for the vector. If you want to write a proper function that constructs a vector out of a single value, you can easily whip up something like this:

```
template <typename T>
std::vector<T> make_vector(T&& value)
{
    return {std::forward<T>(value)};
}
```

You're left with `mbind`. To implement it, it's useful to think of `transform` plus `join` (see figure 10.9).

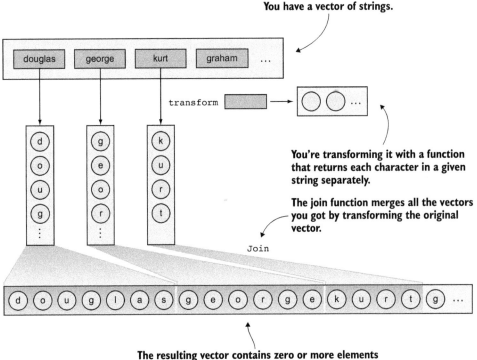

You have a vector of strings.

transform

You're transforming it with a function that returns each character in a given string separately.

The join function merges all the vectors you got by transforming the original vector.

Join

The resulting vector contains zero or more elements for each of the strings in the original vector.

Figure 10.9   The `mbind` function for vectors applies the transformation function to each element in the original vector. The result of each transformation is a vector of elements. All elements from those vectors are collected into a single resulting vector. Unlike `transform`, `mbind` allows you to have not only a single resulting element per input element, but as many as you want.

The `mbind` function (unlike `transform`) wants a function that maps values to instances of the monad—in this case, to an instance of `std::vector`. This means for each element in the original vector, it will return a new vector instead of just a single element.

Listing 10.2 `mbind` **function for vectors**

```
template <typename T, typename F>                    f takes a value of type T and returns
auto mbind(const std::vector<T>& xs, F f)   ◀───     a vector of T or another type.
{
    auto transformed =                               Calls f and yields a range of vectors,
            xs | view::transform(f)                  which you convert to a vector of vectors
               | to_vector;

    return transformed                      You don't want a vector of vectors; you
            | view::join                    want all the values in a single vector.
            | to_vector;
}
```

You've implemented the `mbind` function for vectors. It's not as efficient as it could be, because it saves all intermediary results to temporary vectors; but the main point is to show that `std::vector` is a monad.

> **NOTE** The example defines `mbind` as a function that takes two arguments and returns the result. For convenience, the rest of the chapter uses the `mbind` function with the pipe syntax, because it's more readable. I'll write `xs | mbind(f)` instead of `mbind(xs, f)`. This isn't something you can do out of the box—it requires a bit of boilerplate, as you can see in the `10-monad-vector` and `10-monad-range` examples that accompany this book.

10.4 Range and monad comprehensions

The same approach we used for vectors works for similar collections such as arrays and lists. All these collections are similar in terms of the level of abstraction you're working at. They're flat collections of items of the same type.

You've already seen an abstraction that works over all these types: ranges. You used ranges to implement all previous functions for `std::vector`.

You've seen multiple times that the `transform` function can be useful. And now you have an `mbind` function that's similar but more powerful. The question is whether this additional power is needed. You'll see how it benefits you for other monads later, but let's first investigate how useful it can be for normal collections and ranges.

Let's paint a different picture of what `mbind` does that's more fitting for collection-like structures. And let's start with `transform`, because you know how it works. The `transform` function takes a collection and generates a new one. It does so by traversing the original collection, transforming each element, and putting those transformed elements in the new collection.

With `mbind`, the story is similar but slightly different. I said that it can be seen as a composition of `transform` and `join`. The `transform` function creates a range of new elements for each element in the original collection, and `join` concatenates all those generated ranges. In other words, `mbind` allows you to generate not only a single new element for each element in the original collection, but as many elements as you want: zero or more (see figure 10.10).

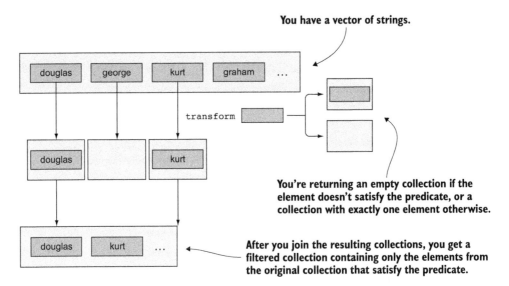

You have a vector of strings.

You're returning an empty collection if the element doesn't satisfy the predicate, or a collection with exactly one element otherwise.

After you join the resulting collections, you get a filtered collection containing only the elements from the original collection that satisfy the predicate.

Figure 10.10   You can easily express filtering with mbind by passing it a transformation function that returns an empty collection if the original element doesn't satisfy the filtering predicate, or a collection containing one element otherwise.

When is this useful? Another function you've seen a few times is filter. It can easily be implemented in terms of mbind. You just need to give mbind a function that will return an empty range if the current element should be filtered out, or a single element range otherwise.

Listing 10.3   Filtering in terms of mbind

```
template <typename C, typename P>
auto filter(const C& collection, P predicate)
{
    return collection
        | mbind([=](auto element) {
            return view::single(element)
                | view::take(predicate(element)
                            ? 1 : 0);
        });
}
```

Creates a range with a single element (constructs the monad instance out of the value) and takes I or 0 elements, depending on whether the current element satisfies the predicate

A few range transformations can be implemented in a similar manner. The list grows if you use mutable function objects. Although the mutable state is discouraged, it should be safe in this case because the mutable data isn't shared (see chapter 5). Obviously, the fact that you can do something doesn't mean you should; the point is to see that you can be expressive with mbind.

The fact that ranges are monads doesn't just let you reimplement range transformations in a *cool* way. It's also the reason you can have range comprehensions.

Imagine you need to generate a list of Pythagorean triples (a sum of squares of two numbers that are equal to the square of the third). To write it with `for` loops, you need to nest three of them. The `mbind` function allows you to perform similar nesting with ranges.

Listing 10.4   Generating Pythagorean triples

Generates an infinite list of integers →

```
view::ints(1)
    | mbind([](int z) {                          For each integer, called z,
        return view::ints(1, z)                  generates a list of integers
            | mbind([z](int y) {                 from l to z and calls them y
                return view::ints(y, z) |
                    view::transform([y,z](int x) {
                        return std::make_tuple(x, y, z);     For each y, generates
                    });                                      integers between y
            });                                              and z
    })
    | filter([] (auto triple) {
        ...
    });              ◄─── You now have a list of triples and must
                         filter out those that aren't Pythagorean.
```

Having flattened-out ranges is useful. The ranges library provides a few special functions you can use to write the same code in a more readable way by combining `for_each` and `yield_if`.

Listing 10.5   Generating Pythagorean triples with range comprehensions

```
view::for_each(view::ints(1), [](int z) {
    return view::for_each(view::ints(1, z), [z](int y) {      Generates (x, y, z)
        return view::for_each(view::ints(y, z), [y,z](int x) {   triples as in the
            return yield_if(                                      previous example
                x * x + y * y == z * z,
                std::make_tuple(x, y, z)        If (x, y, z) is a Pythagorean
            );                                  triple, puts it in the
        });                                     resulting range
    });
});
```

A range comprehension has two components. The first is `for_each`, which traverses any collection you give it and collects all the values yielded from the function you pass to it. If you have multiple nested range comprehensions, all the yielded values are placed consecutively in the resulting range. The range comprehension doesn't generate a range of ranges; it flattens out the result. The second part is `yield_if`. It puts a value in the resulting range if the predicate specified as the first argument holds.

In a nutshell, a range comprehension is nothing more than a `transform` or `mbind` coupled with `filter`. And because these functions exist for any monad, not only for ranges, we can also call them *monad comprehensions*.

10.5   *Failure handling*

At the beginning of this chapter, we touched on functions that communicate errors through the return type, not by throwing exceptions. The main job of a function in FP—in fact, its only job—is to calculate the result and return it. If the function can fail, you can make it either return a value if it has calculated one or return nothing if an error occurs. As you saw in chapter 9, you can do this by making the return value optional.

10.5.1   *std::optional<T> as a monad*

Optionals allow you to express the possibility that a value can be missing. Although this is good by itself, using optionals has a downside: you need constant checks of whether the value is present if you want to use it. For the user_full_name and to_html functions you defined earlier, which return std::optional<std::string>, you get code riddled with checks:

```
std::optional<std::string> current_user_html()
{
    if (!current_login) {
        return {};
    }

    const auto full_name = user_full_name(current_login.value());

    if (!full_name) {
        return {};
    }

    return to_html(full_name.value());
}
```

Imagine you have more functions you need to chain like this. The code will begin to look like old C code, where you had to check errno after almost every function call.

Instead, you'll do something smarter. As soon as you see a value with a context that should be stripped out when calling another function, think of monads. With optional values, the context is the information about whether the value is present. Because the other functions take normal values, this context needs to be stripped out when calling them (see figure 10.11).

And this is exactly what monads allow you to do: compose functions without having to do any extra work to handle the contextual information. std::make_optional is the constructor function for the monad, and mbind is easily defined:

```
template <typename T, typename F>
auto mbind(const std::optional<T>& opt, F f)          Specify the return type, because you're
    -> decltype(f(opt.value()))        ◀────────────  returning just {} if there's no value.
{
    if (opt) {                                        If opt contains a value, transforms it
        return f(opt.value());         ◀────────────  using f and returns its result because it
    } else {                                          already returns an optional value
        return {};                     ◀──────┐  If there's no value, returns an
    }                                         └── empty instance of std::optional
}
```

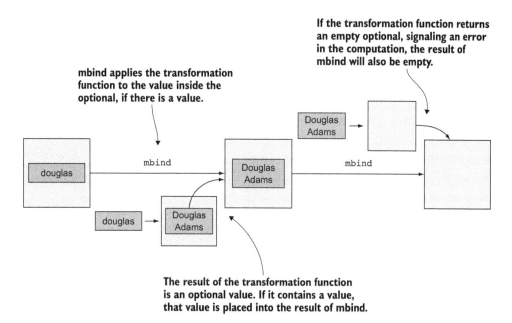

If the transformation function returns an empty optional, signaling an error in the computation, the result of mbind will also be empty.

mbind applies the transformation function to the value inside the optional, if there is a value.

The result of the transformation function is an optional value. If it contains a value, that value is placed into the result of mbind.

Figure 10.11 **To perform error handling with optional values instead of exceptions, you can chain functions that return optional values with** mbind. **The chain will be broken as soon as any of the transformations fails and returns an empty optional. If all the transformations succeed, you'll get an optional containing the resulting value.**

This gives an empty result if the original value is missing or if the function f fails and returns an empty optional. The valid result is returned otherwise. If you chain multiple functions with this approach, you get automatic error handling: the functions will be executed until the first one that fails. If no function fails, you'll get the result.

Now the function becomes much simpler:

```
std::optional<std::string> current_user_html()
{
    return mbind(
            mbind(current_login, user_full_name),
            to_html);
}
```

Alternatively, you can create an mbind transformation that has the same pipe syntax as ranges and makes the code much more readable:

```
std::optional<std::string> current_user_html()
{
    return current_login | mbind(user_full_name)
                         | mbind(to_html);
}
```

This looks exactly like the functor example. In that case, you had ordinary functions and used transform; here, functions return optional values, and you're using mbind.

10.5.2 *expected<T, E> as a monad*

`std::optional` allows you to handle errors, but it doesn't tell you what the error is. With expected<T, E>, you can have both.

As with `std::optional<T>`, if you haven't encountered an error, expected<T, E> contains a value. Otherwise, it contains the information about the error.

Listing 10.6 Composing the `expected` monad

```
template <
    typename T, typename E, typename F,
    typename Ret = typename std::result_of<F(T)>::type
    >
Ret mbind(const expected<T, E>& exp, F f)
{
    if (!exp) {
        return Ret::error(exp.error());
    }

    return f(exp.value());
}
```

f can return a different type, so you need to deduce it so you can return it.

If exp contains an error, passes it on

Otherwise, returns the result f returned

You can easily convert functions not only to tell whether you have the value, but also to contain an error. For the sake of simplicity, let's use integers to denote errors:

```
expected<std::string, int> user_full_name(const std::string& login);
expected<std::string, int> to_html(const std::string& text);
```

The implementation of the current_user_html function doesn't need to change:

```
expected<std::string, int> current_user_html()
{
    return current_login | mbind(user_full_name)
                         | mbind(to_html);
}
```

As before, the function will return a value if no error has occurred. Otherwise, as soon as any of the functions you're binding to returns an error, the execution will stop and return that error to the caller (see figure 10.12).

If the transformation function returned an error, the result of mbind will contain that error.

If you call mbind on an expected that contains an error, mbind won't even invoke the transformation function; it will just forward that error to the result.

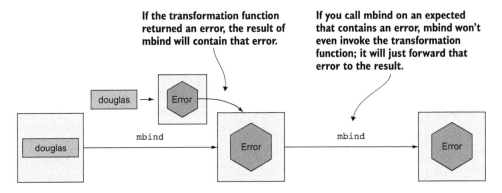

Figure 10.12   When using `expected` for error handling, you can chain multiple transformations that can fail, just as with optional values. As soon as you encounter an error, the transformations will stop, and you'll get that error in the resulting `expected` object. If there is no error, you'll get the transformed value.

It's important to note that for monads, you need one template parameter, and here you have two. You could easily do mbind on the error if you need to perform the transformations on it instead of on the value.

10.5.3 *The Try monad*

The expected type allows you to use anything as the error type. You can use integers as error codes, strings to convey error messages, or some combination of the two. You can also use the same exception class hierarchy you'd use with normal exception handling by specifying the error type as std::exception_ptr.

> **Listing 10.7 Wrapping functions that use exceptions into the expected monad**

f is a function without arguments. To call it with arguments, you can pass a lambda.

```
template <typename F,
         typename Ret = typename std::result_of<F()>::type,
         typename Exp = expected<Ret, std::exception_ptr>
Exp mtry(F f)
{
    try {
        return Exp::success(f());
    }
    catch (...) {
        return Exp::error(std::current_exception());
    }
}
```

If no exception was thrown, returns an instance of "expected" that contains the result of calling f

If any exception is thrown, returns an instance of "expected" that contains a pointer to it

Using exception pointers with the expected monads allows you to easily integrate the existing code that uses exceptions with error handling based on the expected monad. For example, you might want to get the first user in the system. The function that retrieves the list of users can throw an exception, and you also want to throw one if there are no users:

```
auto result = mtry([=] {
        auto users = system.users();

        if (users.empty()) {
            throw std::runtime_error("No users");
        }

        return users[0];
    });
```

The result will be either a value or a pointer to the exception that was thrown.

You can also do it the other way around: if a function returns an instance of expected with a pointer to the exception, you can easily integrate it into the code that uses exceptions. You can create a function that will either return the value stored in the expected object or throw the exception it holds:

```
template <typename T>
T get_or_throw(const expected<T, std::exception_ptr>& exp)
{
```

```
    if (exp) {
        return exp.value();
    } else {
        std::rethrow_exception(exp.error());
    }
}
```

These two functions allow you to have both monadic error handling and exception-based error handling in the same program, and to integrate them nicely.

10.6 *Handling state with monads*

One of the reasons monads are popular in the functional world is that you can implement stateful programs in a pure way. For us, this isn't necessary; we've always had mutable state in C++.

On the other hand, if you want to implement programs by using monads and different monad-transformation chains, it could be useful to be able to track the state of each of those chains. As I've said numerous times, if you want pure functions, they can't have any side effects; you can't change anything from the outside world. How can you change the state, then?

Impure functions can make implicit changes to the state. You don't see what happens and what's changed just by calling the function. If you want to make state changes in a pure way, you need to make every change explicit.

The simplest way is to pass each function the current state along with its regular arguments: the function should return the new state. I talked about this idea in chapter 5, where we entertained the idea of handling mutable state by creating new worlds instead of changing the current one.

Let's see this in an example. You'll reuse the user_full_name and to_html functions, but this time you don't want to handle failures; you want to keep a debugging log of the operations performed. This log is the state you want to change. Instead of using optional or expected, which are union types that can contain either a value or something denoting an error, you want a product type that contains both the value and additional information (the debugging log) at the same time.[1]

The easiest way to do this is to create a class template:

```
template <typename T>
class with_log {
public:
    with_log(T value, std::string log = std::string())
      : m_value(value)
      , m_log(log)
    {
    }

    T value() const { return m_value; }
    std::string log() const { return m_log; }
```

---

[1] In literature, this is usually called a *Writer monad* because you're writing only the contextual information. You aren't using the context in the user_full_name and to_html functions.

```
private:
    T m_value;
    std::string m_log;
};
```

Now you can redefine the `user_full_name` and `to_html` functions to return the values along with the log. Both of them will return the result along with their personal log of performed actions:

```
with_log<std::string> user_full_name(const std::string& login);
with_log<std::string> to_html(const std::string& text);
```

As before, if you want to easily compose these two functions, you need to make a monad out of `with_log` (see figure 10.13). Creating the monad construction function is trivial; either use the `with_log` constructor, or create a `make_with_log` function the same way you wrote `make_vector`.

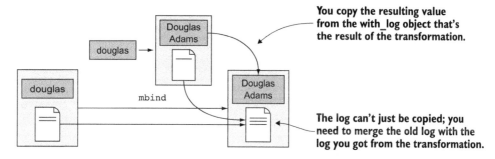

You copy the resulting value from the with_log object that's the result of the transformation.

The log can't just be copied; you need to merge the old log with the log you got from the transformation.

Figure 10.13 Unlike the previous monads, such as `optional` and `expected`, where the result depended only on the last transformation, `with_log` goes a bit further. You're collecting the log from all the transformations performed.

The `mbind` function is where the main magic happens. It should take an instance of `with_log<T>`, which contains the value and the current log (state), a function that transforms the value and returns the transformed value along with the new logging information. `mbind` needs to return the new result along with new logging information appended to the old log.

Listing 10.8 Maintaining the log with `mbind`

```
template <typename T,
          typename F>
          typename Ret = typename std::result_of<F(T)>::type
Ret mbind(const with_log<T1>& val, F f)
{
    const auto result_with_log = f(val.value());
    return Ret(result_with_log.value(),
               val.log() + result_with_log.log());
}
```

Transforms the given value with f, which yields the resulting value and the log string that f generated

You need to return the result value, but not just the log that f returned; concatenate it with the previous log.

This approach to logging has multiple advantages over logging to the standard output. You can have multiple parallel logs—one for each monad transformation chain you create—without the need for any special logging facilities. One function can write to various logs, depending on who called it, and you don't have to specify "this log goes here" and "that log goes there." In addition, this approach to logging lets you keep logs in chains of asynchronous operations without interleaving debugging output of different chains.

10.7   *Concurrency and the continuation monad*

So far, you've seen a few monads. All contained zero or more values, and contextual information. This may induce a mental picture that a monad is some kind of container that knows how to operate on its values, and if you have an instance of that container, you might access those elements when you need them.

This analogy works for many monads, but not all. As you may recall from the monad definition, you can create a monad instance out of a normal value, or perform a transformation on the value already in the monad. You haven't been given a function that can extract the value from inside a monad.

It probably sounds like an oversight to have a container that holds data but doesn't allow you to get that data. After all, you can access all the elements in a vector, a list, an optional, and so forth. Right?

Not really. Although you might not call input streams such as std::cin *containers*, they are. They contain elements of type char. You also have istream_range<T>, which is essentially a container of zero or more values of type T. The difference compared to normal containers is that you don't know their sizes in advance, and you can't access the elements until the user enters them.

From the point of view of the person who writes the code, there isn't much difference. You can easily write a generic function that will perform operations such as filter and transform, which will work for both vector-like containers and input stream-like containers.

But there's a huge difference in executing this code. If you're executing the code on input stream-like containers, program execution will be blocked until the user enters all the required data (see figure 10.14).

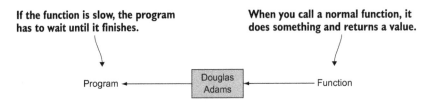

Figure 10.14   When you call a function from the main program, the program is blocked until the function finishes. If the function is slow, the program can be blocked for a long time, and it could use that time to perform other tasks.

In interactive systems, you should never be allowed to block the program. Instead of requesting data and processing it, it's much better to tell the program what to do with it when it becomes available.

Imagine you want to extract the title of a web page. You need to connect to the server on which the page is located, wait for the response, and then parse it to find the title. The operation of connecting to the server and retrieving the page can be slow, and you can't block the program while it finishes.

You should perform the request and then continue with all the other tasks the program needs to perform. When the request is finished and you have the data, then you process it.

You need a handler that will give you access to the data after it becomes available. Let's call it a *future*, because the data isn't available immediately but will become available sometime in the future (see figure 10.15). This idea of future values can be useful for other things as well, so we won't limit the future to containing only strings (the source of a web page); it will be a generic handler `future<T>`.

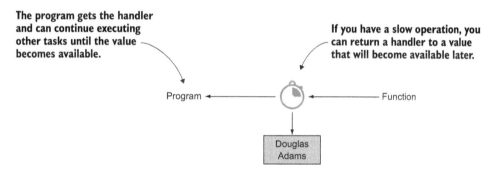

The program gets the handler and can continue executing other tasks until the value becomes available.

If you have a slow operation, you can return a handler to a value that will become available later.

Program ◄────────── 🕐 ◄────────── Function

Douglas Adams

Figure 10.15   Instead of waiting for the slow function to finish, it's better to have that function return a handler you can use to access the value after it's calculated.

To summarize, the handler `future<T>` may not yet contain a value, but the value of type `T` will be in it at some point. With it, you'll be able to design programs that have different components executed concurrently or asynchronously. Any time you have a slow operation, or an operation whose execution time you don't know, you'll make it return a future instead of an ordinary value. A future looks like a container type, but a container whose element you can't get directly—unless the asynchronous operation has finished, and the value is in the container.

10.7.1 Futures as monads

The future object as defined screams, "Monad!" It's a container-like thing that can hold zero or one result, depending on whether the asynchronous operation is finished.

Let's first check whether a future can be a functor. You need to be able to create a `transform` function that takes `future<T1>` and a function `f: T1 → T2`, and it should yield an instance of `future<T2>`.

Conceptually, this shouldn't be a problem. A future is a handler to a future value. If you can get the value when the future arrives, you'll be able to pass it to function f and get the result. At some point in the future, you'll have the transformed value. If you know how to create a handler for it, you can create the transform function for futures, and the future is a functor.

This could be useful when you don't care about the entire result of an asynchronous operation, but need just part of it—as in the previous example, where you wanted to get the title of a web page. If you had a future and the transform function defined for it, you could do it easily:

```
get_page(url) | transform(extract_title)
```

This gives you a future of the string which, when it arrives, will give you only the title of the web page.

If the future is a functor, it's time to move to the next step and check whether it's a monad. Constructing a handler that already contains a value should be easy. The more interesting part is mbind. Let's change the result type of user_full_name and to_html yet again. This time, to get the full name of the user, you need to connect to a server and fetch the data. The operation should be performed asynchronously. Also, imagine to_html is a slow operation that also needs to be asynchronous. Both operations should return futures instead of normal values:

```
future<std::string> user_full_name(const std::string& login);
future<std::string> to_html(const std::string& text);
```

If you used transform to compose these two functions, you'd get a future of a future of a value, which sounds strange. You'd have a handler that will sometime in the future give you another handler that, even later, will give you the value. This becomes even more incomprehensible when you compose more than two asynchronous operations.

This is where you benefit from mbind. As in the previous cases, it allows you to avoid nesting (see figure 10.16). You'll always get a handler to the value, not a handler to a handler to a handler.

The mbind function has to do all the dirty work. It must be able to tell when the future arrives, and then call the transformation function and get the handler to the final result. And, most important: it has to give you the handler to the final result immediately.

With mbind, you can chain as many asynchronous operations as you want. Using the range notation, you get code like this:

```
future<std::string> current_user_html()
{
    return current_user() | mbind(user_full_name)
                          | mbind(to_html);
}
```

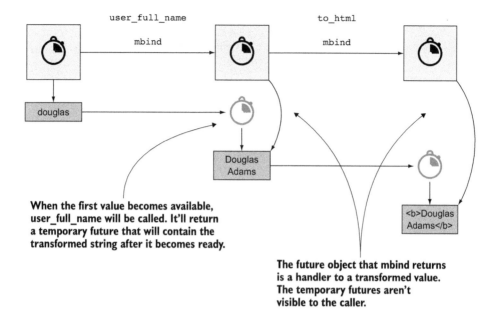

Figure 10.16 Monadic binding allows you to chain multiple asynchronous operations. The result is the future object handling the result of the last asynchronous operation.

In this snippet, three asynchronous operations are chained naturally. Each function continues the work done by the previous one. Therefore, the functions passed to mbind are usually called *continuations*, and the future-value monad you defined is called the *continuation monad*.

The code is localized, readable, and easy to understand. If you wanted to implement the same process by using common approaches such as callback functions or signals and slots, this single function would have to be split into a few separate ones. Every time you call an asynchronous operation, you'd need to create a new function to handle the result.

10.7.2 *Implementations of futures*

Now that you understand the concept of futures, let's analyze what's available in the C++ world. Since C++11, std::future<T> provides a handler for a future value. In addition to a value, std::future can contain an exception if the asynchronous operation failed. In a sense, it's close to a future expected<T, std::exception_ptr> value.

The bad part is that it doesn't have a smart mechanism to attach a continuation. The only way to get the value is through its .get member function, which will block the program execution if the future isn't ready (see figure 10.17). You need to block the main program, spin off a thread that waits for the future to arrive, or poll the future once in a while to check whether it has finished.

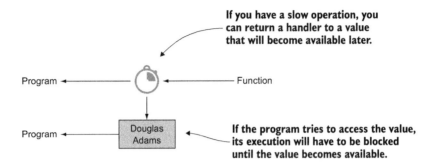

Figure 10.17   One way to access the value from `std::future` is to use the `.get` member function. Unfortunately, this blocks the caller if the future isn't finished. This is useful when you want to perform parallel computations and collect the results before continuing the program, but it's a problem in interactive systems.

All these options are bad. There's a proposal to extend `std::future` with a `.then` member function that can be passed the continuation function to (see figure 10.18). Currently, the proposal is published in the Concurrency TS along with C++17: most standard library vendors will support it, and the extended future class will be accessible as `std::experimental::future`. If you don't have access to a compiler that supports C++17, you can use the `boost::future` class, which already supports continuations.

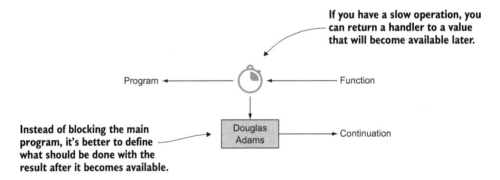

Figure 10.18   Instead of blocking the execution of the program, it's better to attach a continuation function to the `future` object. When the value becomes available, the continuation function will be called to process it.

The `.then` member function behaves similarly to `mbind`, with a slight difference. The monadic bind takes a function whose argument is an ordinary value and whose result is a `future` object, whereas `.then` wants a function whose argument is an already-completed `future` object and that returns a new future. Therefore, `then` isn't exactly the function that makes futures a monad, but it makes implementing the proper `mbind` function trivial.

Listing 10.9 Implementing `mbind` **using the** `.then` **member function**

```
template <typename T, typename F>
auto mbind(const future<T>& future, F f)
{
    return future.then(
            [](future<T> finished) {
                return f(finished.get());
            });
}
```

Takes a function from **T** to a
future instance future<**T2**>

Takes a function from future<**T**> and
returns future<**T2**>. You need to pass
a lambda to extract the value from the
future object before passing it to f.

Doesn't block anything because the
continuation is called only when the result
is ready (or if an exception has occurred)

Outside the usual C++ ecosystem, a few other libraries implement their own futures.
Most of them model the basic concept with the addition of handling and reporting
errors that can occur during asynchronous operations.

The most notable examples outside the standard library and `boost` are the Folly
library's `Future` class and Qt's `QFuture`. Folly provides a clean implementation of the
future concept that can never block (`.get` will throw an exception if the future isn't
ready, instead of blocking). `QFuture` has a way of connecting continuations by using
signals and slots, but it also blocks on `.get` like the future from the standard library.
`QFuture` has additional features that go beyond the basic concept by collecting multiple values over time instead of just a single result. Despite these few differences, all the
classes can be used to chain multiple asynchronous operations using the monadic bind
operation.

10.8 *Monad composition*

So far, you've had an instance of a monadic object, and you used the `mbind` function to
pass it through a monadic function. This yields an instance of the same monadic type,
which you can `mbind` to another function, and so on.

This is analogous to the normal function application, where you pass a value to a
function and get a result that you can pass to another function, and so on. If you remove
the original value from the equation, you get a list of functions that you compose with
one another, and that composition yields a new function.

This is also possible with monads. You can express the binding behavior without the
original instance of the monad, and focus on which monadic functions you want to
compose.

During the course of this chapter, you've seen a few variations of the `user_full_name`
and `to_html` functions. Most of them received a string and returned a string wrapped
in a monadic type. They looked like this (with `M` replaced with `optional`, `expected` or
another wrapper type):

```
user_full_name : std::string → M<std::string>
to_html        : std::string → M<std::string>
```

To create a function that composes these two, the function must receive an instance of M<std::string> representing the user whose name you need. Inside it, you pass the name through two mbind calls:

```
M<std::string> user_html(const M<std::string>& login)
{
    return mbind(
            mbind(login, user_full_name),
            to_html);
}
```

This works but is unnecessarily verbose. It would be easier to say that user_html should be a composition of user_full_name and to_html.

You can create the generic composition function easily. When composing normal functions, you're given two functions: f: T1 → T2 and g: T2 → T3. As the result, you get a function from T1 to T3. With monad composition, things change slightly. The functions don't return normal values, but values wrapped in a monad. Therefore, you'll have f: T1 → M<T2> and g: T2 → M<T3>.

Listing 10.10   *Composing two monad functions*

```
template <typename F, typename G>
auto mcompose(F f, G g) {
    return [=](auto value) {
        return mbind(f(value), g);
    };
}
```

You can now define user_html as follows:

```
auto user_html = mcompose(user_full_name, to_html);
```

The mcompose function can also be used for *simpler* monads such as ranges (and vectors, lists, and arrays). Imagine you have a children function that gives you a range containing all the children of a specified person. It has the right signature for a monad function: it takes a single person_t value and yields a range of person_t. You can create a function that retrieves all grandchildren:

```
auto grandchildren = mcompose(children, children);
```

The mcompose function lets you write short, highly generic code, but there's also one theoretical benefit. As you may recall, I listed three monad rules that weren't intuitive. With this composition function, you can express them in a much nicer way.

If you compose any monadic function with the constructor function for the corresponding monad, you get the same function:

```
mcompose(f, construct) == f
mcompose(construct, f) == f
```

And the associativity law says that if you have three functions f, g, and h that you want to compose, it's irrelevant whether you first compose f and g, and compose the result with h, or you compose g and h, and compose f with the result:

```
mcompose(f, mcompose(g, h)) == mcompose(mcompose(f, g), h)
```

This is also called *Kleisli composition*, and it generally has the same attributes as normal function composition.

> **TIP** For more information and resources about the topics covered in this chapter, see https://forums.manning.com/posts/list/43779.page.

Summary

- Programming patterns are usually connected to object-oriented programming, but the functional programming world is also filled with often-used idioms and abstractions such as the functor and monad.
- Functors are collection-like structures that know how to apply a transformation function on their contents.
- Monads know everything that functors do, but they have two additional operations: they let you create monadic values from normal values, and they can flatten out nested monadic values.
- Functors allow you to easily handle and transform wrapper types, whereas monads let you compose functions that return wrapper types.
- It's often useful to think about monads as boxes. But use the term *box* loosely, to cover cases such as the continuation monad—a box that will eventually contain data.
- You can open a box in the real world to see what's inside, but this isn't the case with monads. In the general case, you can only tell the box what to do with the value(s) it has—you can't always access the value directly.

Template
metaprogramming

This chapter covers

- Manipulating types during compilation

- Using `constexpr-if` to perform branching at compile-time

- Performing static introspection to check for type properties at compile-time

- Using `std::invoke` and `std::apply`

- Creating a DSL to define transactions for data record updates

The normal way to think of programming is that we write code, we compile it, and then the user executes the compiled binary. This is the way programming works for the most part.

With C++, we can also write a different kind of program—one that the compiler executes *while* it compiles our code. This might seem like a strange thing to do (how useful can it be to execute code when we have no input from the user and no data to process?). But the main point of compile-time code execution isn't in processing data at runtime, because most of the data will become available only when we execute the compiled program, but rather in manipulating the things that are available during compilation—types and the generated code.

This is a necessity when writing optimized generic code. We might want to implement an algorithm differently, depending on the features of the type we're given. For example, when working with collections, it's often important to know whether the collection is randomly accessible. Depending on this, we might want to choose a completely different implementation of our algorithm.

The main mechanism for compile-time programming (or metaprogramming) in C++ is templates. Let's look at the definition of the `expected` class template introduced in chapter 9:

```
template<typename T, typename E = std::exception_ptr>
class expected
{
    ...
};
```

This is a template parameterized on two types, `T` and `E`. When we specify these two parameters, we get a concrete type that we can create instances of. For example, if we set `T` to be `std::string` and `E` to be `int`, we'll get a type called `expected<std::string, int>`. If we set both `T` and `E` to be `std::string`, we'll get a different type, `expected<std::string, std::string>`.

These two resulting types are similar and will be implemented in the same way, but they're still two distinct types. We can't convert an instance of one type to the other. Furthermore, these two types will have completely separate implementations in the compiled program binary.

So, we have a thing called `expected` that accepts two types and gives a type as the result. It's like a function that doesn't operate on values, but on the types themselves. We'll call these *metafunctions* in order to differentiate them from ordinary functions.

Metaprogramming with templates (or TMP, template metaprogramming) is a huge topic that deserves a whole book for itself. This chapter covers only some of the parts relevant to this book. We're going to focus on C++17 mostly because it introduced a few features that make writing TMP code much easier.

11.1 Manipulating types at compile-time

Imagine you want to create a generic algorithm that sums all items in a given collection. It should take only the collection as its argument, and it should return the sum of all elements inside the collection. The question is, what will be the return type of this function?

This is easy with `std::accumulate`—the type of the result is the same as the type of the initial value used for accumulation. But here you have a function that takes only the collection and no initial value:

```
template <typename C>
??? sum(const C& collection)
{
    ...
}
```

The most obvious answer is to have the return type be the type of the items contained in the given collection. If you've been given a vector of integers, the result should be an integer. If you have a linked list of doubles, the result should be a double; and for any collection of strings, the result should be a string.

The problem is that you know the type of the collection, not the type of the items contained in it. You need to somehow write a metafunction that will get a collection type and return the type of the contained item.

One thing common to most collections is that you can use iterators to traverse over them. If you dereference an iterator, you get a value of the contained type. If you want to create a variable to store the first element in a collection, you can do it like this:

```
auto value = *begin(collection);
```

The compiler will be able to deduce its type automatically. If you have a collection of integers, `value` will be an `int`, just as you want. The compiler is able to properly deduce the type at the time of compilation. Now you need to use this fact to create a metafunction that does the same.

It's important to note that the compiler doesn't know whether the given collection contains any items at the time of compilation. It can deduce the type of `value` even if the collection can be empty at runtime. Of course, you'll get a runtime error if the collection is empty and you try to dereference the iterator returned by `begin`, but you're not interested in that at this point.

If you have an expression and you want to get its type, you can use the `decltype` specifier. You'll create a metafunction that takes a collection and returns the type of the contained item. You can implement this metafunction as a generic type alias like this:[1]

```
template <typename T>
using contained_type_t = decltype(*begin(T()));
```

Let's dissect this to see what's happening. The template specification tells you that you have a metafunction called `contained_type_t` that takes one argument: the type `T`. This metafunction will return the type of the expression contained in the `decltype` specifier.

When you declared the `value` variable, you had a concrete collection to call `begin` on. Here, you don't have a collection; you just have its type. Therefore, you're creating a default-constructed instance `T()` and passing it to `begin`. The resulting iterator is dereferenced, and the `contained_type_t` metafunction returns the type of the value that the iterator points to.

Unlike the previous code snippet, this won't produce an error at runtime because you're playing with types at compile-time. `decltype` will never execute the code you pass to it; it just returns the type of the expression without evaluating it. Although this sounds great, the metafunction has two significant problems.

First, it relies on `T` being default-constructible. Although all collections in the standard library have default constructors, it's not difficult to imagine a collection-like structure that doesn't. For example, you can see the previously mentioned `expected<T, E>` as a

[1] For more information on type aliases, see http://en.cppreference.com/w/cpp/language/type_alias.

collection that contains zero or one value of type T. And it doesn't have a default constructor. If you want an empty expected<T, E>, you'll need to specify the error explaining why it's empty.

You can't use contained_type_t with it; calling T() will yield a compiler error. To fix this, you need to replace the constructor call with the std::declval<T>() utility metafunction. It takes any type T, be it a collection, an integral type, or any custom type like expected<T, E>, and it *pretends* to create an instance of that type so you can use it in metafunctions when you need values instead of types—which is often the case when you use decltype.

In the original scenario of summing items in a collection, you knew exactly how to implement the summation. The only problem was that you didn't know the return type. The contained_type_t metafunction gives the type of the elements contained in a collection, so you can use it to deduce the return type of the function that sums all items in a collection.

You can use it in the following manner:

```
template <typename C,
          typename R = contained_type_t<C>>
R sum(const C& collection)
{
    ...
}
```

Although we're calling these *metafunctions*, they're nothing more than templates that define something. The metafunctions are *invoked* by instantiating this template. In this case, you instantiate the contained_type_t template for the type of collection C.

11.1.1 Debugging deduced types

The second problem with the implementation of contained_type_t is that it doesn't do what you want. If you try to use it, you'll soon encounter problems. If you try to compile the previous code, you'll get compiler messages hinting that the result of contained_type_t for a std::vector<T> is not T, but something else.

In cases like these—when you expect one type, but the compiler claims to have another—it's useful to be able to check which type you have. You can either rely on the IDE you're using to show the type, which can be imprecise, or you can force the compiler to tell you.

One of the neat tricks you can use is to declare a class template, but not implement it. Whenever you want to check for a specific type, you can try to instantiate that template, and the compiler will report an error specifying exactly which type you passed.

Listing 11.1 Checking which type is deduced by contained_type_t

```
template <typename T>
class error;

error<contained_type_t<std::vector<std::string>>>();
```

This produces a compilation error similar to the following (depending on the compiler you're using):

```
error: invalid use of incomplete type
'class error<const std::string&>'
```

contained_type_t deduced the type to be a constant reference to a string, instead of deducing it to be a string as you wanted—and as auto value would deduce.

This is to be expected, because auto doesn't follow the same deduction rules as decltype. When using decltype, you get the exact type of a given expression, whereas auto tries to be smart and behaves much like the template argument type deduction.

Because you got a constant reference to the type, and you want just the type, you need to remove the reference part of the type and the const qualifier. To remove the const and volatile qualifiers, use the std::remove_cv_t metafunction, and use std::remove_reference_t to remove the reference.

Listing 11.2 Full implementation of the `contained_type_t` metafunction

```
template <typename T>
using contained_type_t =
    std::remove_cv_t<
        std::remove_reference_t<
            decltype(*begin(std::declval<T>()))
        >
    >;
```

If you were to check the result of contained_type_t<std::vector<std::string>> now, you'd get std::string.

The <type_traits> header

Most standard metafunctions are defined in the <type_traits> header. It contains a dozen useful metafunctions for manipulating types and for simulating if statements and logical operations in metaprograms.

Metafunctions that end with _t were introduced in C++14. To perform similar type manipulations on older compilers that support only C++11 features, you need to use more-verbose constructs. Check out http://en.cppreference.com/w/cpp/types/remove_cv for examples of using the regular remove_cv instead of the one with the _t suffix.

Another useful utility when writing and debugging metafunctions is static_assert. Static assertions can ensure that a particular rule holds during compilation time. For example, you could write a series of tests to verify the implementation of contained_type_t:

```
static_assert(
    std::is_same<int, contained_type_t<std::vector<int>>>(),
    "std::vector<int> should contain integers");
static_assert(
```

```
    std::is_same<std::string, contained_type_t<std::list<std::string>>>(),
    "std::list<std::string> should contain strings");
static_assert(
    std::is_same<person_t*, contained_type_t<std::vector<person_t*>>>(),
    "std::vector<person_t> should contain people");
```

`static_assert` expects a `bool` value that can be calculated at compile-time, and it stops the compilation if that value turns out to be `false`. The preceding example checks that the `contained_type_t` metafunction is exactly the type you expected it to be.

You can't compare types by using the operator `==`. You need to use its *meta* equivalent, `std::is_same`. The `std::is_same` metafunction takes two types and returns `true` if the types are identical, or `false` otherwise.

11.1.2 Pattern matching during compilation

Let's see how the previously used metafunctions are implemented. You'll start by implementing your own version of the `is_same` metafunction. It should take two arguments and return `true` if the types are the same, or `false` otherwise. Because you're manipulating types, the metafunction won't return a value—`true` or `false`—but a type—`std::true_type` or `std::false_type`. You can think of these two as `bool` constants for metafunctions.

When defining metafunctions, it's often useful to think about what the result is in the general case, and then cover the specific cases and calculate the results for them. For `is_same`, you have two cases: that you've been given two types and need to return `std::false_type`, and that you've been given the same type for both parameters need to return `std::true_type`. The first case is more general, so let's cover it first:

```
template <typename T1, typename T2>
struct is_same : std::false_type {};
```

This definition creates a metafunction of two arguments that always returns `std::false_type` regardless of what `T1` and `T2` are.

Now the second case:

```
template <typename T>
struct is_same<T, T> : std::true_type {};
```

This is a specialization of the previous template that will be used only if `T1` and `T2` are the same. When the compiler sees `is_same<int, contained_type_t<std::vector<int>>>`, it first calculates the result of the `contained_type_t` metafunction, and that result is `int`. Then, it finds all the definitions of `is_same` that can be applied to `<int, int>` and picks the most specific one (see figure 11.1).

In the preceding implementation, both cases are valid for `<int, int>`—the one that inherits `std::false_type` and the one that inherits `std::true_type`. Because the second is more specialized, it is chosen.

What if you write `is_same<int, std::string>`? The compiler will generate the list of definitions that can be applied to an `int` and a `std::string`. In this case, the specialized definition isn't applicable because there's nothing you can substitute `T` for in

<T, T> to get <int, std::string>. The compiler will pick the only definition it can: the first one that inherits from std::false_type.

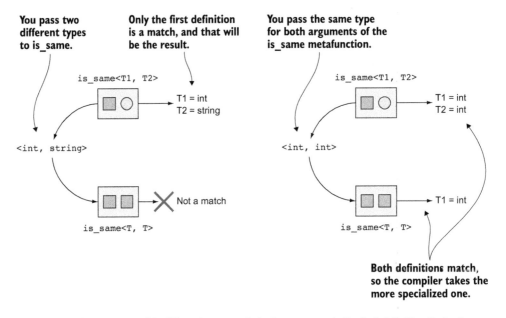

You pass two different types to is_same.

Only the first definition is a match, and that will be the result.

You pass the same type for both arguments of the is_same metafunction.

is_same<T1, T2>

T1 = int
T2 = string

<int, string>

Not a match

is_same<T, T>

is_same<T1, T2>

T1 = int
T2 = int

<int, int>

T1 = int

is_same<T, T>

Both definitions match, so the compiler takes the more specialized one.

Figure 11.1 **When you provide different arguments to** is_same, **only the first definition that returns** false_type **will be a match. If you pass the same type as both parameters, both definitions will be a match, and the more specialized match will win—the one returning** true_type.

is_same is a metafunction that returns a compile-time bool constant. You can implement a function that returns a modified type in a similar way. Let's implement the remove_reference_t function equivalent to the one from the standard library. This time, you have three cases:

- You're given a nonreference type (this is the general case).
- You're given an lvalue reference.
- You're given an rvalue reference.

In the first case, you need to return the type unmodified, whereas you need to strip out the references in the second and third cases.

You can't make the function remove_reference inherit from the result as with is_same. You need the exact type as the result, not a custom type that inherits from the result. To do this, create a structure template that will contain a nested type definition to hold the exact result.

Listing 11.3   Implementation of the remove_reference_t **metafunction**

```
template <typename T>
struct remove_reference {
    using type = T;
};
```

In the general case, remove_reference<T>::type
is type T: it returns the same type it gets.

```
template <typename T>
struct remove_reference<T&> {
    using type = T;
};
```

| **If you get an lvalue reference T&, strip the reference and return T.**

```
template <typename T>
struct remove_reference<T&&> {
    using type = T;
};
```

| **If you get an rvalue reference T&&, strip the reference and return T.**

When you implemented the `contained_type_t` metafunction, you created a template type alias. Here, you use a different approach. A template structure defines a nested alias called `type`. To call the `remove_reference` metafunction and get the resulting type, you need to use more-verbose syntax than with `contained_type_t`. You instantiate the `remove_reference` template and then reach into it to get its nested `type` definition. For this, you need to write `typename remove_reference<T>::type` whenever you want to use it.

Because this is overly verbose, you can create a convenience metafunction `remove_reference_t` to avoid writing `typename ...::type` all the time, similar to what C++ does for metafunctions in the `type_traits` header:

```
template <typename T>
using remove_reference_t<T> =
    typename remove_reference<T>::type;
```

When you use the `remove_reference` template for a specific template argument, the compiler will try to find all definitions that match that argument, and it'll pick up the most specific one.

If you call `remove_reference_t<int>`, the compiler will check which of the preceding definitions can be applied. The first will be a match and will deduce that `T` is `int`. The second and third definitions won't be matches because there's no possible type `T` for which a reference to `T` will be an `int` (`int` isn't a reference type). Because there's only one matching definition, it'll be used, and the result will be `int`.

If you call `remove_reference_t<int&>`, the compiler will again search for all matching definitions. This time, it'll find two. The first definition, as the most general one, will be a match, and it will match `T` to be `int&`. The second definition will also be a match, and it'll match `T&` to be `int&`; that is, it'll match `T` to be `int`. The third definition won't be a match, because it expects an rvalue. Out of the two matches, the second one is more specific, which means `T` (and therefore the result) will be `int`. This process would be similar for `remove_reference_t<int&&>`, with a difference that the second definition wouldn't be a match, but the third one would.

Now that you know how to get the type of an element in a collection, you can finally implement the function that will sum all items in it. Assume the default-constructed value of the item type is the identity element for addition, so you can pass it as the initial value to `std::accumulate`:

```
template <typename C,
        typename R = contained_type_t<C>>
```

```
R sum_iterable(const C& collection)
{
    return std::accumulate(begin(collection),
                           end(collection),
                           R());
}
```

When you call this function on a specific collection, the compiler must deduce the types of C and R. The type C will be deduced as the type of collection you passed to the function.

Because you haven't defined R, it gets a default value specified to be the result of `contained_type_t<C>`. This will be the type of the value you'd get by dereferencing an iterator to collection C, and then stripping the const qualifier and removing the references from it.

11.1.3 *Providing metainformation about types*

The previous examples showed how to find out the type of an element contained in a collection. The problem is, this work is tedious and error prone. Therefore, it's common practice to provide such information in the collection class. For collections, it's customary to provide the type of the contained items as a nested type definition named value_type. You can easily add this information to the implementation of expected:

```
template <typename T, typename E>
class expected {
public:
    using value_type = T;
    ...
};
```

All container classes in the standard library—even `std::optional`—provide this. It's something all well-behaved container classes from third-party libraries should also provide.

With this additional information, you can avoid all the metaprogramming you've seen so far, and write the following:

```
template <typename C,
          typename R = typename C::value_type>
R sum_collection(const C& collection)
{
    return std::accumulate(begin(collection),
                           end(collection),
                           R());
}
```

Using the value_type nested type has an additional benefit in cases where the collection iterator doesn't return an item directly, but instead returns a wrapper type. If you used the contained_type_t metafunction with a collection like this, you'd get the wrapper type as the result, whereas you'd probably want to get the type of the item. By providing the value_type, the collection tells you exactly how it wants you to see the items it contains.

11.2 Checking type properties at compile-time

You've created two sum functions: one that works for collections that have the `value_type` nested type definition, which is the preferred one; and another that works for any iterable collection. It would be nice to be able to detect whether a given collection has a nested `value_type` and act accordingly.

I first need to introduce the strangest metafunction yet—a metafunction that takes an arbitrary number of types and always returns void (see figure 11.2):

```
template <typename...>
using void_t = void;
```

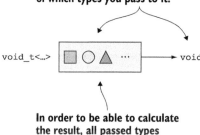

The void_t metafunction takes an arbitrary number of types, but returns void regardless of which types you pass to it.

In order to be able to calculate the result, all passed types need to be valid.

Figure 11.2 The `void_t` metafunction is strange: it ignores all its parameters and always returns `void`. It's useful because it can be evaluated only if the types you pass as its arguments are valid. If they aren't, `void_t` triggers a substitution failure, and the compiler will ignore the definition that used it.

This might look useless, but the result of this metafunction isn't what makes it useful. `void_t` is useful because it allows you to check the validity of given types or expressions in the *substitution failure is not an error* (SFINAE) context at compile-time. SFINAE is a rule that applies during overload resolution for templates. If substituting the template parameter with the deduced type fails, the compiler won't report an error; it'll ignore that particular overload.

> **NOTE** The `void_t` metafunction has been available in the standard library since C++17. If you're using an older compiler, check out http://en.cppreference .com/w/cpp/types/void_t to see how to implement `void_t` for it.

This is where `void_t` comes into play. You can provide it with as many types as you want, and if the types are invalid, the overload in which you're using `void_t` will be ignored. You can easily create a metafunction that checks whether a given type has a nested `value_type`.

Listing 11.4 Metafunction that detects whether a type has a nested `value_type`

```
template <typename C,
          typename = void_t<>>
struct has_value_type
   : std::false_type {};
```

General case: assumes an arbitrary type doesn't have a nested value_type type definition

```
template <typename C>
struct has_value_type<C,
                    void_t<typename C::value_type>>
    : std::true_type {};
```

| Specialized case: considered only if typename C::value_type is an existing type (if C has a nested value_type)

You can now define a function that sums all items in a collection and takes care of whether the collection has a nested value_type:

```
template <typename C>
auto sum(const C& collection)
{
    if constexpr (has_value_type<C>()) {
        return sum_collection(collection);
    } else {
        return sum_iterable(collection);
    }
}
```

If a given collection doesn't have a nested value_type, you can't call sum_collection on it. The compiler would try to deduce the template parameters and fail.

This is where constexpr-if comes into play. The regular if statement checks its condition at runtime and requires both branches to be compilable. constexpr-if, on the other hand, requires both branches to have a valid syntax but won't compile both branches. Calling sum_collection on a collection that doesn't have a nested value_type would yield an error; but the compiler will see only the else branch in that case, because has_value_type<C>() will be false.

What happens if you pass something that doesn't have a value_type type and also isn't iterable to sum? You'll get a compilation error that sum_iterable can't be called on that type. It'd be nicer if you guarded against that just as you guarded against calling sum_collection when it's not applicable.

You need to check whether a collection is iterable—whether you can call begin and end on it, and whether you can dereference the iterator returned by begin. You don't care whether end can be dereferenced, because it can be a special sentinel type (see chapter 7).

You can use void_t for this as well. Although void_t checks for validity of types, it can also be used to check expressions with a little help from decltype and std::declval.

Listing 11.5 Metafunction that detects whether a type is iterable

```
template <typename C,
          typename = void_t<>>
struct is_iterable
    : std::false_type {};
```

| The general case: assumes an arbitrary type isn't iterable

```
template <typename C>
struct is_iterable<
    C, void_t<decltype(*begin(std::declval<C>())),
            decltype(end(std::declval<C>()))>>
    : std::true_type {};
```

| Specialized case: considered only if C is iterable, and if its begin iterator can be dereferenced

You can now define a complete sum function that checks for validity of the collection type before calling any of the functions on that collection:

```
template <typename C>
auto sum(const C& collection)
{
    if constexpr (has_value_type<C>()) {
        return sum_collection(collection);
    } else if constexpr (is_iterable<C>()) {
        return sum_iterable(collection);
    } else {
        // do nothing
    }
}
```

The function properly guards all its calls, and you can even choose to handle the case when you're given a type that doesn't look like a collection. You could even report a compilation error in this case (check out the 11-contained-type accompanying code example).

11.3 *Making curried functions*

In chapter 4, I talked about currying and how to use it to improve APIs in projects. I mentioned that in this chapter, you were going to implement a generic function that turns any callable into its curried version.

As a reminder, currying allows you to treat multi-argument functions as unary functions. Instead of having a function that you call with n arguments and that gives you a result, you have a unary function that returns another unary function that returns yet another unary function, and so on, until all n arguments are defined and the last function can give you the result.

Let's recall the example from chapter 4. The function print_person had three arguments, the person to print, the output stream to print to, and the format:

```
void print_person(const person_t& person,
                  std::ostream& out,
                  person_t::output_format_t format);
```

When you implemented the curried version by hand, it became a chain of nested lambdas, and each lambda had to capture all the previously defined arguments:

```
auto print_person_cd(const person_t& person)
{
    return [&](std::ostream& out) {
        return [&](person_t::output_format_t format) {
            print_person(person, out, format);
        };
    };
}
```

The curried version required you to pass arguments one by one because, as I said, all curried functions are unary:

```
print_person_cd(martha)(std::cout)(person_t::full_name);
```

It can be tedious to write all those parentheses, so let's relax this. You'll allow the user to specify multiple arguments at the same time. Keep in mind that this is syntactic sugar; the curried function is still a unary function, and you're just making it more convenient to use.

The curried function needs to be a function object with state because it has to remember the original function and all the previously given arguments. It'll store copies of all the captured arguments in `std::tuple`. For this, you need to use `std::decay_t` to make sure the type parameters for the tuple are not references but actual value types:

```cpp
template <typename Function, typename... CapturedArgs>
class curried {
private:
    using CapturedArgsTuple = std::tuple<
        std::decay_t<CapturedArgs>...>;

    template <typename... Args>
    static auto capture_by_copy(Args&&... args)
    {
        return std::tuple<std::decay_t<Args>...>(
            std::forward<Args>(args)...);
    }


public:
    curried(Function, CapturedArgs... args)
        : m_function(function)
        , m_captured(capture_by_copy(std::move(args)...))
    {
    }

    curried(Function, std::tuple<CapturedArgs...> args)
        : m_function(function)
        , m_captured(std::move(args))
    {
    }

    ...

private:
    Function m_function;
    std::tuple<CapturedArgs...> m_captured;
};
```

So far, you have a class that can store a callable object and an arbitrary number of function arguments. The only thing left to do is to make this class a function object—to add the call operator.

The call operator needs to cover two cases:

- The user provided all remaining arguments to call the original function, in which case you should call it and return the result.
- You still don't have all the arguments to call the function, so you can return a new curried function object.

To test whether you have a sufficient number of arguments, you're going to use the `std::is_invocable_v` metafunction. It accepts a callable object type and a list of argument types, and returns whether that object can be invoked with arguments of the specified types.

To check whether `Function` can be called only with the arguments captured so far, write the following:

```
std::is_invocable_v<Function, CapturedArgs...>
```

In the call operator, you need to check whether the function is callable not only with the captured arguments, but also with the newly defined ones. You have to use `constexpr-if` here because the call operator can return different types depending on whether it returns the result or a new instance of the curried function object:

```
template <typename... NewArgs>
auto operator()(NewArgs&&... args) const
{
    auto new_args = capture_by_copy(std::forward<NewArgs>(args)...);

    if constexpr(std::is_invocable_v<
            Function, CapturedArgs..., NewArgs...>) {
        ...
    } else {
        ...
    }
}
```

In the `else` branch, you need to return a new instance of `curried` that contains the same function that the current instance does, but with newly specified arguments added to the tuple `m_captured`.

11.3.1 *Calling all callables*

The `then` branch needs to evaluate the function for the given arguments. The usual way to call functions is with the regular call syntax, so you might want to try this as well.

The problem is, a few things in C++ look like functions but can't be called as such: pointers to member functions and member variables. When you have a type like `person_t` with a member function `name`, you can get a pointer to that member function with `&person_t::name`. But you can't call this pointer to a function as you can with pointers to normal functions, because you'd get a compiler error:

```
&person_t::name(martha);
```

This is an unfortunate limitation of the C++ core language. Every member function is just like an ordinary function, where the first argument is the implicit `this` pointer. But you still can't call it as a function. The same goes for member variables. They can be seen as functions that take an instance of a class and return a value stored in its member variable. Because of this language limitation, it's not easy to write generic code that can work with all callables—with both function objects and pointers to member functions and variables.

std::invoke was added to the standard library as a remedy for this limitation of the language. With std::invoke, you can call any callable object regardless of whether it allows the usual call syntax. Whereas the previous snippet would produce a compilation error, the following will compile and do exactly what's expected:

```
std::invoke(&person_t::name, martha);
```

The syntax for std::invoke is simple. The first argument is the callable object, which is followed by the arguments that will be passed to that callable object:

```
std::less<>(12, 14)        std::invoke(std::less<>, 12, 14)
fmin(42, 6)                std::invoke(fmin, 42, 6)
martha.name()              std::invoke(&person_t::name, martha)
pair.first                 std::invoke(&pair<int,int>::first, pair)
```

Using std::invoke makes sense only in generic code—when you don't know exactly the type of the callable object. Every time you implement a higher-order function that takes another function as its argument, or when you have a class such as curried that stores a callable of an arbitrary type, you shouldn't use the normal function call syntax, but should use std::invoke instead.

For curried, you can't use std::invoke directly, because you have a callable and a std::tuple containing the arguments you need to pass to the callable. You don't have the individual arguments. You'll use a helper function called std::apply, instead. It behaves similarly to std::invoke (and is usually implemented using std::invoke), with a slight difference: instead of accepting individual arguments, it accepts a tuple containing the arguments—exactly what you need in this case.

Listing 11.6   Complete implementation of `curried`

```
template <typename Function, typename... CapturedArgs>
class curried {
private:
    using CapturedArgsTuple =
        std::tuple<std::decay_t<CapturedArgs>...>;

    template <typename... Args>
    static auto capture_by_copy(Args&&... args)
    {
        return std::tuple<std::decay_t<Args>...>(
                std::forward<Args>(args)...);
    }

public:
    curried(Function function, CapturedArgs... args)
        : m_function(function)
        , m_captured(capture_by_copy(std::move(args)...))
    {
    }

    curried(Function function,
            std::tuple<CapturedArgs...> args)
        : m_function(function)
```

```
                , m_captured(std::move(args))
    {
    }

    template <typename... NewArgs>
    auto operator()(NewArgs&&... args) const
    {
        auto new_args = capture_by_copy(
                std::forward<NewArgs>(args)...);

        auto all_args = std::tuple_cat(
                m_captured, std::move(new_args));

        if constexpr(std::is_invocable_v<Function,
                CapturedArgs..., NewArgs...>) {

            return std::apply(m_function, all_args);

        } else {
            return curried<Function,
                        CapturedArgs...,
                        NewArgs...>(
                    m_function, all_args);
        }
    }

private:
    Function m_function;
    std::tuple<CapturedArgs...> m_captured;
};
```

- Creates a tuple out of the new arguments
- Concatenates the previously collected arguments with the new ones
- If you can call m_function with the given arguments, do so.
- Otherwise, return a new curried instance with all the arguments so far stored inside.

An important thing to note is that the call operator returns different types depending on the branch of constexpr-if that was taken.

You can now easily create a curried version of print_person like so:

```
auto print_person_cd = curried{print_person};
```

Because you're storing the arguments by value, if you want to pass a noncopyable object (for example, an output stream) when calling the curried function, or if you want to avoid copying for performance reasons (for example, copying a person_t instance), you can pass the argument in a reference wrapper:

```
print_person_cd(std::cref(martha))(std::ref(std::cout))(person_t::name_only);
```

This will call the print_person function and pass it a const reference to martha and a mutable reference to std::cout. In addition, person_t::name_only will be passed by value.

This implementation of currying works for ordinary functions, for pointers to member functions, for normal and generic lambdas, for classes with the call operator—both generic and not—and even for classes with multiple different overloads of the call operator.

11.4 *DSL building blocks*

Until now, we've been focused mainly on writing generally useful utilities that make code shorter and safer. Sometimes these utilities are overly generic, and you might require something more specific.

You may notice patterns in a project: things you do over and over, with minor differences. But they don't look generic enough to warrant creating a library like ranges that the whole world would find useful. The problems you're solving may seem overly domain specific. Still, following the *don't-repeat-yourself* mantra, you should do something.

Imagine the following scenario. You have a set of records, and when you update them, you need to update all fields of a record in a single transaction. If any of the updates fail, the record must remain unchanged. You could implement a transaction system and put `start-transaction` and `end-transaction` all over the code. This is error-prone—you might forget to end a transaction, or you might accidentally change a record without starting the transaction. It would be much nicer to create a more convenient syntax that was less error-prone and saved you from thinking about transactions.

This is a perfect case for creating a small *domain-specific language* (DSL). The language only needs to allow you to define the record updates in a nice way, and nothing else. It doesn't have to be generic. It's meant to be used only in this small domain—the domain of transactional record updates. When you define what needs to be updated, the implementation of the DSL should handle the transaction.

You might want to create something that looks like this:

```
with(martha) (
    name = "Martha",
    surname = "Jones",
    age = 42
);
```

It's obvious that this isn't *normal* C++—no curly braces or semicolons. But it can be valid C++ if you're willing to spend time to implement the DSL. The implementation won't be pretty, but the point is to hide the complexity from the main code—to make writing the main program logic as easy as possible, while sacrificing the under-the-hood parts that most people never see.

Let's investigate the syntax in this example:

- You have a `function` (or a type) called `with`. You know it's a function because you're calling it with the argument `martha`.
- The result of this call is another function that needs to accept an arbitrary number of arguments. You might need to update more fields at the same time.

You also have the entities `name` and `surname`, which have the assignment operator defined on them. The results of these assignments are passed to the function returned by `with(martha)`.

When implementing a DSL like this, the best approach is to start from the innermost elements and create all the types needed to represent an abstract syntax tree (AST) of the syntax you want to implement (see figure 11.3). In this case, you need to start from the `name` and `surname` entities. Obviously, they're meant to represent the members of the `person` record. When you want to change a class member, you need to either declare that member as `public` or go through a setter member function.

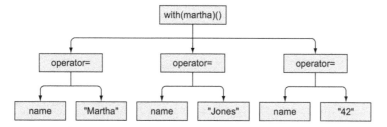

Figure 11.3   **The abstract syntax tree you want to model contains three levels: the object you're updating, a list of updates that need to be performed (if each update contains two items, the field that should be updated), and the new value the field should have.**

You need to create a simple structure that can store either a pointer to a member or a pointer to a member function. You can do this by creating a dummy structure `field` that can hold anything:

```
template <typename Member>
struct field {
field(Member member)
        : member(member)
    {
    }

    Member member;
};
```

With this, you can provide fields for your types. You can see how to define the fields for a type in the accompanying code example `11-dsl`.

   With the AST node to hold a pointer to the member or a setter member function, you can move on to implementing the syntax it needs to support. From the preceding example, you see that `field` needs the assignment operator defined on it. Unlike a regular assignment operator, this one can't change any data—it only needs to return another AST node named `update` that defines one update operation. This node will be able to store the member pointer and the new value:

```
template <typename Member, typename Value>
struct update {
    update(Member member, Value value)
        : member(member)
        , value(value)
    {
    }

    Member member;
```

```
    Value value;
};

template <typename Member>
struct field {
    …

    template <typename Value>
    update<Member, Value> operator=(const Value& value) const
    {
        return update{member, value};
    }
};
```

That leaves the main node: the `with` function. It takes an instance of a `person` record and returns a function object representing a transaction that accepts a list of updates that need to be performed. Therefore, let's call this function object `transaction`. It'll store a reference to the record so it can change the original one, and the list of `update` instances will be passed to the call operator of `transaction`. The call operator will return a `bool` value indicating whether the transaction was successful:

```
template <typename Record>
class transaction {
public:
    transaction(Record& record)
        : m_record(record)
    {
    }

    template <typename... Updates>
    bool operator()(Updates... updates)
    {
        …
    }

private:
    Record& m_record;
};

template <typename Record>
auto with(Record& record)
{
    return transaction(record);
}
```

You have all the required AST nodes, which means you only need to implement the DSL behavior.

Consider what a transaction means to you. If you're working with a database, you must start the transaction and commit it when all updates are processed. If you needed to send all updates to your records over the network to keep the distributed data synchronized, you could wait for all the updates to be applied and then send the new record over the network.

To keep the things simple, let's consider the C++ structure that members update as a transaction. If an exception occurs while changing the data, or if a setter function returns `false`, you'll consider that the update failed, and you'll cancel the transaction. The easiest way to implement this is the *copy-and-swap* idiom introduced in chapter 9. Create a copy of the current record, perform all the changes on it, and swap with the original record if all updates were successful.

Listing 11.7 Implementation of the call operator for the transaction

```
template <typename Record>
class transaction {
public:
    transaction(Record& record)
        : m_record(record)
    {
    }

    template <typename... Updates>
    bool operator()(Updates... updates)
    {
        auto temp = m_record;            // Creates a temporary copy to perform updates on

        if (all(updates(temp)...)) {     // Applies all the updates. If all updates are successful, swaps the temporary copy with the original record and returns true.
            std::swap(m_record, temp);
            return true;
        }

        return false;
    }

private:
    template <typename... Updates>
    bool all(Updates... results) const  // Collects all the results of different updates, and returns true if all of them succeeded
    {
        return (... && results);
    }

    Record &m_record;
};
```

You call all updates on the temporary copy. If any of the updates returns `false` or throws an exception, the original record will remain unchanged.

The only thing left to implement is the call operator for the `update` node. It has three cases:

- You have a pointer to a member variable that you can change directly.
- You have an ordinary setter function.
- You have a setter function that returns a `bool` value indicating whether the update succeeded.

You've seen that you can use std::is_invocable to test whether a given function can be called with a specific set of arguments that you can use to check whether you have a setter function or a pointer to a member variable. The novelty here is that you also want to differentiate between setters that return void and those that return bool (or another type convertible to bool). You can do this with std::is_invocable_r, which checks whether the function can be called as well as whether it'll return a desired type.

Listing 11.8   Full implementation of the update structure

```
template <typename Member, typename Value>
struct update {
    update(Member member, Value value)
        : member(member)
        , value(value)
    {
    }

    template <typename Record>
    bool operator()(Record& record)
    {
        if constexpr (std::is_invocable_r<
                bool, Member, Record, Value>()) {
            return std::invoke(member, record, value);

        } else if constexpr (std::is_invocable<
                Member, Record, Value>()) {
            std::invoke(member, record, value);
            return true;

        } else {
            std::invoke(member, record) = value;
            return true;
        }
    }

    Member member;
    Value value;
};
```

- If the Member callable object returns a bool when you pass it a record and a new value, you have a setter function that might fail.
- If the result type isn't bool or convertible to bool, invoke the setter function and return true.
- If you have a pointer to a member variable, set it and return true.

C++ brings a lot to the table when implementing DSLs—operator overloading and variadic templates being the main two features. With these, you can develop complex DSLs.

The main problem is that implementing all the necessary structures to represent AST nodes can be tedious work and requires a lot of boilerplate code. Although this significant downside makes DSLs in C++ not as popular as they might be, DSLs offer two huge benefits: you can write concise main program logic, and you can switch between different meanings of transactions without altering the main program logic. For example, if you decided to serialize all your records to a database, you'd just need to reimplement the call operator of the transaction class, and the rest of the program would suddenly start saving data to the database without your having to change a single line of the main program logic.

TIP For more information and resources about the topics in this chapter, see https://forums.manning.com/posts/list/43780.page.

Summary

- Templates give you a Turing-complete programming language that is executed during program compilation. This was discovered accidentally by Erwin Unruh, who created a C++ program that prints the first 10 prime numbers during compilation—as compilation errors.
- TMP is not only a Turing-complete language; it's also a pure functional language. All variables are immutable, and there's no mutable state in any form.
- The `type_traits` header contains many useful metafunctions for type manipulation.
- From time to time, because of limitations or missing features in the core programming language, workarounds are added to the standard library. For example, `std::invoke` allows you to call all function-like objects, even those that don't support the regular function-call syntax.
- DSLs are tedious to write but let you significantly simplify the main program logic. Ranges are also DSLs, in a sense; they define an AST for defining range transformations using the pipe syntax.

Functional design
for concurrent systems

The biggest problem in software development is handling complexity. Software systems tend to grow significantly over time and quickly outgrow original designs. When the features we need implement collide with the design, we must either reimplement significant portions of the system or introduce horrible quick-and-dirty hacks to make things work.

This problem with complexity becomes more evident in software that has different parts executing concurrently—from the simplest interactive user applications to network services and distributed software systems.

A large fraction of the flaws in software development are due to programmers not fully understanding all the possible states their code may execute in. In a multithreaded environment, the lack of understanding and the resulting problems are greatly amplified, almost to the point of panic if you are paying attention.

—John Carmack[1]

Most problems come from the entanglement of different system components. Having separate components that access and mutate the same data requires synchronizing that access. This synchronization is traditionally handled with mutexes or similar synchronization primitives, which works but also introduces significant scalability problems and kills concurrency.

One approach to solving the problem of shared mutable data is to have no mutable data whatsoever. But there's another option: to have mutable data but never share it. We focused on the former in the chapter 5, and we're now going to talk about the latter.

12.1 *The actor model: Thinking in components*

In this chapter, you'll see how to design software as a set of isolated, separate components. We first need to discuss this in the context of object-oriented design so you can later see how to make the design functional.

When designing classes, we tend to create getter and setter functions—getters to retrieve information about an object, and setters to change attributes of an object in a valid way that won't violate the class invariants. Many object-oriented design proponents consider this approach to be contrary to the philosophy of OO. They tend to call it *procedural* programming because we still think in algorithm steps, and the objects serve as containers and validators for the data.

Step one in the transformation of a successful procedural developer into a successful object developer is a lobotomy.

—David West[2]

Instead, we should stop thinking about what data an object contains, and instead think about what it can do. As an example, consider a class that represents a person. We'd usually implement it by creating getters and setters for the name, surname, age, and other attributes. Then we'd do something like this:

```
douglas.set_age(42);
```

And this shows the problem. We've designed a class to be a data container instead of designing it to behave like a person. Can we force a human being to be 42 years old? No. We can't change the age of a person, and we shouldn't design our classes to allow us to do so.

---

[1] John Carmack, "In-Depth: Functional Programming in C++," *#altdevblogaday*, April 30, 2012, reprinted on *Gamasutra*, http://mng.bz/OAzP.

[2] David West, *Object Thinking* (Microsoft Press, 2004).

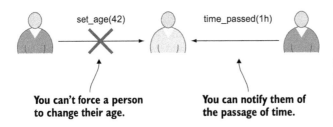

Figure 12.1 **We can't set the attributes of real-life objects. We can send them messages and let the objects react to those messages.**

You can't force a person to change their age.

You can notify them of the passage of time.

We should design classes to have a set of actions or tasks they can perform, and then add the data necessary to implement those actions. In the case of the class that models a person, instead of having a setter for the age, we'd create an action that tells the person that some time has passed, and the object should react appropriately (see figure 12.1). Instead of `set_age`, the object could have a member function `time_passed`:

```
void time_passed(const std::chrono::duration& time);
```

When notified that the specified time has passed, the person object would be able to increase its age and perform other related changes. For example, if relevant to our system, the person's height or hair color could be changed as a result of the person getting older. Therefore, instead of having getters and setters, we should have only a set of tasks that the object knows how to perform.

> *Don't ask for the information you need to do the work; ask the object that has the information to do the work for you.*

> —Allen Holub[3]

If we continue to model the person object after real-life people, we'll also come to realize that multiple person objects shouldn't have any shared data. Real people *share* data by talking to each other; they don't have shared variables that everyone can access and change.

This is the idea behind *actors*. In the actor model, actors are completely isolated entities that share nothing but can send messages to one another. The minimum that an actor class should have is a way to receive and send messages (see figure 12.2).

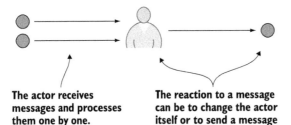

Figure 12.2 **An actor is an isolated component that can receive and send messages. It processes the messages serially; for each message, it can change its state or behavior, or it can send a new message to another actor in the system.**

The actor receives messages and processes them one by one.

The reaction to a message can be to change the actor itself or to send a message to another actor.

Traditionally, actors can send and receive different types of messages, and each actor can choose which actor to send the message to. Also, communication should be asynchronous.

---

3   Allen Holub, *Holub on Patterns: Learning Design Patterns by Looking at Code* (Apress, 2004).

Actor frameworks for C++

You can find a complete implementation of the traditional actor model for C++ at http://actor-framework.org and use it in your projects. The C++ Actor Framework has an impressive set of features. The actors are lightweight concurrent processes (much lighter-weight than threads), and it's network-transparent, meaning you can distribute actors over multiple separate machines and your program will work without the need to change your code. Although traditional actors aren't easily composed, they can easily be made to fit into the design covered in this chapter.

An alternative to the C++ Actor Framework is the SObjectizer library (https://sourceforge .net/projects/sobjectizer). It often provides better performance, but it has no built-in support for distributing actors across separate processes.

In this chapter, we'll define a more rudimentary actor compared to actors as specified by the actor model and actors in the C++ Actor Framework, because we want to focus more on the software design than on implementing a true actor model (see figure 12.3). Although the design of actors presented in this chapter differs from the design of actors in the traditional actor model, the concepts presented are applicable with traditional actors.

You'll design actors as follows:

- Actors can receive only messages of a single type and send messages of a single (not necessarily the same) type. If you need to support multiple different types for input or output messages, you can use `std::variant` or `std::any`, as shown in chapter 9.
- Instead of allowing each actor to choose to whom to send a message, you'll leave this choice to an external controller so you can compose the actors in a functional way. The external controller will schedule which sources an actor should listen to.
- You'll leave it up to the external controller to decide which messages should be processed asynchronously and which shouldn't.

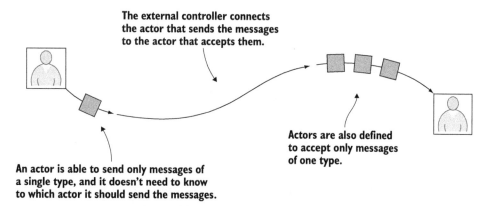

The external controller connects the actor that sends the messages to the actor that accepts them.

Actors are also defined to accept only messages of one type.

An actor is able to send only messages of a single type, and it doesn't need to know to which actor it should send the messages.

Figure 12.3 You'll use simplified typed actors that don't need to care about who sends the message to whom: that will be left to an external controller.

NOTE Most software systems nowadays use or implement some kind of event loop that can be used to asynchronously deliver messages, so we won't concern ourselves with implementing such a system. We'll focus on a software design that can easily be adapted to work on any event-based system.

The following listing shows the actor interface.

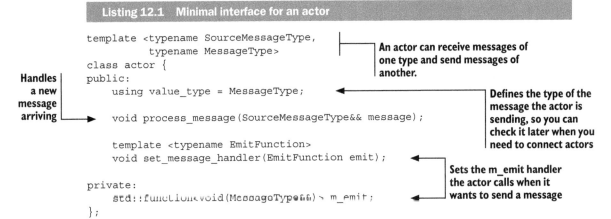

Listing 12.1   Minimal interface for an actor

```
template <typename SourceMessageType,
          typename MessageType>                         An actor can receive messages of
class actor {                                           one type and send messages of
public:                                                 another.
    using value_type = MessageType;

    void process_message(SourceMessageType&& message);

    template <typename EmitFunction>
    void set_message_handler(EmitFunction emit);

private:
    std::function<void(MessageType&&)> m_emit;
};
```

Handles a new message arriving → (points to process_message)

Defines the type of the message the actor is sending, so you can check it later when you need to connect actors → (points to value_type)

Sets the m_emit handler the actor calls when it wants to send a message → (points to set_message_handler and m_emit)

This interface clearly states that an actor only knows how to receive a message and how to send a message onward. It can have as much private data as it needs to perform its work, but none of it should ever be available to the outside world. Because the data can't be shared, you have no need for any synchronization on it.

It's important to note that there can be actors that just receive messages (usually called *sinks*), actors that just send messages (usually called *sources*), and general actors that do both.

12.2   *Creating a simple message source*

In this chapter, you're going to create a small web service that receives and processes bookmarks (see example:bookmarks-service). Clients will be able to connect to it and send JSON input that defines a bookmark like this:

```
{ "FirstURL": "https://isocpp.org/", "Text": "Standard C++" }
```

To do this, you need a few external libraries. For network communication, you'll use the Boost.Asio library (http://mng.bz/d62x); and for working with JSON, you'll use Niels Lohmann's JSON library, JSON for Modern C++ (https://github.com/nlohmann/json).

You'll first create an actor that listens for incoming network connections, and collect the messages clients send to the service. To make the protocol as simple as possible, messages will be line-based; each message needs to have only one newline character in it, at the end of the message.

This actor is the source actor. It receives messages from the outside world (entities that aren't part of your service) and is the source of those messages, as far as your service is concerned. The rest of the system doesn't need to be concerned about where messages come from, so you can consider the client connections to be an integral part of this source actor.

The service (see figure 12.4) will have an interface similar to actor, with the exception that you don't need the process_message function because this is a source actor. It doesn't receive messages from other actors in the system (as I said, it gets the messages from external entities—the clients—which aren't considered actors in this service); the service actor just sends the messages.

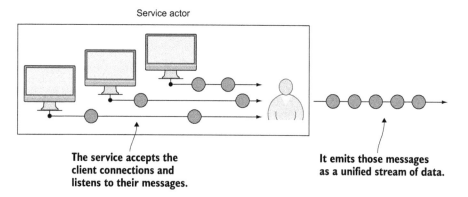

The service accepts the client connections and listens to their messages.

It emits those messages as a unified stream of data.

Figure 12.4 The service actor listens for client connections and for their messages. This part is hidden from the rest of the program, which just knows a stream of strings is arriving from somewhere.

Listing 12.2 Service to listen for client connections

```
class service {
public:
    using value_type = std::string;        Reads client input line by line,
                                            so sent messages are strings

    explicit service(
            boost::asio::io_service& service,
            unsigned short port = 42042)                  Creates the service that
        : m_acceptor(service,                             listens at the specified
            tcp::endpoint(tcp::v4(), port))               port (by default, 42042)
        , m_socket(service)
    {
    }

    service(const service& other) = delete;     Disables copying,
    service(service&& other) = default;          but allows moves

    template <typename EmitFunction>
    void set_message_handler(EmitFunction emit)
    {
                                                     No point accepting
        m_emit = emit;                               connections from clients
        do_accept();                                 until someone registers
    }                                                to listen to messages
private:                                             from message_service.
```

```
void do_accept()
{
    m_acceptor.async_accept(
        m_socket,
        [this](const error_code& error) {
            if (!error) {
                make_shared_session(
                        std::move(m_socket),
                        m_emit
                    )->start();

            } else {
                std::cerr << error.message() << std::endl;

            }

            // Listening to another client
            do_accept();
        });
}

tcp::acceptor m_acceptor;
tcp::socket m_socket;
std::function<void(std::string&&)> m_emit;
};
```

> Creates and starts the session for the incoming client. When the session object reads a message from a client, it's passed to m_emit. make_shared_session creates a shared pointer to a session object instance.

The service is mostly easy to understand. The only part that's more difficult is the do_ accept function, because of the Boost.Asio callback-based API. In a nutshell, it does the following:

- m_acceptor.async_accept schedules the lambda passed to it to be executed when a new client appears.
- The lambda checks whether the client has connected successfully. If so, it creates a new session for the client.
- You want to be able to accept multiple clients, so you call do_accept again.

The session object does most of the work. It needs to read the messages from the client one by one, and notify the service of them, so that the service can act as the source of messages for the rest of the program.

The session object also needs to keep its own lifetime. As soon as an error occurs and the client disconnects, the session should destroy itself. You'll use a trick here; the session object will inherit from std::enable_shared_from_this. This will allow a session instance that's managed by std::shared_ptr to safely create additional shared pointers to itself. Having a shared pointer to the session allows you to keep the session object alive for as long as there are parts of the system that use the session (see figure 12.5).

You'll capture the shared pointer to the session in the lambdas that process connection events. As long as there's an event the session is waiting for, the session object won't be deleted, because the lambda that handles that event will hold an instance of the shared pointer. When there are no more events you want to process, the object will be deleted.

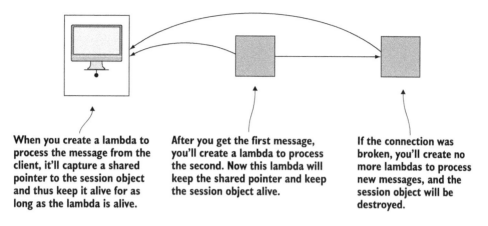

When you create a lambda to process the message from the client, it'll capture a shared pointer to the session object and thus keep it alive for as long as the lambda is alive.

After you get the first message, you'll create a lambda to process the second. Now this lambda will keep the shared pointer and keep the session object alive.

If the connection was broken, you'll create no more lambdas to process new messages, and the session object will be destroyed.

Figure 12.5 You capture the shared pointer to the session object in the lambda that will process when new data arrives from the client. The session object will be kept alive as long as the client keeps the connection alive.

Listing 12.3 Reading and emitting messages

```
template <typename EmitFunction>
class session:
    public std::enable_shared_from_this<session<EmitFunction>> {
public:
    session(tcp::socket&& socket, EmitFunction emit)
        : m_socket(std::move(socket))
        , m_emit(emit)
    {
    }

    void start()
    {
        do_read();
    }

private:
    using shared_session =
        std::enable_shared_from_this<session<EmitFunction>>;

    void do_read()
    {
        auto self = shared_session::shared_from_this();          ◄── Creates another pointer that has shared ownership of this session

        boost::asio::async_read_until(
            m_socket, m_data, '\n',                               ── Schedules a lambda to be executed when you reach the newline character in the input
            [this, self](const error_code& error,
                         std::size_t size) {

                if (!error) {                                     ── You should have encountered an error, or you can read the line and send it to whoever registered to listen for messages.
                    std::istream is(&m_data);
                    std::string line;
                    std::getline(is, line);
                    m_emit(std::move(line));
```

```
                         do_read();
                 }
          });
   }

   tcp::socket m_socket;
   boost::asio::streambuf m_data;
   EmitFunction m_emit;
};
```

If you've read the message successfully, schedule to read the next one.

Although the users of the `service` class won't know the `session` object exists, it will send messages to them.

12.3   Modeling reactive streams as monads

You've created a service that emits messages of type `std::string`. It can emit as many messages as it wants—zero or more. This kind of looks like a singly linked list: you have a collection of values of some type, and you can traverse it element by element until you reach the end. The only difference is that with lists, you already have all the values to traverse over, whereas in this case the values aren't yet known—they arrive from time to time.

As you may recall, you saw something similar in chapter 10. You had futures and the continuation monad. A future is a container-like structure that contains a value of a given type at some point in time. Your service is similar, except it's not limited to a single value, but sends new values from time to time (see figure 12.6). We'll call structures like these *asynchronous*, or *reactive*, streams. It's important to note that this isn't the same as `future<list<T>>`—that would mean you'd get all values at a single point in time.

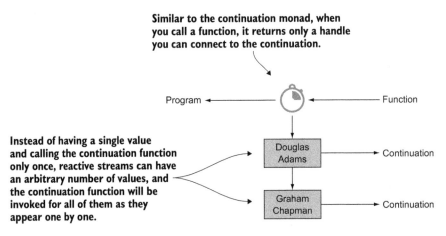

Figure 12.6   Unlike the continuation monad, which calls the continuation function only once, reactive streams can have an arbitrary number of values. The continuation function is called for each new value that arrives.

Reactive streams look like collections. They contain items of the same type; it's just that not all items are available at once. You saw a type that behaved in a similar way in chapter 7: the input stream. You used the input stream with the ranges library and performed transformations on it:

```
auto words = istream_range<std::string>(std::cin)
             | view::transform(string_to_lower);
```

You created the same transformations on futures and optionals. You probably see where I'm going with this; you were able to create the same transformations for all monads we covered. The important question is whether reactive streams are monads.

Conceptually, they seem to be. Let's recap what's required for something to be a monad:

- It must be a generic type.
- You need a constructor—a function that creates an instance of a reactive stream that contains a given value.
- You need the transform function—a function that returns a reactive stream that emits transformed values coming from the source stream.
- You need a `join` function that takes all messages from all given streams and emits them one by one.
- You need for it to obey the monad laws (proving this is outside the scope of this book).

The first item is satisfied: reactive streams are generic types parameterized on the type of the messages the stream is emitting (`value_type`). In the following sections, you'll make reactive streams a monad by doing the following:

- Creating a stream transformation actor
- Creating an actor that creates a stream of given values
- Creating an actor that can listen to multiple streams at once and emit the messages coming from them

12.3.1 *Creating a sink to receive messages*

Before implementing all the functions to show that reactive streams are a monad, let's first implement a simple sink object you can use to test the service. The sink is an actor that only receives messages but doesn't send them (see figure 12.7). You therefore don't need the `set_message_handler` function; you just need to define what `process_message` does. You'll create a generic sink that will execute any given function every time a new message appears.

Listing 12.4   Implementation of the sink object

```
namespace detail {
    template <typename Sender,
              typename Function,
              typename MessageType = typename Sender::value_type>
    class sink_impl {
    public:
        sink_impl(Sender&& sender, Function function)
            : m_sender(std::move(sender))
            , m_function(function)
        {
            m_sender.set_message_handler(
                [this](MessageType&& message)
                {
                    process_message(
                        std::move(message));
                }
            );
        }

        void process_message(MessageType&& message) const
        {
            std::invoke(m_function,
                std::move(message));
        }

    private:
        Sender m_sender;
        Function m_function;
    };
}
```

When the sink is constructed, it connects to its assigned sender automatically.

When you get a message, you pass it on to the function defined by the user.

Single-owner design

One of the things you'll notice in this chapter is that `std::move` and rvalue references are used often. For example, `sink_impl` takes the `sender` object as an rvalue reference. The `sink` object becomes the sole owner of the sender you assign to it. In a similar manner, other actors become owners of their respective senders.

This implies that the data-flow pipeline will own all the actors in it, and when the pipeline is destroyed, all the actors will be as well. Also, the messages will be passed on through different actors by using rvalue references to indicate that only one actor has access to a message at any point in time. This design is simple and easy to reason about, which is why I think it's the best approach to demonstrate the concept of actors and the data-flow design.

The downside is that you can't have multiple components in your system listen to a single actor, nor can you share actors between different data flows in the system. This can be easily fixed by allowing shared ownership of actors (`std::shared_ptr` would be a perfect choice) and allowing each sender to have multiple listeners by keeping a collection of message-handler functions rather than having only one.

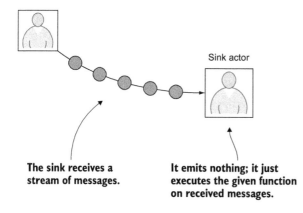

Figure 12.7 The sink actor calls a function for each message it receives. It emits nothing. You can use it to print out all the messages you receive to `std::cerr` or do something more advanced such as saving the messages to a file or a database.

The sink receives a stream of messages.

It emits nothing; it just executes the given function on received messages.

Now you need a function that creates an instance of `sink_impl`, given a sender and a function:

```
template <typename Sender, typename Function>
auto sink(Sender&& sender, Function&& function)
{
    return detail::sink_impl<Sender, Function>(
        std::forward<Sender>(sender),
        std::forward<Function>(function));
}
```

You can easily test whether the service object works by connecting it to a sink that writes all messages to `cerr`.

Listing 12.5 Starting the service

```
int main(int argc, char* argv[])
{
    boost::asio::io_service event_loop;

    auto pipeline =
        sink(service(event_loop),
            [](const auto& message) {
                std::cerr << message << std::endl;
            });

    event_loop.run();
}
```

`io_service` is a class in Boost.Asio that handles the event loop. It listens to events and calls the appropriate callback lambdas for them.

Creates the service and connects the sink to it

Starts to process events

C++17 and class template argument deduction

C++17, which is required to compile the examples in this chapter, supports class template deduction. It isn't strictly necessary to create the `sink` function; you could name the class `sink`, and the preceding code would still work.

The reason for separating `sink` and `sink_impl` is to be able to support the range-like syntax on reactive streams. You'll have two `sink` functions that return different types depending on the number of arguments passed. This would be more difficult to achieve if `sink` weren't a proper function.

This looks similar to calling the `for_each` algorithm on a collection: you pass it a collection and a function that's executed for each item of the collection. This syntax is awkward, so you'll replace it with pipe-based notation—the same as the ranges library uses.

To do so, you need a `sink` function that takes only the function that will be invoked on each message, without taking the sender object as well. It must return a temporary helper object holding that function. The instance of the `sink_impl` class will be created by the pipe operator when you specify the sender. You can think of this as a partial function application—you bind the second argument and leave the first one to be defined later. The only difference is that you specify the first argument by using the pipe syntax instead of using the normal function call syntax you used with partial function application in chapter 4:

```
namespace detail {
    template <typename Function>
    struct sink_helper {
        Function function;
    };
}

template <typename Sender, typename Function>
auto operator| (Sender&& sender,
                detail::sink_helper<Function> sink)
{
    return detail::sink_impl<Sender, Function>(
        std::forward<Sender>(sender), sink.function);
}
```

You'll define an `operator|` for each transformation you create, in a way similar to this. Each will accept any sender as the first argument and a `_helper` class that defines the transformation. You can make the main program more readable:

```
auto sink_to_cerr =
    sink([](const auto& message) {
        std::cerr << message << std::endl;
    });

auto pipeline = service(event_loop) | sink_to_cerr;
```

Now you have a nice way to test whether the service works properly. Whatever stream you have, you can write all its messages to `cerr`. You can compile the program, start it, and use `telnet` or a similar application to test simple textual connections to connect to your program on port 42042. Each message any client sends will automatically appear on the output of the server.

12.3.2 *Transforming reactive streams*

Let's return to making reactive streams a monad. The most important task is to create the `transform` stream modifier. It should take a reactive stream and an arbitrary function, and it needs to return a new stream—one that emits the messages from the original stream, but transformed using the given function.

In other words, the `transform` modifier will be a proper actor that both receives and sends messages. For each message it receives, it'll call the given transformation function and emit the result it produces as a message (see figure 12.8).

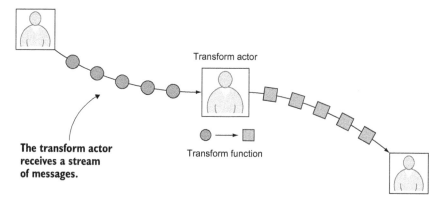

The transform actor receives a stream of messages.

Transform actor

Transform function

Figure 12.8   Similar to ranges, `transform` on reactive streams applies the given transformation function on each message it receives, and it sends the function result to the next actor.

Listing 12.6   Transform stream modifier implementation

```
namespace detail {
    template <
        typename Sender,
        typename Transformation,
        typename SourceMessageType =
            typename Sender::value_type,
        typename MessageType =
            decltype(std::declval<Transformation>()(
                std::declval<SourceMessageType>()))>
    class transform_impl {
    public:
        using value_type = MessageType;

        transform_impl(Sender&& sender, Transformation transformation)
            : m_sender(std::move(sender))
            , m_transformation(transformation)
        {
        }

        template <typename EmitFunction>
        void set_message_handler(EmitFunction emit)
        {
            m_emit = emit;
            m_sender.set_message_handler(
                [this](SourceMessageType&& message) {
                    process_message(
                        std::move(message));
                });
        }
```

To properly define the message receiving and sending functions, you need the types of the messages you receive and the type of the messages you send.

When an actor is interested in messages, connect to the actor that will send the messages.

```
        void process_message(SourceMessageType&& message) const
        {
            m_emit(std::invoke(m_transformation,
                               std::move(message)));
        }

    private:
        Sender m_sender;
        Transformation m_transformation;
        std::function<void(MessageType&&)> m_emit;
    };
}
```

> When you receive a message, transform it with the given function and send the result to the actor that listens to you.

One thing worth noting here is that unlike the `sink` actor, `transform` doesn't immediately connect to its sender. If you don't have anyone to send messages to, there's no reason you should process them. You'll start listening to the messages coming from the sender only when the `set_message_handler` function is called—when you get someone to listen to your messages.

After you create all the helpers and the pipe operator, you can use the `transform` modifier the same way you'd use it with ranges. For example, to trim messages before printing them out, do this:

```
auto pipeline =
    service(event_loop)
    | transform(trim)
    | sink_to_cerr;
```

This is starting to look similar to ranges. And that is the main point: reactive streams let you think about software as a collection of input streams, the transformations you need to perform on them, and where you should put the results—just as you can do with ranges.

12.3.3 *Creating a stream of given values*

The `transform` function made reactive streams a functor. To make it a proper monad, you need a way to construct the stream out of a value, and you need the `join` function.

First, let's create the easier of the two. Given a value or a list of values (for convenience), you want to create a stream that emits them. This stream doesn't accept any messages, but only emits them, just like the `service` you saw before.

You don't need to listen for messages coming from other actors. The user must be able to specify the values upon construction, store them, and, when an actor starts listening to the messages from this class, send the values to it:

```
template <typename T>
class values {
public:
    using value_type = T;

    explicit values(std::initializer_list<T> values)
        : m_values(values)
    {
    }
```

```
template <typename EmitFunction>
void set_message_handler(EmitFunction emit)
{
    m_emit = emit;
    std::for_each(m_values.cbegin(), m_values.cend(),
                  [&](T value) { m_emit(std::move(value)); });
}

private:
    std::vector<T> m_values;
    std::function<void(T&&)> m_emit;
};
```

This class can be used as a monad constructor for reactive streams. You can easily test whether this works by passing the values directly to a `sink` object:

```
auto pipeline = values{42} | sink_to_cerr;
```

This creates a stream containing a single value. When you connect `sink_to_cerr` to the stream, it'll print that value to `std::cerr`.

12.3.4 Joining a stream of streams

The last thing you need to do to make reactive streams a monad is define a `join` function. Say you want a few ports for your service to listen on. You'd like to create a `service` instance for each port and then join the messages from all those instances into a single unified stream.

You want to be able to do something like this:

```
auto pipeline =
    values{42042, 42043, 42044}
    | transform([&](int port) {
          return service(event_loop, port);
      })
    | join()
    | sink_to_cerr;
```

This might seem difficult, but with all the things you've learned, it's easy. The implementation is similar to `transform`. Both `join` and `transform` receive messages of one type and emit messages of a different type. The only difference is that in the case of `join`, you're receiving messages that are new streams. You listen to messages from those streams and then pass them on.

Listing 12.7 Implementing the `join` transformation

```
namespace detail {
    template <
        typename Sender,
        typename SourceMessageType =           ┐ Type of the streams
            typename Sender::value_type,        ┘ you need to listen to
        typename MessageType =
            typename SourceMessageType::value_type>  ┐ Type of the messages sent by
    class join_impl {                                │ the streams you're listening
    public:                                          │ to—the messages you need
                                                     │ to pass on to listeners
```

```
        using value_type = MessageType;

        ...

        void process_message(SourceMessageType&& source)
        {
            m_sources.emplace_back(std::move(source));
            m_sources.back().set_message_handler(m_emit);
        }

    private:
        Sender m_sender;
        std::function<void(MessageType&&)> m_emit;
        std::list<SourceMessageType> m_sources;
    };
}
```

> **When you get a new stream to listen to, store it, and forward its messages as your own.**

> **Saves all the streams you listen to, to expand their lifetimes. Uses a list to minimize the number of reallocations.**

Now that you have both `join` and `transform`, you can finally say that reactive streams are monads.

12.4   *Filtering reactive streams*

So far, we've shown that reactive streams with the transformations we created are monads, and we've tried to make them look like ranges as much as possible. Let's implement another useful function that you used with ranges.

In the previous examples, you wrote all the messages coming from a client to the error output. Say you want to ignore some of them. For example, you want to filter out empty messages and messages starting with the pound symbol (#), because they represent comments in the data the client is sending.

You want to do something like this:

```
auto pipeline =
    service(event_loop)
    | transform(trim)
    | filter([](const std::string& message) {
        return message.length() > 0 &&
                message[0] != '#';
    })
    | sink_to_cerr;
```

You need to create a new stream modifier similar to `transform`. It'll receive messages and emit only those that satisfy the given predicate. The main difference is that unlike `transform` and `join`, filtering listens for and emits the same type of messages.

> **Listing 12.8   Transformation actor that filters messages in a stream**

```
template <typename Sender,
          typename Predicate,
          typename MessageType =
              typename Sender::value_type>
class filter_impl {
public:
    using value_type = MessageType;
```

> **You're receiving the same type of message you're sending.**

```
...
        void process_message(MessageType&& message) const
        {
            if (std::invoke(m_predicate, message)) {
                m_emit(std::move(message));
            }
        }

    private:
        Sender m_sender;
        Predicate m_predicate;
        std::function<void(MessageType&&)> m_emit;
    };
```

> When you receive a message, checks whether it satisfies the predicate, and if so passes it on

Filtering is useful whenever you want to discard invalid data, or data you have no interest in.

12.5 Error handling in reactive streams

Because you're trying to implement a web service that receives JSON-formatted messages, you need to be able to handle parsing errors. We discussed a few ways to perform error handling in a functional way in chapters 9 and 10. There's optional<T>, which you can leave empty when you want to denote an error in a computation. You can also use expected<T, E> when you want to tell exactly which error has occurred.

The library we're using to handle JSON input is heavily exception based. Because of this, we'll use expected<T, E> for error handling. The type T will be the type of the message you're sending, and E will be a pointer to an exception (std::exception_ptr). Every message will contain either a value or a pointer to an exception.

To wrap the functions that throw exceptions into code that uses expected for error handling, you'll use the mtry function defined in chapter 10. As a quick reminder, mtry is a helper function used to convert functions that throw exceptions into functions that return an instance of expected<T, std::exception_ptr>. You can give any callable object to mtry, and that object will be executed. If everything goes well, you'll get a value wrapped in an expected object. If an exception is thrown, you'll get an expected object containing a pointer to that exception.

With mtry, you can wrap the json::parse function and use transform to parse all messages you receive from the client into JSON objects. You'll get a stream of expected_json objects (expected<json, std::exception_ptr>).

Listing 12.9 Parsing strings into JSON objects

```
auto pipeline =
    service(event_loop)
    | transform(trim)
    | filter([](const std::string& message) {
          return message.length() > 0 &&
                 message[0] != '#';
      })
```

> Tries to parse each string received. The result is either a JSON object or a pointer to an exception (or, specifically expected<json, std::exception_ptr>).

```
    | transform([](const std::string& message) {
          return mtry([&] {
              return json::parse(message);
          });
      })
    | sink_to_cerr;
```

You need to extract the data from each JSON object into a proper structure. You'll define a structure to hold the URL and text of a bookmark, and create a function that takes a JSON object and gives you a bookmark if the object contains required data, or an error if it doesn't:

```
struct bookmark_t {
    std::string url;
    std::string text;
};

using expected_bookmark = expected<bookmark_t, std::exception_ptr>;

expected_bookmark bookmark_from_json(const json& data)
{
    return mtry([&] {
        return bookmark_t{data.at("FirstURL"), data.at("Text")};
    });
}
```

The JSON library will throw an exception if you try to access something with the at function and it's not found. Because of this, you need to wrap it into mtry just as you did with json::parse. Now you can continue processing the messages.

So far, you've parsed the strings and gotten expected<json, ...>. You need to skip the invalid values and try to create the bookmark_t values from the valid JSON objects. Further, because the conversion to bookmark_t can fail, you also need to skip all the failed values. You can use a combination of transform and filter for this:

```
auto pipeline =
    service(event_loop)
    | transform(trim)
    | filter(...)

    | transform([](const std::string& message) {      ◄───── Gets only valid
          return mtry([&] {                                   JSON objects
              return json::parse(message);
          });
      })
    | filter(&expected_json::is_valid)
    | transform(&expected_json::get)

    | transform(bookmark_from_json)      ◄───── Gets only valid
    | filter(&expected_bookmark::is_valid)        bookmarks
    | transform(&expected_bookmark::get)

    | sink_to_cerr;
```

The preceding pattern is clear: perform a transformation that can fail, filter out all the invalid results, and extract the value from the `expected` object for further processing. The problem is that it's overly verbose. But that's not the main problem. A bigger issue is that you forget the error as soon as you encountered it. If you wanted to forget errors, you wouldn't use `expected`; you'd use `optional`.

This is where the example starts to be more interesting. You got a stream of values, and each value is an instance of the `expected` monad. So far, you've treated only streams as monads, and you've treated all the messages as normal values. Will this code become more readable if you treat `expected` as a monad, which it is?

Instead of doing the whole `transform-filter-transform` shebang, let's transform the instances of expected in a monadic manner. If you look at the signature of the `bookmark_from_json` function, you'll see that it takes a value and gives an instance of the `expected` monad. You've seen that you can compose functions like these with monadic composition: `mbind`.

Listing 12.10 Treating `expected` as a monad

```
auto pipeline =
    service(event_loop)
    | transform(trim)
    | filter(…)

    | transform([](const std::string& message) {        // Until this point, you had a
        return mtry([&] {                                // stream of normal values.
            return json::parse(message);                 // Here you get a stream of
        });                                              // expected instances: a
    })                                                   // monad inside a monad.

    | transform([](const auto& exp_json) {               // If you can use mbind to
        return mbind(exp_json, bookmark_from_json);      // transform instances of
    })                                                   // expected, you can lift it
                                                         // with transform to work
                                                         // on streams of expected
                                                         // objects.
    …                                                    // You can concatenate as many fallible
    | sink_to_cerr;                                      // transformations as you want.
```

This is a nice example of how lifting and monadic bind can work together. You started with a function that works on normal values of `json` type, bound it so it can be used with `expected_json`, and then lifted it to work on streams of `expected_json` objects.

12.6 *Replying to the client*

The service implemented so far receives requests from the client but never replies. This might be useful if you wanted to store the bookmarks the clients send you—instead of `sink_to_cerr`, you could write the bookmarks to a database.

It's more often the case that you need to send some kind of reply to the client, at least to confirm you've received the message. At first glance, this seems like a problem, given the design of the service. You've collected all messages into a single stream—your main program doesn't even know that clients exist.

You have two choices. One is to go back to the drawing board. The other is to listen to that voice in the back of your head that whispers, "Monads. You know this be done with monads." Instead of deleting everything you've implemented so far, let's listen to that voice.

If you want to respond to a client instead of writing the bookmarks to `std::cerr` or to a database, you need to know which client sent which message. The only component in the system that can tell you is the service object. You somehow need to pass the information about the client through the whole pipeline—from `service(event_loop)` up to the sink object—without it being modified in any of the steps.

Instead of the service object sending messages containing only strings, it needs to send messages that contain strings and a pointer to the socket you can use to further communicate with the client. Because the socket needs to be passed through all the transformations while the message type changes, you'll create a class template to keep the socket pointer along with a message.

Listing 12.11   Structure to hold a socket along with the message

```
template <typename MessageType>
struct with_client {
    MessageType value;
    tcp::socket* socket;

    void reply(const std::string& message) const
    {
        // Copy and retain the message until the async_write
        // finishes its asynchronous operation
        auto sptr = std::make_shared<std::string>(message);
        boost::asio::async_write(
            *socket,
            boost::asio::buffer(*sptr, sptr->length()),
            [sptr](auto, auto) {});
    }
};
```

To simplify the main program so as not to have any dependency on Boost.Asio, you also create a `reply` member function (see the full implementation in the accompanying `examplebookmark-service-with-reply`), which you can use to send messages to the client.

`with_client` is a generic type that holds extra information. You've learned that you should think *functor* and *monad* every time you see something like this. It's easy to create the required functions to show that `with_client` is a monad.

> ### Join function for with_client
>
> The only function that deserves a bit of consideration is `join`. If you have a `with_client` nested inside another `with_client`, you'll have one value and two pointers to a socket, but you only need the value with a single socket after the join.

You can choose to always keep the socket from the innermost instance of `with_client` if it's not null, or to always keep the socket from the outermost instance. In your use case, whatever you do, you always want to reply to the client that initiated the connection, which means you need to keep the outermost socket.

Alternatively, you could change the `with_client` class to keep not only one socket, but a collection of sockets. In that case, joining a nested instance of `with_client` would need to merge these two collections.

If you change the service to emit messages of type `with_client<std::string>` instead of plain strings, what else should you change in order for the program to compile? Obviously, you need to change the sink. It must send the messages to the client instead of writing them to `std::cerr`. The sink will receive messages of type `with_client<expected_bookmark>`. It needs to check whether the `expected` object contains an error, and then act accordingly:

```
auto pipeline =
    service(event_loop)
        …

    | sink([](const auto& message) {
        const auto exp_bookmark = message.value;

        if (!exp_bookmark) {
            message.reply("ERROR: Request not understood\n");
            return;
        }

        if (exp_bookmark->text.find("C++") != std::string::npos) {
            message.reply("OK: " + to_string(exp_bookmark.get()) +
                          "\n");
        } else {
            message.reply("ERROR: Not a C++-related link\n");
        }
    });
```

If any error occurs while you parse the bookmarks, you notify the client. Also, because you want to accept only C++-related bookmarks, you report an error if the text of the bookmark doesn't contain C++.

You've changed the service, and you've changed the sink to be able to reply to the client. What else needs changing?

You could change all the transformations one by one until you make them all understand the newly introduced `with_client` type. But you can be smarter than that. Just as you handled fallible transformations with `mbind` instead of passing each message through a `transform-filter-transform` chain of modifiers, you should try to do something similar here.

This is another level of monads. You have a stream (which is a monad) of `with_client` values (which is also a monad), each of which contains an `expected<T, E>` value (a third nested monad). You just need to lift everything one level further.

You want to redefine the `transform` and `filter` functions implemented for your reactive streams that reside in the `reactive::operators` namespace (see the example `bookmark-service-with-reply`) to work on a reactive stream of `with_client` values:

```
auto transform = [](auto f) {
        return reactive::operators::transform(lift_with_client(f));
    };
auto filter = [](auto f) {
        return reactive::operators::filter(apply_with_client(f));
    };
```

`lift_with_client` is a simple function that lifts any function from T1 to T2 to a function from `with_client<T1>` to `with_client<T2>`. And `apply_with_client` does something similar, but returns an unwrapped result value instead of putting it into the `with_client` object.

This is everything you need to do. The rest of the code will continue functioning without any changes. The code in the following listing is available in example:bookmark-service-with-reply/main.cpp.

Listing 12.12   Final version of the server

```
auto transform = [](auto f) {
        return reactive::operators::transform(lift_with_client(f));
    };
auto filter = [](auto f) {
        return reactive::operators::filter(apply_with_client(f));
    };

boost::asio::io_service event_loop;

auto pipeline =
    service(event_loop)
    | transform(trim)

    | filter([](const std::string& message) {
          return message.length() > 0 && message[0] != '#';
      })

    | transform([](const std::string& message) {
          return mtry([&] { return json::parse(message); });
      })

    | transform([](const auto& exp) {
          return mbind(exp, bookmark_from_json);
      })

    | sink([](const auto& message) {
          const auto exp_bookmark = message.value;
```

```
    if (!exp_bookmark) {
        message.reply("ERROR: Request not understood\n");
        return;
    }

    if (exp_bookmark->text.find("C++") != std::string::npos) {
        message.reply("OK: " + to_string(exp_bookmark.get()) +
                      "\n");
    } else {
        message.reply("ERROR: Not a C++-related link\n");
    }
});
```

```
std::cerr << "Service is running...\n";
event_loop.run();
```

This shows the power of using generic abstractions such as functors and monads. You've managed to dig through the whole processing line just by changing a few things and leaving the main program logic intact.

12.7 *Creating actors with a mutable state*

Although you should always try not to have any mutable state, in some situations it's useful. It may have gone unnoticed until this point, but you've already created one transformation that has a mutable state: the `join` transformation. It keeps a list of all sources whose messages it forwards.

In this case, having mutable state in the `join` transformation is an implementation detail—you need to keep the sources alive. But in some situations, explicitly stateful actors are necessary.

To keep the service responsive, you can't give the same priority to all messages. Say you have a client that's trying to perform a denial-of-service (DoS) attack by flooding you with messages so you become unable to reply to other clients.

There are various approaches to dealing with problems like these. One of the simpler techniques is message throttling. When you accept a message from the client to process, you reject all subsequent messages until a certain predefined time interval has passed. For example, you might define a throttle of 1 second, which would mean after you accept a message from a client, you'll ignore that client for 1 second.

To do so, you can create an actor that accepts messages and remembers the client that sent the message, along with the absolute time when you'll start accepting messages from that client again. This requires the actor to have mutable state; it needs to remember and update timeouts for each client.

In ordinary concurrent software systems, having mutable state would require synchronization. This isn't the case in actor-based systems. An actor is a single-threaded component completely isolated from all other actors. The state you want to mutate can't be mutated from different concurrent processes. Because you don't share any resources, you don't need to do any synchronization.

As previously mentioned, the actors in the bookmarks service example are oversimplified. You can handle quite a few clients at the same time, but you're still doing all the processing in a single thread. And you use asynchronous messaging only in the places where you communicate with the client (in the parts of the code that uses Boost.Asio).

In the general actor model, each actor lives in a separate process or a thread (or in something even more lightweight that behaves like a thread). Because all actors have their own little world where time passes independently of the time of other actors, there can be no synchronous messages.

All actors need their own message queues to which you can add as many messages as you want. The actor (as a single-threaded component) will process the messages in the queue one by one.

In the example implementation, messages are synchronous. Calling m_emit in one of the actors will immediately call the process_message function in another. If you wanted to create a multithreaded system, you'd have to make these calls indirect. You'd need a message-processing loop in each thread, and that loop would have to deliver the messages to the right actor.

The change in the infrastructure wouldn't be trivial, but the concept of an actor being an isolated component that receives and sends messages wouldn't change. Only the message delivery mechanism would.

Although the underlying implementation would change, the design of the software wouldn't need to. While designing the message pipeline, you didn't rely on your system being single-threaded. You designed it as a set of isolated components that process each other's messages—you didn't require any of those messages to be delivered immediately. The message pipeline you designed can stay completely intact, both conceptually and code-wise, even if you completely revamp the underlying system.

12.8   *Writing distributed systems with actors*

There's another benefit of designing concurrent software systems as a set of actors that send messages to one another. I said that all actors are isolated; they share nothing, not even timelines. The only thing that's guaranteed is that the messages an actor has in its queue are processed in the order they were sent.

Actors don't care whether they live in the same thread, a different thread in the same process, a different process on the same computer, or in different computers, as long as they can send messages to one another. One implication that follows from this is that you can easily scale the bookmark service horizontally without needing to change its main logic. Each of the actors you created can live on a separate computer and send messages over the network.

Just as switching from a single-threaded to a multithreaded system did not incur any changes to the main program logic, switching an ordinary system based on actors and reactive streams to a distributed system will also leave it intact. The only necessary change is in the message-delivery system. With multithreaded execution, you had to create message-processing loops in each thread and know how to deliver the right messages to the right loop, and therefore to the right actor. In distributed systems, the story is the same—but you have another level of indirection. The messages need to be able not only to travel between threads, but also to be serialized for sending over the network.

TIP For more information and resources about the topics covered in this chapter, see https://forums.manning.com/posts/list/43781.page.

Summary

- Most C++ programmers write procedural code. I recommend reading *Object Thinking* by David West (Microsoft Press, 2004) to help you start writing better object-oriented code. It's beneficial even when you're doing functional programming.
- Humans tend to achieve grand things when they talk to one another. We don't have a shared mind, but the ability to communicate helps us achieve complex goals. This is the reasoning that led to the invention of the actor model.
- Monads can cooperate well. You shouldn't be afraid to stack them on each other.
- You can implement transformations for reactive streams similar to those for input ranges. You can't implement things such as sorting on them, because for sorting you need random access to all elements, and you don't even know how many elements a reactive stream will have—they're potentially infinite.
- Just like futures, common implementations of reactive streams aren't limited to sending values; they can also send special messages such as "stream ended." This can be useful for more efficient memory handling: you can destroy a stream when you know it won't send you any more messages.

Testing and debugging

This chapter covers

- Avoiding runtime errors by moving them to compile-time
- Understanding the benefits of pure functions in unit testing
- Automatically generating test cases for pure functions
- Testing code by comparing against existing solutions
- Testing monad-based concurrent systems

Computers are becoming omnipresent. We have smart watches, TVs, toasters, and more. Consequences of bugs in software today range from minor annoyances to serious problems, including identity theft and even danger to our lives.

Therefore, it's more important than ever that the software we write is correct: that it does exactly what it should and doesn't contain bugs. Although this sounds like a no-brainer—because who in their right mind would want to write bug-ridden software?—it's widely accepted that all nontrivial programs contain bugs. We are so accustomed to this fact that we tend to subconsciously develop workarounds to avoid the bugs we discover in programs we're using.

Although this is the sad truth, it's not an excuse for not trying to write correct programs. The issue is that this isn't easy to do.

Most features of higher-level programming languages arc introduced with this issue in mind. This is especially true for C++, where most recent evolution has focused on making safe programs easier to write—or, to be more precise, to make it easier for programmers to avoid common programming mistakes.

We've seen safety improvements in dynamic memory management with smart pointers, automatic type deduction with `auto` to shorten code and avoid accidental implicit casts, and monads such as `std::future` to make it easier to develop correct concurrent programs without bothering with low-level concurrency primitives such as mutexes. We've also seen the push toward stronger type-based programming with the algebraic data types `std::optional` and `std::variant`, units and user-defined literals (`std::chrono::duration`, for example), and so forth.

13.1 Is the program that compiles correct?

All these features exist to help us avoid common programming mistakes and move error detection from runtime to compilation time. One of the most famous examples of how a simple error can create a huge loss was the Mars Climate Orbiter bug; most of the code assumed distances were measured in metric units, but part of the code used imperial (English) units.

> *The MCO MIB has determined that the root cause for the loss of the MCO spacecraft was the failure to use metric units in the coding of a ground software file, "Small Forces," used in trajectory models. Specifically, thruster performance data in English units instead of metric units was used in the software application code titled SM_FORCES (small forces).*
>
> —NASA,[1]

This error could have been avoided if the code had used stronger typing instead of raw values. You can easily create a type to handle distances that forces a certain measurement unit:

```
template <typename Representation,
          typename Ratio = std::ratio<1>
class distance {
    ...
};
```

This type would allow you to create different types for different measurement units, and to represent the number of those units with an arbitrary numeric type—integers, floating-point numbers, or a special type you created. If you assume that meters are the default, you can create others (rounded-up miles to meters for simplicity):

```
template <typename Representation>
using meters = distance<Representation>;
```

---

[1] NASA, "Mars Climate Orbiter Mishap Investigation Board Phase I Report," November 10, 1999, http://mng.bz/YOl7..

```
template <typename Representation>
using kilometers = distance<Representation, std::kilo>;

template <typename Representation>
using centimeters = distance<Representation, std::centi>;

template <typename Representation>
using miles = distance<Representation, std::ratio<1609>>;
```

You can also make these easier to use by creating user-defined literals for them:

```
constexpr kilometers<long double> operator ""_km(long double distance)
{
    return kilometers<long double>(distance);
}
```

```
... // And similar for other units
```

Now you can write a program using any unit you want. But if you try to mix and match different units, you'll get a compilation error because the types don't match:

```
auto distance = 42.0_km + 1.5_mi; // error!
```

You could provide conversion functions to make this more usable, but you've achieved the main goal: a small, zero-cost abstraction that moves the error from runtime to compilation time. This makes a huge difference during the software development cycle—the difference between losing a space probe and detecting the bug long before the probe is even scheduled for launch.

By using the higher-level abstractions covered in this book, you can move many common software bugs to compilation time. For this reason, some people say that after you successfully compile a functional program, it's bound to work correctly.

Obviously, all nontrivial programs have bugs, and this applies to FP-style programs as well. But the shorter the code (and, as you've seen, FP and the abstractions it introduces allow you to write significantly shorter code compared to the usual imperative approach), the fewer places you can make mistakes. And by making as many mistakes as possible detectable at compile-time, you significantly reduce the number of runtime errors.

13.2 *Unit testing and pure functions*

Although you should always try to write code in a way that makes potential programming errors detectable during compilation, it isn't always possible. Programs need to process real data during runtime, and you could still make logic errors or produce incorrect results.

For this reason, you need automatic tests for your software. Automatic tests are also useful for regression testing when you change existing code.

At the lowest level of testing are *unit tests*. The goal of unit testing is to isolate small parts of a program and test them individually to assure their correctness. You're testing the correctness of the units themselves, not how they integrate with one another.

The good thing is that unit testing in functional programming is similar to unit testing of imperative programs. You can use the same libraries you're accustomed to while writing standard unit tests. The only difference is that testing pure functions is a bit easier.

Traditionally, a unit test for a stateful object consists of setting up the object state, performing an action on that object, and checking the result. Imagine you have a class that handles a textual file. It might have several member functions, including one that counts the number of lines in the file the same way you counted the lines in chapter 1— by counting the number of newline characters in the file:

```
class textual_file {
public:
    int line_count() const;

    ...

};
```

To create a unit test for this function, you need to create several files, create instances of `textual_file` for all of them, and check the result of the `line_count` function.

This is a common approach if a class you're testing has state. You have to initialize the state, and only then you can perform the test. You often need to perform the same test with various states the class can be in.

This often means in order to write a good test, you need to know which parts of the class state can influence the test you're writing. For example, the state for the `textual_file` class might include a flag to tell you whether the file is writable. You need to know its internals to be able to tell that this flag has no influence on the result of `line_count`, or you have to create tests that cover both writable and read-only files.

This becomes much simpler when testing pure functions. The function result can depend only on the arguments you pass in to the function. If you don't add superfluous arguments to functions just for the fun of it, you can assume that all arguments are used to calculate the result.

You don't need to set up any external state before running tests, and you can write tests without considering how the function you're testing is implemented. This decoupling of a function and the external state also tends to make the function more general, which increases reusability and allows testing of the same function in various contexts.

Consider the following pure function:

```
template <typename Iter, typename End>
int count_lines(const Iter& begin, const End& end)
{
    using std::count;
    return count(begin, end, '\n');
}
```

As a pure function, it doesn't need any external state to calculate the result, it doesn't use anything besides its arguments, and it doesn't modify the arguments.

When testing, you can call this function without any previous preparations, and you can call it on several types—from lists and vectors, to ranges and input streams:

```
std::string s = "Hello\nworld\n";
assert(count_lines(begin(s), end(s)) == 2);
```
├ **Testing with a string**

```
auto r = s | view::transform([](char c) { return toupper(c); });
assert(count_lines(begin(r), end(r)) == 2);
```
| Testing with
   a range

```
std::istrstream ss("Hello\nworld\n");
assert(count_lines(std::istreambuf_iterator<char>(ss),
                   std::istreambuf_iterator<char>()) == 2);
```
| Testing with an input
   stream (instead of
   being limited to files)

```
std::forward_list<char> l;
assert(count_lines(begin(l), end(l)) == 0);
```
| Testing with a singly
   linked list

If you were so inclined, you could implement overloads that would be more comfortable to use, instead of having to call count_lines with pairs of iterators. Those would be one-line wrappers and not something that would require thorough testing.

Your task when writing unit tests is to isolate small parts of the program and test them individually. Every pure function is already an isolated part of the program. This, along with the fact that pure functions are easy to test, makes each pure function a perfect candidate for a unit.

13.3 *Automatically generating tests*

Although unit tests are useful (and necessary), their main problem is that you have to write them by hand. This makes them error-prone, because you might make coding errors in the tests, and you're at risk of writing incorrect or incomplete tests. Just as it is harder to find spelling errors in your own writing than in somebody else's, it's more difficult to write tests for your own code; you're likely to skip the same corner cases you forgot to cover in the implementation. It would be much more convenient if the tests could be automatically generated based on what you're testing.

13.3.1 *Generating test cases*

When implementing the count_lines function, you have its specification: given a collection of characters, return the number of newlines in that collection. What's the inverse problem of counting lines? Given a number, generate all collections whose line counts are equal to the given number. This yields a function like the following (covering only strings as the collection type):

```
std::vector<std::string> generate_test_cases(int line_count);
```

If these problems are the inverse of one another, then for any collection generated by generate_test_cases(line_count), the count_lines function needs to return the same value line_count passed to generate_test_cases. And this must be true for any value of line_count, from zero to infinity. You could write this rule as follows:

```
for (int line_count : view::ints(0)) {
    for (const auto& test : generate_test_cases(line_count)) {
        assert(count_lines(test) == line_count);
    }
}
```

This would be a perfect test, but it has one *small* problem. The number of cases you're testing is infinite, because you're traversing the range of all integers starting with zero.

And for each of them, you can have an infinite number of strings that have the given number of newlines.

Because you can't check all of these, you need to generate a subset of problems and check whether the rule holds for that subset. Generating a single example of a string that has a given number of newlines is trivial. You can generate it by creating a sufficient number of random strings and concatenate them by putting a newline between each two. Each string will have a random length and random characters inside—you must just make sure they don't contain newlines:

```
std::string generate_test_case(int line_count)
{
    std::string result;

    for (int i = 0; i < line_count; ++i) {
        result += generate_random_string() + '\n';
    }

    result += generate_random_string();
    return result;
}
```

This generates a single test case: a single string that contains exactly line_count number of newlines. You can define the function that returns an infinite range of these examples:

```
auto generate_test_cases(int line_count)
{
    return view::generate(std::bind(generate_test_case, line_count));
}
```

Now you need to limit the number of tests you're performing. Instead of covering all integers, and processing an infinite number of collections for each, you can add predefined limits.

> **Listing 13.1 Testing count_lines on a set of randomly generated tests**

```
for (int line_count :
        view::ints(0, MAX_NEWLINE_COUNT)) {        ← Instead of covering all integers, checks
    for (const auto& test :                          only up to a predefined value
            generate_test_cases(line_count)      ←
            | view::take(TEST_CASES_PER_LINE_COUNT)) {   Specifies the number of test
        assert(line_count ==                             cases for each number of lines
            count_lines(begin(test), end(test)));
    }
}
```

Although this covers only a subset of all possible inputs, each time the tests are run, a new set of random examples is generated. With each new run, the space of inputs for which you've checked correctness is expanded.

The downside of the randomness is that the tests might fail in some invocations, and not in others. This could lead to the wrong implication: you might assume that when the tests fail, the last change you made to the program is at fault. To remedy this, it's

always a good idea to write out the seed you used for the random-number generator
to the test output so that you can later easily reproduce the error and find the software
revision in which it was introduced.

13.3.2 *Property-based testing*

Sometimes you have problems for which checks are already known or are much simpler
than the problem. Imagine you want to test a function that reverses the order of the
items in a vector:

```
template <typename T>
std::vector<T> reverse(const std::vector<T>& xs);
```

You could create a few test cases and check whether `reverse` works correctly for them.
But, again, this covers only a small number of cases. You could try to find rules that
apply to the `reverse` function.

First, let's find the inverse problem of reversing a given collection xs. You need to
find all collections that, when reversed, give that original collection xs. There exists
only one, and it's `reverse(xs)`. Reversing a collection is the inverse problem of itself:

```
xs == reverse(reverse(xs));
```

This needs to hold for any collection xs that you can think of. You can also add a few
more properties of the `reverse` function:

- The number of elements in the reversed collection needs to be the same as the
  number of elements in the original collection.
- The first element of a collection needs to be the same as the last element in the
  reversed collection.
- The last element of a collection needs to be the same as the first element in the
  reversed collection.

All these need to hold for any collection. You can generate as many random collections
as you want, and check that all these rules hold for them.

Listing 13.2   Generating test cases and checking that properties hold

```
for (const auto& xs : generate_random_collections()) {
    const auto rev_xs = reverse(xs);

    assert(xs == reverse(rev_xs));          ◄─── If you reverse a collection two times,
                                                 you get the original collection.

    assert(xs.length() == rev_xs.length()); ◄─── The original and reversed collections
                                                 must have the same number of elements.

    assert(xs.front() == rev_xs.back());    ┌─── The first element in the original
    assert(xs.back()  == rev_xs.front());   │    collection is the same as the last element
}                                           └─── of the reversed collection, and vice versa.
```

As in the previous case, where you checked the `count_lines` function for correctness,
you'll check a different part of the function input space with each new run of the tests.
The difference here is that you don't need to create a smart generator function for the

test examples. Any randomly generated example has to satisfy all the properties of the `reverse` function.

You can do the same for other problems—problems that aren't the inverse of themselves, but that still have properties that need to hold. Imagine you need to test whether a sorting function works correctly. There are more than a few ways to implement sorting; some are more efficient when sorting in-memory data, and some are better when sorting data on storage devices. But all of them need to follow the same rules:

- The original collection must have the same number of elements as the sorted one.
- The minimum element of the original collection must be the same as the first element in the sorted collection.
- The maximum element of the original collection must be the same as the last element in the sorted collection.
- Each element in a sorted collection must be greater or equal to its predecessor.
- Sorting a reversed collection should give the same result as sorting the collection without reversing it.

You've generated a set of properties that you can easily check (this list isn't extensive but is sufficient for demonstration purposes).

Listing 13.3 Generating test cases and checking sorting properties

```
for (const auto& xs : generate_random_collections()) {
    const auto sorted_xs = sort(xs);

    assert(xs.length() == sorted_xs.length());

    assert(min_element(begin(xs), end(xs)) ==
        sorted_xs.front());
    assert(max_element(begin(xs), end(xs)) ==
        sorted_xs.back());

    assert(is_sorted(begin(sorted_xs),
            end(sorted_xs)));

    assert(sorted_xs == sort(reverse(xs)));
}
```

Annotations:
- Checks that the sorted collection has the same number of elements as the original
- Checks that the smallest and largest elements in the original collection are the first and last elements in the sorted collection
- Checks that each element in the sorted collection is greater than or equal to its predecessor
- Checks that sorting a reversed list yields the same result as sorting the original list (assuming total ordering of elements)

When you define a set of properties for a function and implement checks for them, you can generate random input and feed it to the checks. If any of the properties fail on any of the cases, you know you have a buggy implementation.

13.3.3 *Comparative testing*

So far, you've seen how to automatically generate tests for functions for which you know how to solve the inverse problem, and how to test function properties that need to hold regardless of the data provided to the function. There's a third option, in which randomly generated tests can improve your unit tests.

Imagine you want to test the implementation of the bitmapped vector trie (BVT) data structure from chapter 8. You designed it to be an immutable (persistent) data structure. It looks and behaves like the standard vector, with one exception: it's optimized for copies and doesn't allow in-place mutation.

The easiest way to test a structure like this is to test it against the structure it aims to mimic—against a normal vector. You need to test all operations you defined on your structure and compare the result with the same or equivalent operation performed on the standard vector. To do so, you need to be able to convert between the standard vector and a BVT vector, and to be able to check whether a given BVT and standard vectors contain the same data.

Then you can create a set of rules to check against. Again, these rules must hold for any random collection of data. The first thing to check is that the BVT constructed from a standard vector contains the same data as that vector, and vice versa. Next, test all the operations—perform them on both the BVT and the standard vector, and check whether the resulting collections also hold the same data.

Listing 13.4   Generating test cases and comparing BVT and vector

```
for (const auto& xs : generate_random_vectors()) {
    const BVT bvt_xs(xs);

    assert(xs == bvt_xs);          If both collections support iterators, this
                                   is trivial to implement with std::equal.

    {
        auto xs_copy = xs;                           Because BVT is immutable, you need to
        xs_copy.push_back(42);                       simulate that behavior with the standard
        assert(xs_copy == bvt_xs.push_back(42));     vector as well. First create a copy, and
    }                                                then modify it.

    if (xs.length() > 0) {
        auto xs_copy = xs;
        xs_copy.pop_back();
        assert(xs_copy == bvt_xs.pop_back());
    }

    ...
}
```

These approaches to automatic test generation aren't exclusive. You can use them together to test a single function.

For example, to test a custom implementation of the sort algorithm, you can use all three approaches:

- For each sorted vector, create an unsorted vector by shuffling it. Sorting the shuffled version must return the original vector.
- Test against a few properties that all sorting implementations must have, which you've already seen.
- Generate random data, and sort it with your sorting algorithm and `std::sort` to make sure they give the same output.

When you get a list of checks, you can feed them as many randomly generated examples as you want. Again, if any of the checks fail, your implementation isn't correct.

13.4 *Testing monad-based concurrent systems*

You saw the implementation of a simple web service in chapter 12. That implementation was based mostly on reactive streams, and you used a couple of other monadic structures: `expected<T, E>` to handle errors, and `with_socket<T>` to transfer the socket pointer through the program logic so you could send a reply to the clients.

This monadic data-flow software design has a few benefits you've already seen. It's composable; you split the program logic into a set of completely isolated range-like transformations that can easily be reused in other parts of the same program or in other programs.

Another big benefit is that you modified the original server implementation to be able to reply to the client without changing a single line in the main program logic—in the data-flow pipeline. You lifted the transformations up one level, to teach them how to handle the `with_socket<T>` type, and everything else just worked.

In this section, you're going to use the fact that all monadic structures are alike—they all have `mbind`, `transform`, and `join` defined on them. If you base your logic on these functions (or functions built on top of them), you can freely switch between monads without changing the main program logic, so you can implement tests for your program. One of the main problems when testing concurrent software systems, or software that has parts executed asynchronously from the main program, is that it isn't easy to write tests to cover all possible interactions between concurrent processes in the system. If two concurrent processes need to talk to each other or share the same data, a lot can change if in some situations one of them takes more time to finish than expected.

Simulating this during testing is hard, and it's almost impossible to detect all the problems that are exposed in production. Furthermore, replicating a problem detected in production can be a real pain, because it's difficult to replicate the same timings of all processes.

In the design of the small web service, you never made any assumptions (explicit or implicit) about how much time any of the transformations took. You didn't even assume the transformations were synchronous.

The only thing you assumed was that you had a stream of messages coming from a client. Although this stream was asynchronous, the defined data flow had no need for it to be—it had to work even for synchronous streams of data—for ranges.

As a short reminder, this is what the data flow pipeline looked like:

```
auto pipeline =
    source
    | transform(trim)

    | filter([](const std::string& message) {
          return message.length() > 0 && message[0] != '#';
      })

    | transform([](const std::string& message) {
          return mtry([&] { return json::parse(message); });
```

```
    })

    | transform([](const auto& exp) {
          return mbind(exp, bookmark_from_json);
      })

    | sink([](const auto& message) {
        const auto exp_bookmark = message.value;

        if (!exp_bookmark) {
            message.reply("ERROR: Request not understood\n");
            return;
        }

        if (exp_bookmark->text.find("C++") != std::string::npos) {
            message.reply("OK: " + to_string(exp_bookmark.get()) +
                          "\n");
        } else {
            message.reply("ERROR: Not a C++-related link\n");
        }
    });
```

A stream of strings comes from the source, and you parse them into bookmarks. If you got this code without being given any sort of context, the first thing you'd think isn't that the source is a service based on Boost.Asio, but that it's some kind of collection, and that you're using the range-v3 library to process it.

This is the primary benefit of this design when testing is concerned: you can switch asynchronicity on and off as you please. When the system runs, you'll use reactive streams, and when you need to test the main logic of the system, you'll be able to use normal data collections.

Let's see what you need to change to make a test program from the web service. Because you don't need the service component when testing the pipeline, you can strip out all the code that uses Boost.Asio. The only thing that needs to remain is the wrapper type you use to send the messages back to the client. Because you no longer have clients, instead of a pointer to the socket, you'll store the expected reply message in that type. Then, when the pipeline calls the `reply` member function, you'll check whether you got the message you expected:

```
template <typename MessageType>
struct with_expected_reply {
    MessageType value;
    std::string expected_reply;

    void reply(const std::string& message) const
    {
        REQUIRE(message == expected_reply);
    }
};
```

Just like `with_socket`, this structure carries the message along with contextual information. You can use this class as a drop-in replacement for `with_socket`; as far as the data-flow pipeline is concerned, nothing has changed.

The next step is to redefine the pipeline transformations to use the transformations from the range library instead of the transformations from the simple reactive streams library. Again, you don't need to change the pipeline; you'll just change the definitions of `transform` and `filter` from the original program. They need to lift the range transformations to work with `with_expected_reply<T>`:

```
auto transform = [](auto f) {
    return view::transform(lift_with_expected_reply(f));
};
auto filter = [](auto f) {
    return view::filter(apply_with_expected_reply(f));
};
```

You also need to define the `sink` transformation, because ranges don't have it. The sink transformation should call the given function on each value from the source range. You can use `view::transform` for this, but with a slight change. The function you passed to `sink` returns void, and you can't pass it to `view::transform` directly because it would result in a range of `void`s. You'll need to wrap the transformation function in a function that returns an actual value:

```
auto sink = [](auto f) {
    return view::transform([f](auto&& ws) {
        f(ws);
        return ws.expected_reply;
    });
};
```

That's all. You can now create a vector of `with_expected_reply<std::string>` instances and pass it through the pipeline. As each item in the collection is processed, it tests whether the reply was correct. For a full implementation of this example, check out the accompanying example bookmark-service-testing.

It's important to note that this is just the test for the main program logic. It doesn't relieve you from writing tests for the service component, and for the individual transformation components such as `filter` and `transform`. Usually, tests for small components like these are easy to write, and most bugs don't arise from the component implementation, but from different components' interaction. And this interaction is exactly what you simplified the testing for.

> **TIP** For more information and resources about the topics in this chapter, see https://forums.manning.com/posts/list/43782.page.

Summary

- Every pure function is a good candidate to be unit tested. You know what it uses to calculate the result, and you know it doesn't change any external state—its only effect is that it returns a result.
- One of the most famous libraries that does property-checking against a randomly generated data set is Haskell's QuickCheck. It inspired similar projects for many programming languages, including C++.
- By changing the random function, you can change which types of tests are more often performed. For example, when generating random strings, you can favor shorter strings by using a random function with normal distribution and with mean zero.
- Fuzzing is another testing method that uses random data. The idea is to test whether software works correctly given invalid (random) input. It's highly useful for programs that accept unstructured input
- Remembering the initial random seed allows you to replicate tests that have failed.
- Correctly designed monadic systems should work without problems if the continuation monad or reactive streams are replaced with normal values and normal data collections. This allows you to switch on and off concurrency and asynchronous execution on the fly. You can use this switch during testing.

index

H

head function 40
higher-order functions 22
  writing 38–44

I

ifstream class (std::) 5
immutable states 110–113
immutable vector-like data structures *See* bitmapped
      vector tries
imperative programming 3–8
increment (++) operator 145
infinite ranges 151–154
infix operators 84
inheritance, sum types through 176–179
input ranges 151–152
input stream-like containers 218
internal const-ness 116
ints, ranges (view::) 153
invoking metafunctions 229
invoke function (std::) 240
is_invocable_v metafunction (std::) 239
is_invocable_r metafunction (std::) 246
is_same metafunction (std::) 230
istream_range 154
istreambuf_iterator (std::) 5
item views 128

J

join
  for streams 262
  view::join, ranges 206
JSON 252

L

lambdas 54–61
  as alternative for std::bind 83–85
  creating arbitrary member variables in 59–60
  generalized lambda capture 60
  generic 60–61
  overview of 56–59
  syntax of 55–56
lazy copying *See* copy-on-write
lazy evaluation 122–141
  as optimization technique 126–133
    dynamic programming 131–133

for sorting collections 126–127
  item views in user interfaces 128
  pruning recursion trees by caching function
      results 129–131
  C++ and 123–126
  expression templates 136–141
  lazy string concatenation 136–141
  memoization 133–136
  of range values 147–149
lazy quicksort algorithm 128
lazy_string_concat_helper class 140
lazy_val 123–126
left associativity 30
left fold 30
less-than (<) operator 176
Levenshtein distance 132
lexicographical comparison 175
lifting
  functions 95–98
  overview of 13
line_count function 277
lists
  adding elements to and removing from end
      of lists 161
  adding elements to and removing from middle
      of lists 162
  adding elements to and removing from start
      of lists 159–160
  immutable linked lists 159–164
  list (std::) 101
  memory management 163–165
logical const-ness 116
logical operators 65

M

Mach7 library 196–198
make_curried function 88
  implementation 238–241
make_memoized function 133–136
map 6
max_element algorithm (std::) 104
mbind function (monadic bind) 206
mcompose function (monad composition) 224
member variables in lambdas 59–60
memoization 123, 133–136
messages
  creating simple sources of 252–256
  creating sinks to receive 257–260

V

values
  creating streams of 262–263
  mutating through ranges 149–151
  optional values
    as a functor 201
    as a range 202
    as a monad 212
    optional (std::) 184
variant (std::) 179
views *See* ranges, views
visit function (std::) 195
void_t metafunction (std::) 235

W

web_page socket 179
wildcards in lambda captures 56
with_client class 269
word frequencies 154–157
wrapping function objects with std::function 68–69
Writer monad 216

Y

yield_if, ranges 211

Z

zip function, ranges (view::) 153